D1707183

Far Left of Center

Far Left of Center
The American Radical Left Today

Harvey Klehr

Transaction Books
New Brunswick (U.S.A.) and Oxford (U.K.)

This study by Professor Harvey Klehr of Emory University, Atlanta, Georgia, was made possible by a grant from the Anti-Defamation League of B'nai B'rith.

Library of Congress Catalog Number: 87-31424
ISBN: 0-88738-217-7
Printed in the United States of America

Library of Congress Cataloging-in-Publication Data

Klehr, Harvey:
   The American radical left.
   Includes bibliographies and index.
   1. Communism—United States.   2. Communist Party
of the United States of America.   I. Title.
HX86.K59   1988   324.273'7   87-31424
ISBN 0-88738-217-7

For my uncle and aunt—
Samuel and Ronnie Brummer

Contents

Acknowledgments

This book would never have been written without the help and support of a number of people. It was commissioned by the Anti-Defamation League of B'nai B'rith. I am grateful to the ADL for its assistance and commitment to the values of a democratic society. Of the ADL's fine staff Irwin Suall, David Lowe, Jerome Bakst, Mortimer Kass, Justin Finger, Gail Gans, Alan Schwartz and Mira Boland were particularly helpful. David Evanier was a unique source of assistance, insight and encouragement. Without the courage and vision of the late Nathan Perlmutter, National Director of the ADL, this project would not have been possible.

My faculty colleagues at Emory University, including Tom Walker, Tom Remington, Eleanor Main, and Juan DelAguila were useful sounding boards. I am also appreciative of the assistance of Dean David Minter and Micheal Giles.

Finally, my wife Elizabeth and my children, Benjamin, Gabriel and Joshua, were constant reminders that there is more to life than left-wing political sects.

Introduction

Histories of various American radical groups abound. The Communist Party has been the subject of dozens of monographs, and writers like Theodore Draper, Irving Howe and Lewis Coser have chronicled its turbulent life in distinguished books. Similarly, the tiny Trotskyist movement in the United States has been minutely examined. Accounts of the New Left, although less voluminous, have also been written.

Very little information is available, however, about the radical left today. Many people assume, erroneously, that with the collapse of the New Left in the early 1970s, American radicalism disappeared. Except when some shocking incident—a shootout in Greensboro, North Carolina or an armored car holdup and murder in New York—catapults a radical group into the headlines, the activities of the far left are generally ignored.

The 1980s have not, it is true, been good years for radicals in the United States or, indeed, in the democratic world. Their ideologies, particularly Marxism–Leninism, have been discredited, their tactics and visions have been repudiated by most of their fellow citizens and they have been plagued by internal problems. Still, the history of American radicalism does suggest that such movements have rebounded from similar depressions in the past.

Moreover, while many of the Marxist–Leninist groups in this country are quite small, they often have an impact far out of proportion to their size because of their ability to convince well-meaning people to support their activities in connection with some of the causes they exploit, ranging from peace to civil rights. Through the use of front groups, radical organizations can achieve a respectability and a hearing that would be denied them if people knew what they really stood for. It is not the purpose of this book to suggest that these groups be denied the protections of the Constitution or to suggest curtailment of their legal rights. It is to describe the origins and policies of these groups so that people can know what they stand for.

The radical left in America often suggests that anyone who disagrees with or criticizes its positions and tactics is guilty of McCarthyism. To expose an organization's ties to the Communist Party or to the Workers World Party is not McCarthyism, however, any more than it would be to uncover the unsavory ties between a respectable business and the underworld.

Most of the organizations discussed in this book are hostile to democratic values and institutions both in theory and practice. They admire and support Marxist–Leninist regimes that have destroyed or trampled on democratic freedoms. It is sometimes argued that hostility to communism is an unhealthy American obsession. Given the historical record, it is hard to understand why any American or anyone concerned about democracy, freedom and liberty would be anything but hostile to communism.

Wherever they have come to power communist regimes have left behind a trail of blood and slaughter dwarfed only by fascists—and it is arguable about which kind of regime has killed more people. Every communist regime has brutally suppressed dissenters of all stripes, from political heretics to religious believers. Every communist regime has crushed freedom of the press. Every one has unleashed secret police against its own population. Every one has purged its own ranks, destroying more of its own members than any enemy ever had. Every one has stripped scholars, artists and teachers of the right to pursue the truth and has brazenly rewritten history.

There are democratic socialists in the United States who have vigorously and continuously denounced Marxism–Leninism and those regimes founded on its principles. This book is not about them. These include organizations such as Social Democratics–USA, formerly led by the late Bayard Rustin, and Democratic Socialists of America, led by Michael Harrington, which are committed to democratic values and democratic society. My focus is, rather, on those groups whose denunciations of American society and political life go hand–in–hand with testimonials to some of the most repressive regimes in the world.

In the last several years in the United States we have once again been reminded of the dangers of right–wing extremism as a result of the activities of groups that spout Nazi rhetoric, profess allegiance to philosophies blaming the world's ills on Jews, threaten violence and even engage in it. Such organizations as The Order, Aryan Nations, and Posse Comitatus have engaged in bank robberies, murdered a Jewish radio personality in Denver and declared war on the "Zionist Occupation Government" of the United States.

It is important not to minimize this danger from the ultraright. It is real and needs to be combatted. At the same time, however, it is imperative that we recognize the dangers arising from the radical left. The far left poses a different kind of danger but one that is overlooked or minimized to the peril of the security and best interests of the American public.

Part of my concern about the policies and views of the extremist left stems from its hostility to the interests of Jews. There is a very good historical reason why Jews have been more sensitive to antisemitism of the right than of the left. For centuries in Europe, the major source of hostility to Jews came from the defenders of traditional, feudal society. Beginning with the French Revolution, support for Jewish emancipation came from the political left. Not all on the left, however, had any great affection for Jews. Some believed that Jews had an obligation to disappear as Jews in return for integration into Western political culture.

In fact, blatant antisemitism has also emanated from the socialist movement. The most famous radical antisemite was Karl Marx himself, whose works and letters are filled with slurs and epithets against his one-time coreligionists (both he and his father had been baptized). Marx attacked Jews as the very symbols of capitalism, whose religion was business and huckstering. "What is the profane basis of Judaism?" Marx asked. His answer was that it was "practical need, self-interest. What is the worldly cult of the Jew? Huckstering. What is his worldly god? Money." While he believed that Jews should be given civil and political rights, Marx also looked forward to their disappearance as a community when socialism replaced capitalism: "In the final analysis, the emancipation of the Jews is the emancipation of mankind from Judaism."[1] To be sure, the democratic socialist movement has always contained important forces friendly to Jewish interests, but antisemitic strains have also remained powerful among radicals.

Communist regimes have been the most potent source of left–wing antisemitism in recent decades. The Soviet Union's destruction of Jewish culture and attacks on Jews go well back into Stalin's dictatorship and continued right up to his death, with the infamous "doctors' plot." Today, Jews face persecution for pursuing their cultural heritage, and suffer systematic exclusion from access to higher education and sensitive positions. Officially sanctioned government publications contain classical antisemitic stereotypes, caricatures, and slurs. The regime also has published scurrilous antisemitic tracts under the guise of anti–Zionism. The Soviet bloc was one of the prime sponsors of the infamous "Zionism is racism" resolution passed by the United Nations a decade ago and was actually the original source of the charge.

This book is not intended to provide an history of the American radical left. Its aim, rather, is to describe and analyze the contemporary radical left, illustrating its values, policies and organizational relationships, while providing only enough historical background to illustrate the group's political trajectory. Some of these extremist groups camouflage their views. They may have one agenda for public consumption while many of their activities reflect another line. Occasionally, some prominent individuals may give these organizations respectability by associating with their activities. Because many of them are obscure, however, their full agenda may not be known by those to whom they appeal for support and assistance, be it economic, political or intellectual.

The first section deals with the Communist Party of the United States of

America (CPUSA) and its varied front groups. The Party is the largest and most influential Marxist–Leninist group in the United States. Its membership is only about fifteen thousand but it has been growing steadily in recent years. Moreover, the CPUSA, unlike its competitors on the radical left, has a foothold in the labor movement, a foothold on campuses and one in the black community. Much of its most effective work is done by one or another of its many front groups, ranging from the National Alliance against Racist and Political Repression, to Women for Racial and Economic Equality, to the US Peace Council or Labor Research Association. While no respectable American politician would consider lending his name to Nazi propaganda, some of them—including several congressmen—routinely endorse and assist such Communist Party fronts. To anyone concerned about human rights, the activities of the Communist Party—tied to and controlled by the Kremlin—should be as objectionable as those of the extreme right.

The second section of the book deals with the various Trotskyist, Maoist and other Marxist–Leninist organizations in the US. These sects tend to be quite small, usually with fewer than a thousand members. Most trace their origins to some theoretical fissure within the communist movement. While they rarely have much influence on public policy or politicians, they sometimes are capable of fomenting public turmoil, disruption or violence. Moreover, many have developed ties to extremist Arab groups, thereby generating mutual support for anti-Israel activity. Far more militant than the CPUSA, these radical sects often provide the footsoldiers for demonstrations. Also included in this section are the tiny terrorist offshoots of the New Left. Such groups as the John Brown Anti-Klan Committee and the Weathermen, although nearly extinct now, provided the core of the terrorist component of the American radical left.

The final part of the book deals with organizations that, while eschewing formal ties to Marxist–Leninist parties and without being under the control of such parties, work in coalitions with them toward some of the same objectives. Many of them have especially targeted Israel as a danger to world peace and security. They also share a hostility for American domestic and foreign policy—an animus which translates into support for Marxist revolutionary regimes abroad. Included among these groups are the Committee in Solidarity with the People of El Salvador, Mobilization for Survival, National Lawyers Guild, and Clergy and Laity Concerned.

It is hoped that this book will contribute to greater public understanding of the nature of the radical left and the challenge it poses to all democratically minded Americans.

Note

1. *Karl Marx: Early Writings,* translated and edited by T.B. Bottomore (New York: McGraw-Hill, 1964), p. 34.

Part I

The Communist Party of the United States

Introduction

The Communist Party of the United States of America (CPUSA) is the oldest, largest, wealthiest, best–organized, and most effective Marxist–Leninist group in America. The Party has a number of advantages its competitors lack. At one time it did play an important role in American politics and had a substantial membership. Even when it was reduced to a bare fraction of its prior membership, it retained a base and contacts in a number of larger organizations. Many of its activists occupy secure jobs in American society and the Party does not suffer from the same organizational instability that afflicts many smaller sects largely composed of veterans of the New Left of the 1960s. Finally, the Party enjoys the use of the Soviet franchise for the United States, a gift that severely limits its organizational growth but that also ensures stability and offers a variety of ideological and personal rewards to Party members and leaders. While other Marxist–Leninist sects hitch their ideological wagons to such obscure or bizarre Marxist carts as that of Albania or North Korea or the Gang of Four, the CPUSA remains securely tied to the stable, orthodox and powerful Marxism–Leninism of the Soviet Union.

The CPUSA is presently enjoying its most prosperous era in many a year. And yet, compared to its impact on American life during the 1930s when a considerable number of the Party's leaders first rose to prominence, its present state is hardly robust. Many of the Party's programs and tactics of today are echoes of the past and reflect an effort to recreate the Popular Front era when American communism appeared to be on the way to becoming a major actor in American politics.

Nonetheless, the significance of the Communist Party in America today rests, not on the Party itself, but with its peripheral organizations. By itself, it is not a robust organization. It has, however, the ability to involve people outside of its membership in its activities. It is able to build successful fronts to advance its aims.

The communist movement in America has always been a hostage to Soviet fortunes. It was born largely in response to the Russian Revolution and the desire of some American socialists to emulate the revolutionary militancy and commitment of the Bolshevik Party that had made that revolution possible. In 1919 two separate Communist Parties were formed. Their differences were less ideological than tactical. Both were overwhelmingly dominated by recent immigrants, although one, led by John Reed, was slightly more "American" in tone. The early years of American communism are a complex story of amalgamations and splits, followed by more unifications and more splits. For the first several years, much activity took place "underground," as members met in secret and leaders assumed pseudonyms and skulked about the country to avoid government surveillance and prosecution.

When a unified Communist Party, called the Workers Party, emerged from underground in the early 1920s, it was a small group. The various communist parties had claimed more than fifty thousand members in 1919; by the early 1920s there were barely fifteen thousand. Nor did the Party prosper during America's Jazz Age. In 1929 Party membership was down to some seventy-five hundred. As a result of painful experiences with communist "rule or ruin" tactics, few liberals or radicals were anxious to cooperate with the Party. Nor did the Depression immediately initiate an improvement in Party fortunes. The crash coincided with the initiation of a new policy ordered by the Communist International, or Comintern, the directing body of the world revolution, which was headquartered in Moscow. That policy, demanding ultrarevolutionary tactics and rhetoric and refusing to allow coalitions with other groups unless the Communist Party dominated the coalition, also required the Party to set up separate trade unions to compete with the American Federation of Labor. Its militant policy allowed the CPUSA to garner impressive publicity as a result of a series of dramatic confrontations with authorities in places like Gastonia, North Carolina and Harlan County, Kentucky,but it also failed to result in an influx of new members. As late as 1933, after four years of the worst depression in American history there were only fifteen thousand Party members, no more than there had been in the early 1920s.

The CPUSA's surrender of its autonomy to the Comintern, which was dominated by the Soviet Union, was not imposed by terror or the Red Army. In the early days, the Comintern had been the only body with the authority to end the squabbling among the contentious party factions. The enormous prestige of the Soviet Union among radicals gave its representatives pride of place and convinced many that they knew how more backward or immature or less sophisticated radicals could emulate their success. By 1929 Comintern decisions were so slavishly followed that it could expel Party leader Jay Lovestone from his own organization just months after he had won internal elections with 90 percent of the vote. Only two hundred fifty communists remained loyal to Lovestone; the rest obediantly followed the Comintern.

When the Communist Party won some measure of influence in American life, it did so not mainly because of any special merit of its own (although that certainly was a contributing factor), but because a Comintern decision allowed the Party to adopt a more realistic appraisal of American political life. Concerned about the growth of Nazi Germany and its own policies which precluded communist alliances to fight against it, the Comintern adopted the Popular Front tactic in 1935. Over the next few years the CPUSA moved cautiously towards support for Franklin Roosevelt and the New Deal, albeit without many corresponding gestures by the New Dealers. Communists jettisoned their revolutionary rhetoric and attacks on reformers. They presented themselves as the most ardent defenders of American liberalism and reformism. They worked tirelessly to help build the Congress of Industrial Organizations (CIO). In dozens of other organizations they established congenial relations with non–communists. Party leader Earl Browder proclaimed that "Communism is Twentieth-Century Americanism" and, attracted by the Party's new image and reputation as the most stalwart foe of fascism, new members flocked to join. By 1939 Party membership was approaching one hundred thousand and there was scarcely an organization committed to some liberal goal which did not have some communist representation.

The Nazi–Soviet pact in August 1939 offered striking confirmation that American communist fortunes were hostage to Soviet foreign policy. Within a few months the CPUSA totally reversed its views. Heretofore the most dedicated opponent of fascism, it now professed neutrality in the conflict between fascism and the allies. For several years the most fervent supporter of Franklin Roosevelt, it now denounced him in the most vitriolic and extreme language imaginable. Membership plummeted and would doubtless have continued to do so had not Hitler's invasion of the Soviet Union in 1941 enabled the Party to once again reverse itself and parade under more acceptable banners.

The American–Soviet alliance during World War II allowed the CPUSA to regain some of the ground it had lost after the pact. As the war neared its end, however, and American–Soviet tensions grew, the Party began to revert to a more adversarial position. In 1943 Joseph Stalin had abolished the Comintern in deference to his allies' resentment at an organization formally dedicated to their elimination. Emboldened by Stalin's step and the promise of postwar great power cooperation, Party leader Earl Browder formally dissolved the CPUSA in 1944 and replaced it with a political association designed to work within the two–party system. The Soviet Union, however, sponsored an attack on Browder the following year and he was duly expelled from the reconstituted CPUSA.

The CPUSA remained an important actor in the American political system during the last half of the 1940s and the first part of the 1950s, but mostly as an object of attack. As the Cold War developed, attacks on domestic communists intensified. Over one hundred Party leaders were prosecuted for violating the Smith Act, accused of conspiring to teach and advocate the overthrow of the government by force and violence. A stream of congressional legislation did everything but formally outlaw the Party. Congressional investigations spotlighted hundreds of communists and exposed many to private economic and social sanctions. A series of sensational revelations about Soviet espionage contributed to the odium heaped upon communists.

Not unexpectedly, such pressures took a heavy toll on Party members. In response to government prosecution, the Party sent hundreds of cadres underground to avoid arrest. Those suspected of weaknesses were dropped from the rolls. Thousands more resigned to avoid trouble. By 1956 there were no more than twenty thousand in the Party and it was largely isolated from the American mainstream. As the McCarthy period came to a close, the Communist Party's health got worse, not better. Nikita Khruschev's revelations in 1956 of Stalin's crimes shocked many communists who had refused to believe the same stories told by many other observers for more than twenty years and called into question the moral authority of the Soviet Union. The simultaneous disclosures of Soviet antisemitism and the destruction of Yiddish culture sent shockwaves through the Party's Jewish members. And, finally, the Soviet invasion of Hungary to suppress an indigenous workers' revolution compounded the confusion and demoralization among Party members. An attempt to reform and democratize the Party and move it away from total dependence on the Soviet Union came to naught; most of those sympathetic to reform were so disgusted that they simply quit. By the end of 1958 there were only three thousand Party members.

From this low point the communists had nowhere to go but up. They nonetheless remained a miniscule organization for more than a decade, discredited by their history, tactics and blind adherence to Soviet dogma. The New Left of the 1960s self consciously rejected the old left which the Party had represented. When the New Left moved in the direction of Marxism–Leninism later in the decade, it was attracted not to the stodgy image of the Soviet Union but the more romantic societies of Cuba and China. For its part, the CPUSA kept at arms length from the youth movement and the black power movement, regarding many of their manifestations as anarchic or Maoist. Having seemingly lost its historical chance during the depression, the CPUSA also looked like it had missed the opportunity to take advantage of the radicalism of the 1960s. Dominated by aging veterans of the 1930s, it appeared to be a tired, over–the–hill and dated organization.

While it would be misleading to claim that the CPUSA has made some sort of miraculous recovery or that it has achieved even a fraction of the influence it wielded in the 1930s, it is true that it has made major strides in the past fifteen years. Membership began to increase in the 1970s, partly as a result of the return of some people who had once been Party members and now felt safe rejoining. A trickle of 1960s activists found their way to the Party, some, like Angela Davis, the children of Party members or sympathizers, others convinced that the CPUSA offered a kind of stability lacking in many of the New Left groupings.

1

Party Structure and Strategy

The exact number of Party members is not clear. In the past decade the CPUSA has given wildly varying figures and made improbable claims. Party spokesmen have given figures ranging from fifteen thousand to twenty thousand in the past decade, although in 1979 one Party enthusiast reported, rather improbably that somewhere between thirty thousand and eighty thousand people were members. Most recently, Gus Hall, the Party's general secretary, gave a figure of twenty thousand. Other estimates are considerably lower—and probably more accurate. The FBI, which closely monitors Party activity, estimated that membership was around forty-two hundred in 1975. Party sources told a reporter from one radical publication in 1983 that membership was at its highest level in years—ten thousand.[1]

Much of the Party's growth appears to have come since it held an Extraordinary Party Conference in 1982 that was consciously modeled on a similar gathering held in 1933. The earlier gathering was called in response to the Party's sluggish growth in the face of the depression and concluded with a call to turn the Party's attention to industrial concentration and Party recruitment. The modern gathering came after years of complaints that the CPUSA was not taking advantage of objective opportunities for growth. At its twenty-second convention in Detroit, held in August 1979, for instance, the Party was urged to focus on industrial recruitment and work. "With the present size of the party," went one complaint by the leadership, "there are limitations on what we can do or contribute." Both the Central Committee and Party leaders harped continuously on the theme that it was time for a mass communist party.[2] Four years later, the Party's 23rd convention once again stressed industrial concentration and asserted that with its cadre core in place, it was now ready to become a mass party.[3]

After the Extraordinary Party Conference a thousand new members were recruited, the largest influx since the beginning of the Cold War.

Numerous Party conferences were held and regional Party schools organized.[4] In one key state, Ohio, membership rose by 30 percent in the last half of 1982. Yet, it was still under a thousand, two–thirds of it concentrated in the northeast portion of the state.[5]

What kinds of people are members of the Communist Party? What groups does the Party appeal to? In recent years the CPUSA has not provided a public breakdown of its membership. Some information can be gleaned indirectly from figures that the Party provides about the delegates to its conventions. Most key Party personnel would be delegates and the percentages reported by the Party at least suggest the image of itself that the Party wants to project.

At three recent conventions the number of delegates has ranged from 357 to 426. In 1979 40 percent were women, 24 percent black, 4 percent Chicano, 2 percent Puerto Rican, 2 percent Native American, 1 percent Asian–Pacific Islander; 26 percent workers, 45 percent trade unionists and 53 percent had been in the CPUSA for ten years or less. In 1983 43 percent were women, 17 percent black, 7 percent Chicano, Mexican or Puerto Rican, and 17 percent other racial and ethnic minorities. Twenty-one percent had been Party members for less than 5 years and 32 percent were union members. Thirty-two percent were between the ages of eighteen and thirty-four and 25 percent were over sixty-five. If these figures can be trusted it appears that the Party's gains in recruiting in recent years resulted in a dilution of its black, industrial union base.[6]

The CPUSA regards certain groups as its natural constituency. Marxist–Leninist theory provides that not all potential recruits are equally valuable. The decisive revolutionary class in modern capitalist society is supposed to be the proletariat and the key to the growth and health of a communist party is its success in recruiting members of that class. Additionally, the CPUSA has placed great stress over the years in recruiting blacks, chicanos and other "oppressed minorities" that it contends are central to the American working class. By these criteria, the Party has not been uniformly happy about the nature of its recent growth.

In October 1983 Gus Hall, the Party's general secretary, complained that efforts on "industrial concentration have actually diminished." Many Party clubs did not make such work a priority and limited it to distributing the *Daily World* at plant gates. In fact, the size of the Party in both the auto and steel industries has declined in recent years and in Michigan the industrial concentration policy has been fraught with problems. Hall attributed part of the problem to a tendency in the Party to downplay the class struggle and the role of the working class.[7]

Much of the blame for this state of affairs has been laid on the party clubs. The club is the basic unit of the Party; each member belongs to one. They are supposed to meet every two weeks and direct Party efforts. Vir-

tually all Party clubs are community-based, rather than organized by industry. At the 22nd Convention in 1979 the clubs were indicted as the weak
link in the Party's efforts, accused of often failing to lead struggles. Four
years later there was criticism that they were too much like discussion
groups and not action-oriented. Many clubs were practically invisible due
to members' fears of public exposure as communists.

Those clubs that are active participate in a variety of activities. One
Daily World report on some exemplary clubs noted that one in Pittsburgh
campaigned for a local Consumer Party, one of whose candidates for
county commissioner was in the Young Communist League. A Detroit
club focused its work among the unemployed. It held regular discussion
groups for non-party allies, sent a bulletin with information and its views
on current events to numerous people and regularly distributed the *Daily
World*. A Cleveland club met every two weeks and regularly had eight to
ten people attending. The Simon Bolivar Club in a Mexican neighborhood
in Chicago had been active in the mayoral campaign. The key to a successful communist club, according to Party leaders, is that it "must have
contact with masses."[8]

There are regional and state organizations above the clubs. The Party
also has a Central Committee of 83 members and a National Council of
107. While the Central Committee is technically the directing force of the
Party between conventions, real power is vested in a smaller Political Bureau. A Central Review Commission handles Party discipline.

Party leadership is a combination of aging veterans and some new recruits. Gus Hall has been general secretary and the acknowledged Party
leader since 1959. Born to Finnish immigrants and charter members of the
Communist movement, Hall has been a Party activist since his teens. He is
an alumnus of the Lenin School in Moscow and has held important Party
posts since the 1930s. Henry Winston, the Party's national chairman until
his death late in 1986, was a prominent leader of the Young Communist
League in the 1930s. Other Party leaders include James Jackson, a prominent spokesman on black issues and secretary of the Central Committee
and the Politburo, Arnold Bechetti, national organization secretary and
Sid Taylor, treasurer. Key Party commissions and their chairs include Afro-
American (Charlene Mitchell), Political Action (Si Gerson), Labor (George
Meyers), Economics (Victor Perlo), International Affairs (Lee Dlugin), Jew-
ish Affairs (Lew Moroze). Party leaders in key states include Jarvis Tyner
(New York), Rich Nagin (Ohio), Sam Webb (Michigan), Ted Pearson (Illi-
nois). Those Party leaders identified by the *Daily World* recently as mem-
bers of the Politburo are Hall, Jackson, Mitchell, John Pittman, Helen
Winter, Daniel Rubin, Louis Diskin, Myers, Bechetti, Mike Zagarell and
James West.

Communist Party finances have always been one of the murkier areas of

Party life. Until the 1930s the Soviet Union subsidized various activities. Members' dues did not begin to cover the considerable costs of Party activities even in the 1930s when membership was at its height. The Party raised large amounts of money from wealthy sympathizers and relied on frequent fundraising from within its own ranks.

The Party today provides very little public information about its finances. It reported that its 1984 presidential campaign had cost $500,000 by mid-October. A high-tech drive to modernize the printing equipment of the *Daily World,* conducted in 1983, had a goal of $500,000 and raised $600,000, half of it from non-members.[9] The yearly *Daily World* fundraising drive in 1985 was set at $250,000. The Party has additional financial obligations, ranging from salaries for functionaries to expenses for the activities it undertakes.

Some portion of these expenses are met by dues and contributions. The CPUSA has been exempted from reporting individual contributions to its political campaigns as required by federal law on the grounds that contributors could face harassment. The Party also receives some money from estates of members; in one notable case recently, it decided not to fight for some $700,000 when a dying man changed his will to give his money to relatives. The source of other substantial sums of money is much murkier. The FBI has charged in public testimony that the "KGB has clandestinely transferred funds to the CPUSA."[10] According to one historical account, a top–ranking American party leader, Morris Childs, regularly served as a courier to bring Soviet money to the CPUSA as late as the 1960s.[11]

The Communist Party is committed to the ideals of Marxism–Leninism, including the principle of democratic centralism. In theory, this guarantees full internal democracy and control of leadership by the membership with complete obedience by the members after a decision has been reached. In practice, democratic centralism has led to the withering away of democracy in every Communist Party in the world. The Party leadership is a self–perpetuating oligarchy and does not lightly tolerate dissent from its policies. The CPUSA has, however, had some difficulties in imposing its views on lower Party units. Some have resisted the leadership's policies. In 1975, for example, Gus Hall complained that some "sectarian" comrades were opposed to forming coalitions in unions to help elect insurgent candidates, preferring the purity of opposition.[12] On one occasion, the Party's Auto Commission released an attack on a United Auto Workers' program for dealing with the crisis in the industry. Only after the *Daily World* published the denunciation did Party leaders discover that some members of the commission, including Sam Webb, Party leader in Michigan, had not been consulted about it. An embarrassed Hall admitted that the attack damaged party activities in the UAW and was not fair to the union's proposal.[13] The episode seems to indicate that some Party members are far more militant and confrontational than the Party leaders feel is currently opportune and that the CPUSA occasionally fails to rein in such enthusiasms. On the other hand, many Party clubs have been reluctant or afraid to become too visible and have therefore not taken as public a role as the Party would like.

While the CPUSA trumpets its internal democracy, in fact dissenters rarely survive in the party for very long. During discussions about the Party's basic program, for example, individual clubs are encouraged to submit modifications and changes are made, often to strengthen particular sections or to emphasize a connection that has not been made forcefully enough. Challenges to the Party's core positions, however, are not lightly taken. In December 1973 the Central Committee expelled long-time California Party leaders Al Richmond and Dorothy Healey for their opposition to the Soviet invasion of Czechoslovakia and the principles of democratic centralism.[14] A few years later Peggy Dennis, widow of a former Party general secretary and herself a fifty year Party veteran, resigned with a withering blast at the Party leadership for its treatment of Richmond and Healey. They had been expelled after resigning. Other Party members were removed for associating with excommunists. Dissenting members were not allowed to present their cases to leading Party bodies or given an opportunity to rebut accusations against them.[15]

The Party's struggle to build up its membership faces other obstacles besides the low base from which it operates. The Communist Party remains anathema to most Americans and membership can result in social or economic pressures. One Party recruiting brochure assures prospective members that the Party tries "to guarantee the full privacy and security of every worker" to protect members from reprisals from employers.[16] At Party conventions cameramen and photographers are prevented from obtaining pictures of most ordinary delegates. Many of its members conceal their membership, some because they fear exposure and others for tactical reasons, since they are more effective in their activity if their true allegiance is unknown. Much of the Party's activity takes place in the shadows and it carefully husbands important material that would shed light on its structure and membership.

By itself the CPUSA can hardly hope to achieve a major impact on American life. Its membership is quite small. Its candidates for public office rarely gain more than a minute fraction of the popular vote. Gus Hall has been the Party's candidate for president in the last four elections; his vote totals have gone from 25,595 in 1972 to 58,992 in 1976 to 45,023 in 1980 to 35,561 in 1984. Since numerous states have requirements which effectively debar most third parties from the ballot, the Party insists that its vote underestimates its support. Local Party candidates occasionally draw higher percentages of the vote—one, running against Speaker of the House Tip O'Neill in 1984, got 6 percent—but only a handful of avowed communists have ever been elected to public office in the United States and by any criteria the Party is a minimal electoral force by itself.

Ever since the 1930s the CPUSA has recognized the strength of the two-party system. Like most third parties it has had to balance its distaste for the major parties with its desire to avoid isolation. Since so many of the people whom the Party hopes to attract or to ally itself with, such as blacks or the working class, remain committed to the Democratic Party, the CPUSA has faced a dilemma. If it remains totally opposed to the Democratic Party it risks not only isolation but also charges that it weakens the most "progressive" forces in the Democratic Party by denying them its help. Late in 1987 the Party leadership announced that it would not run a presidential candidate in the 1988 election.

The CPUSA's ultimate goal is a mass Communist Party. That possibility is presently a utopian dream. Its long-term goal is a new leftist anti-monopoly party in which it would have a major role. While it detects signs that such a grouping is in formation, the Party recognizes the need to act in the present. Thus, it has given indirect support to the Democratic Party as the only practical alternative to Reaganism. It should be emphasized that the Democratic Party has not sought or been asked if it wants that support and with few exceptions, most of the support is merely rhetorical. The CPUSA has nonetheless been criticized as reformist by other radical groups because of its willingness to cooperate with some segments of the Democratic Party.

The anti-monopoly party that the CPUSA has in mind is intended to be anti-racist and anti anti-communist, but not necessarily socialist.[17] It would encompass unionists, family farmers, blacks, peace forces, chicanos, the elderly and other groups presumed discontented with or frozen out of the two-party system. While committed to such a party, the CPUSA has not been enthusiastic about the third parties which have arisen in recent years. Gus Hall was critical of the Citizens Party on the grounds that it was a middle-class organization and he denounced John Anderson for his conservatism. On the other hand, he insisted that an anti-monopoly party need not take a stand on socialism since a socialist party— the CPUSA— already exists. It would have to be a coalition of various elements.[18] In the spring of 1985 Gus Hall told a gathering of Party leaders that in the future communists would run for office on "slates organized by left-progressive-communist electoral fronts, as well as on the C.P. ticket."[19] In 1985 the communists organized a People Before Profits ticket for municipal elections in New York City. Although dominated by the CPUSA and led by Jarvis Tyner, it included non-communists.

The CPUSA has persistently denounced the Republican Party as the representative of America's monopolists. In 1976 Gerald Ford was de-nounced as a reactionary while Ronald Reagan was tarred as a fascist. By 1984 Gus Hall fulminated that Reagan was a front man for right-wingers and organizations dominated by "fascist-minded individuals" who had taken over the Republican Party. These forces were entertaining the idea of a "ruling class dictatorship."[20] The Republican Party platform was "the most war-oriented, anti-labor, racist platform in the history of US pol-itics."[21]

The Democratic Party is regarded as only marginally better. It is al-legedly dominated by servants of monopoly capital and filled with enemies of detente. In 1976 the Party harshly attacked Jimmy Carter as a racist fronting for George Wallace.[22] Nonetheless, there are two factors which led the CPUSA to view the Democratic Party as the lesser of two evils in 1984 and persuaded it to offer at least indirect support. First, the Party's the-oretical journal argued that the Republican ultraright was "creating the atmosphere in which fascist ideas germinate and grow." A Reagan victory would strengthen these forces and their anti-democratic views. This helped to persuade the Party that the real competitors in the 1984 election were not Reagan and Mondale but monopoly capital and its enemies.[23]

The second factor leading to a more benign view of the Democratic Party was the belief that the core of a genuine anti-monopoly people's party was coalescing within it and the CPUSA could not afford to isolate itself from this development. Gus Hall argued that the CPUSA had no illusions that the Democratic Party could become a progressive organization but that most people the Party wished to attract to an anti-monopoly party still believed that it offered a viable alternative. Since the CPUSA did not wish to break with its putative allies, it respected their decision.[24]

At its 1982 Extraordinary Conference the CPUSA, while reaffirming its belief in the strategy of an anti-monopoly party, called for the tactics of an all-people's front to defeat Reagan. This involved a recognition that even an anti-monopoly position was unrealistic and that some monopolists and their allies were opposed to the administration. This theoretical twist al-lowed the CPUSA to regard a coalition with the Democratic Party as positive step.[25]

The core of that anti-monopoly party that so mesmerized the CPUSA was clearly the Rainbow Coalition of Jesse Jackson. The *Daily World* had welcomed the Jackson candidacy, "whatever weaknesses he may have," because of his positions and the impact it would have on the growth of an independent party.[26] Angela Davis saw the platform demands made by Jackson playing a "historic role in moving the candidates in a more pro-gressive direction."[27]

While the CPUSA was enthusiastic about Jackson's candidacy, it was reluctant to denounce Walter Mondale, the frontrunner for the nomination, as totally inadequate, since he was the man around whom the Party believed the anti-Reagan people's front would have to coalesce. At the Party's 23rd convention in November 1983, a resolution from the floor urged Party members to try to get their union locals to endorse Jackson. it was defeated after opposition from the Party leadership but received a large number of votes.[28] Several communists and Party sympathizers played key roles in Jackson's campaign, including Kevin Mercadel, the CP's Harlem organizer, and Anne Braden of the Southern Organizing Committee for Economic and Social Justice.[29]

The Party thus ran its own presidential ticket in the elections but insisted that the most important goal was the defeat of Reagan—an implicit admission that the lesser evil was the election of Walter Mondale. Party spokesmen offered various rationalizations for this seeming contradiction, noting that the communist vote had never yet made a difference in a national election and that the Hall-Davis ticket would not drain votes away from the Democrats. On the other hand, they asserted, by pressuring the Democrats from the left, the communists prevented them from moving towards Reagan, forced sharper attention to the real issues and hence contributed to Reagan's defeat.[30]

For the communists the virtues of this posture were that it enabled the Party to claim victory no matter what happened. If Reagan had lost the election, the communists could claim to have contributed to his downfall. When he won, they insisted that Mondale's rout was a consequence of his trying to ape Reagan. But even the massive Reagan landslide did not dismay the CPUSA. In November 1983 Gus Hall rashly declared that "without question he'll (Reagan) be defeated."[31] He also predicted that in one year, the American people would be celebrating a great victory or "they will be miserable and in mourning over an unthinkable four more deadly years of ruinous Reaganism."[32] Yet, Hall interpreted the Reagan landslide to mean "no swing to the right and no new political realignment." Reagan's victory had occured because people perceived that the presidency was a figurehead and that real power now lay with Congress.[33] After years of dire warnings about the consequences of the president's reelection, the CPUSA optimistically decided that it did not matter. In a post-election report to the Party's Central Committee, Hall admitted that the results were a "setback" but saw no swing to the right. At the same meeting Henry Winston gave the CPUSA credit for blocking a big right-wing victory through its "all-out mobilization" prior to election day.[34]

The CPUSA's extraordinary optimism about its tactics and strategy is linked to its equally optimistic assessment about the failure of capitalism. Ever since its founding more than sixty years ago, the CPUSA has been predicting the imminent demise of capitalism. With the exception of a few short interludes, it has seen every economic downturn as a confirmation of the inherent instability of the system and minimized recoveries as merely temporary and incomplete reversals. In communist eyes, American capitalism in the past decade has been in one long crisis.

Current Party doctrine holds that the US economy has entered a new phase of development in recent years, "a phase of contraction and decline." To the general crisis of world capitalism, there has been added a structural crisis caused by advanced technology which has devastated old industries in the Frostbelt. On top of this the CPUSA also perceives a cyclical crisis caused by the gap between productive capacity and workers' purchasing power.[35]

As the crisis of capitalism deepens, the communists believe, the class struggle in the United States will continue to heat up. As it does, the role of unions in transforming American capitalism will once again become crucial. True to the tenets of Marxism, the CPUSA has always seen trade unions and their members as the essential element in any fundamental transformation of capitalism.

For years, the Party has deplored the "reactionary" and anti-communist role played by the AFL-CIO. In the mid-1970s Gus Hall lamented that despite the "objective conditions" which favored union militancy, trade union leaders were the worst "mob of totally case-hardened reactionary toadying bootlickers" he had ever seen; they were "more completely class-collaborationist, racist, red-baiting and corrupt than any in the history of the AFL-CIO."[36] By 1976, however, the greater willingness of unions to participate in Democratic Party politics, the death of George Meany and a growing militancy among some union officials and staffers increased Party hopes that the union movement would become more amenable to cooperation.

The Party has focused its efforts on creating a Center-Left coalition in the union movement, an alliance similar to the one it believes existed in the 1940s in the CIO between Phil Murray and the communist-led unions. The Left would incude such unions as the United Electrical Workers and the West Coast longshoremen, in both of which the CPUSA has long enjoyed some influence. The center would encompass unions ranging from the United Auto Workers and the Machinists to the American Federation of State, County and Municipal Workers (AFSCME) unions generally regarded as being on the left of the AFL-CIO. By 1979 Hall saw the growth of a healthy left-wing sector in the unions and the explosive growth of center forces breaking away from the worst forms of class-collaboration such as anti-communism. The center forces were often tainted by their backward position on such issues as working in the Democratic Party, or racism. The left, meanwhile, was often impatient with compromise and susceptible to the blandishments of the "phony left"—small Maoist or Trotskyist sects. Nonetheless, the CPUSA saw great promise for the future in the growth of these two tendencies.[37]

One of the constants of communist policy throughout the world has always been its stress on creating or capturing organizations with specific goals. For every person willing to join a Communist Party, there are dozens who are willing to join an organization devoted to some worthy end, be it peace or civil rights or economic justice or the advancement of some particular group. If these organizations can be controlled by communists they can advance the Party's program far more effectively than the Party itself since they do not carry an open communist stigma. The Party has called such organizations, largely composed of non-communists but controlled by the Party, mass organizations or auxiliaries or transmission belts. Less charitable observers have called them fronts.

To further its aims over the years, the CPUSA has created numerous front groups. Nominally independent, they help the Party to reach out to non-communists and to overcome its isolation. People who would find it politically inexpedient or risky to embrace the Communist Party can embrace the more protected front group. On the other hand, the fronts can also be useful in helping to ensnare people innocent of the group's true committments and loyalties. The significance of the CPUSA in American political life today derives from its ability to operate successful fronts, since the Party itself remains a pariah in most circles.

For years the Party was isolated from the American labor movement. In the late 1940s the CIO had expelled communist-dominated unions from its ranks and most of them had withered away. The merged AFL-CIO was fiercely anti-communist. Many of the staunchest anti-communists were socialists and ex-socialists like Walter Reuther who carried the scars of many a battle with communists for control of their own unions. George Meany was adamantly opposed to communists; his advisor on international affairs, Jay Lovestone, was himself the one-time leader of the American Communist Party who had been deposed by Stalin.

In the last decade the CPUSA has made modest strides in the labor movement. One of its long-time front organizations, the Labor Research Association (LRA), has played a key role in this emergence. LRA was founded in the 1920s by Grace Hutchins, Anna Rochester, Solon DeLeon, Alexander Trachtenberg and Robert Dunn, all communists. It put out an annual labor fact book that endorsed whatever the current party line happened to be.[38] *Economic Notes*, LRA's monthly publication, today avoids crude communist propaganda and poses as a disinterested research organization. One editorial declared that "as a research and educational institution servicing US trade unions, LRA has no sectarian interest."[39] Nonetheless it supports Party positions and expounds Party analyses, often without identifying them as such. A lead article in one issue by Victor Perlo, the Party's chief economist, omits mention of his affiliation.[40] One entire issue devoted to the dangers of nuclear war blames the United States for the arms race and denies that the Soviet Union poses any danger to America. The American government is taxed with opposing all the constructive efforts made by the Soviet Union to achieve peace.[41]

LRA apparently believes that whatever economic problems exist in the world are due to capitalist depredations. In the Soviet Union, where there is public ownership of industry "unemployment and poverty do not exist."[42] At one LRA-sponsored meeting James Pinto, Director of Coordinated Bargaining of the International Association of Machinists complained that US-based multinational banks prefer to give loans to dictatorial governments because they are regarded as more stable. The report of Pinto's speech suggested that neither he nor his fellow-conferees had Poland in mind.[43]

After a long period of isolation, the LRA has been able in recent years to attract leading trade unionists to its dinners and conferences. By avoiding explicit identification with the Communist Party and camouflaging its true colors, it has been able to gain support that would never be given otherwise. For example, in December 1982, LRA held a banquet to honor the Congressional Black Caucus. Eight hundred people attended, including six congressmen, six members of the New York State legislature and three city council members. Thirty unions were represented. Among the speakers were Frank Chapman of the National Alliance Against Racism and Repression, another Party-dominated organization, Fred Dube, representing the African National Congress (he became a controversial figure because of his course at SUNY-Stony Brook which depicted Zionism as a form of racism), and Representative John Conyers, who gave the major address.[44]

The sponsors of an LRA event in 1983 illustrated LRA's new respectability and its ability to hide its origins. They included a number of major union officials and politicians. Additional sponsors were long-time Party stalwarts Jane Benedict, Angela Davis, Ernest DeMaio, Fred Gaboury and Esther Jackson.[45] Many of the same people were sponsors of LRA's 1985 Labor Awards Luncheon, leading Greg Tarpinian to boast that "no similar function attracts so much active support from such a broad array of labor and political leaders."[46]

LRA has also sponsored two conferences on the need for trade union unity against multinational corporations. The first one, held in New York in June 1982 included among the sponsors a number of prominent trade union officials.

LRA also runs labor education classes in conjunction with the Coalition of Black Trade Unionists and the Coalition of Labor Union Women. One example of LRA's activities in the organized labor movement is that the Iowa Federation of Labor sent free copies of *Economic Notes* to all state legislators for three months in 1983.[47] Gregory Tarpinian is LRA's director and editor of its newsletter, *Economic Notes.*

A newer Party front group is Trade Unionists for Action and Democracy (TUAD), which was founded in 1970. One Party journalist admitted that "communists, in unity with other left forces, supported the founding" in unity with other left forces, supported the founding" at a Chicago conference that drew nine hundred people.[48] Its goal was to build a united front with non-party workers, but in 1974 George Meyers, the Party's labor czar, complained that it was floundering in several key cities because of its isolation from local unions, involvement in united fronts with small left sects and the tendency of Party units to ignore it.[49] Its leaders have included Rayfield Mooty, Fred Gaboury and Bill Scott. In 1981 its co-chairmen were Lew Moye, a St. Louis auto worker, and Lance Cohn, a Chicago teacher. It publishes *Labor Today.*

Another focus of Party effort is the publication of shop papers, issued to workers in a given plant or industry. *Bullseye* has been given to workers at the US Repeating Arms Corporation in New Haven for thirteen years. Other papers put out by local clubs include the *Jefferson Worker* in Detroit, *Fightback* in St. Louis and *Chrysler Worker* in Warren, all distributed at Chrysler plants, the *LTV Steelworker* in Chicago, *Common Sense* for Cleveland teachers, and *Flightline* for Boeing workers in Seattle.[50]

Notes

1. For a variety of Party claims see the *Saturday Review World,* February 23, 1974, *Wall Street Journal,* October 29, 1976, *New York Times,* January 25, 1979, August 25, 1979, February 27, 1981, *Washington Post* October 19, 1984. The FBI estimate is in the *Christian Science Monitor,* July 25, 1975. See also Walter and Miriam Schneir, "The Socialist Workers: Square Target of the FBI," *Nation,* September 25, 1976 and *Frontline,* November 28, 1983.
2. "Draft Main Political Resolution [II]," *Political Affairs,* June 1979; Arnold Bechetti, "CPUSA Convention—A Signal Event," *Political Affairs,* November 1979.
3. *Frontline,* November 28, 1983.
4. Arnold Bechetti, "Communists Are Working-Class Activists," *Political Affairs,* December 1983.
5. *Cincinnati Enquirer,* January 3, 1983.
6. Bechetti, "CPUSA Convention"; John Pittman, "For Peace, Jobs, and Equality," *World Marxist Review,* February 1984.
7. Gus Hall, "Industrial Concentration: Our Constant Course," *Political Affairs,* November 1983.

8. *Daily World,* October 27, 1983.
9. *Daily World,* November 17, 1983.
10. *FBI Oversight and Authorization,* Hearings Before the Subcommittee on Security and Terrorism, Senate Committee on the Judiciary, 98th Congress, 1st Session, February 2, 1983, p. 36.
11. David Garrow, *The FBI and Dr. Martin Luther King Jr.* (New York: Norton, 1981), pp. 35-43.
12. Gus Hall, "On Mass Movements," *Political Affairs,* January 1975.
13. *Daily World,* July 21, 1983; Hall, "Industrial Concentration," *op. cit.*
14. *Daily World,* January 10, 1974.
15. Peggy Dennis, *The Autobiography of an American Communist* (Westport: Lawrence Hill, 1977).
16. *Join Us to Build A Better USA,* Communist Party, 1984.
17. *Daily World,* July 1, 1975.
18. Gus Hall, "The Challenge of the 1980 Elections," *Political Affairs,* December 1979; "Critical Issues of the 1980 Campaign," *Political Affairs,* July 1980. Hall also noted that some of those active in the Citizens Party got "their political training in the Communist Party."
19. *Daily World,* June 6, 1985.
20. Gus Hall, *The New Danger: Reaganism's Alliance with Ultra-Right and Fascist Forces* (Hall-Davis Campaign '84). Among the extremist groups that Hall identified as having captured the Republican convention was the American Political Science Association.
21. *New York Times,* September 23, 1984.
22. *Daily World,* April 10, 1976, and October 14, 1976.
23. "Reaganism and Extremism— A New Threat," *Political Affairs,* October 1984.
24. Gus Hall, "1984 Elections: The Final Lap," *Political Affairs,* July 1984.
25. *Daily World,* December 27, 1984.
26. *Daily World,* November 4, 1983.
27. *New York Times,* August 19, 1984.
28. *Frontline,* November 28, 1983.
29. Manning Marable, "Jackson and the Rise of the Rainbow Coalition," *New Left Review,* January-February 1985.
30. *Daily World,* April 4, 1984.
31. *Frontline,* November 28, 1983.
32. *Daily World,* November 17, 1983.
33. *Daily World,* November 9, 1984.
34. *Daily World,* December 20, 1984.
35. Pittman, "For Peace, Jobs, and Equality," *World Marxist Review,* February 1984.
36. *Daily World,* July 20, 1974.
37. Gus Hall, "Class Struggle is the Pivot," *Political Affairs,* October 1979; Bechetti, "CPUSA Convention," op. cit.
38. Harvey Klehr, *The Heyday of American Communism: The Depression Decade* (New York: Basic Books, 1984), p. 476n.
39. "Editorial," *Economic Notes,* July-August 1982.
40. Victor Perlo, "The Reagan Budget," *Economic Notes,* March 1983.
41. See *Economic Notes* for June 1983.
42. Ibid.
43. James Pinto, "From Conference Reports," *Economic Notes,* July-August 1982.

44. "LRA Honors Black Caucus," *Economic Notes,* December 1982.
45. *Daily World,* September 29, 1983.
46. *Economic Notes,* January 1986.
47. *Economic Notes,* April 1983.
48. George Morris, "Sixty Years of Communist Trade Union Work," *Political Affairs,* August-September 1979.
49. *Daily World,* June 28, 1975, George Meyers, "Build the Rank-and-File Movement," *Political Affairs,* August 1974.
50. *Daily World,* January 16, 1986.

2

International Affairs and Peace

Ever since its beginnings the CPUSA has been a faithful handmaiden of Soviet policies. For more than sixty years the Party has looked to the USSR as the model of a socialist society and a guide to the policies it ought to pursue. The CPUSA has removed leaders who incurred Soviet displeasure and it has altered its views to accomodate changes in Soviet foreign policy. Those who have criticized Soviet policy have been unable to remain in the CPUSA; those who remain are cheerleaders for every twist and turn in the foreign and even domestic policy of another nation.

The CPUSA is not bashful about its loyalty to the Soviet Union. On one of his frequent visits there in 1976, Gus Hall proudly averred that the Soviet Communist Party "serves as the working pattern for the revolutionary movements throughout the world."[1] Hall has admitted that the Party's close association with the USSR causes political problems in the United States but has insisted that it would be opportunistic to surrender to anti-Sovietism.

The schisms and debates in the world communist movement during the past two decades have largely bypassed the CPUSA. Maoism and Eurocommunism have both been bluntly condemned and denounced in no uncertain terms. There does not seem to have been a lenghty or robust internal debate about either one. A small group of Maoists were expelled from the CPUSA in the early 1960s. The CPUSA has steadfastly denounced Maoism for both domestic and foreign heresies, the most serious being its hostility to the Soviet Union. The Party's 21st convention in 1975 endorsed a Soviet-sponsored call for convening all Communist parties to read China out of the world movement.[2]

Unlike many European Communist Parties that have criticized various aspects of Soviet policy, the CPUSA demanded adherence to "proletarian internationalism." Hall denounced Spanish Communist leader Santiago Carillo for slandering the Soviet Union and accused him of abandoning Marxism-Leninism.[3] He also castigated the French and Italian communists who had the temerity to criticize the USSR for its activities in Poland and Afghanistan. In the real world, Hall lectured them, there were only two sides—the Soviet Union and the imperialists.[4]

Both Gus Hall and the CPUSA have been faithful to that credo. No Soviet action is too unseemly to prevent the CPUSA from defending it. Soviet attacks on dissidents have been justified, defended and even applauded. After Soviet police broke up an abstract art show, Hall noted that "a socialist society has the right to ask its artists in every field to reflect the reality of that society and to enrich and inspire" its people. He did admit that attaining correct guidelines was a problem but his argument accepted the right of a socialist state—but not a capitalist one—to impose requirements of both form and method on art.[5] The *Daily World* justified the deportation of Alexander Solzhenitsyn on the grounds that he was an instrument of cold warriors anxious to sabotage detente.[6] Talking to the bourgeois media, Gus Hall allowed that he privately thought it wrong to expel the writer (and that Soviet Jews should be allowed to emigrate) but that the CPUSA avoided taking a position on these issues because they involved internal Soviet practices.[7] Those who criticize Soviet human rights policies are accused of being motivated by a desire to poison relations between the two countries.[8]

The CPUSA admits, in general terms, that there are problems in the Soviet Union. The Party denies, however, that they are systemic. Victor Perlo argued that the USSR is dealing with the difficulties of the transition from the early stages of socialism to building an advanced socialist economy. While America's problems were those of a system in decline, Russia's were those of a system of growth.[9] The Party's logic is exactly the same as when it defended each and every one of Joseph Stalin's crimes; by definition, what the Soviet Union does is progressive and in the interests of mankind.

By the same criteria, the CPUSA supports the policies of Soviet allies and proxies. The Party applauded the collapse of the South Vietnamese government and supported the brutal and genocidal Pol Pot regime in Cambodia—until the Cambodians fell out with the Soviet-backed Vietnamese, at which point it praised Vietnam for saving Cambodia from the horrors of Pol Pot. When several well-known anti-Vietnam war activists criticized the Vietnamese government for its barbaric human rights violations, the CPUSA denounced them and praised the regime for conducting one of the "most tolerant, even gentle" revolutions in history.[10] Cuban troops "help safeguard" Angola's freedom.[11] South Korea is a "terrorist dictatorship" while North Korea is "one of the most advanced and progressive of Asian states."[12] Charter 77, the democratic rights group repressed by the Czech government, was actually an effort by outsiders to interfere in internal Czech politics.[13] The Soviet invasion of Afghanistan was not an invasion; criticisms by the Carter administration were lies on a scale not seen "since Hitler and Goebbels."[14]

In a 1984 interview with the *New York Times*, Gus Hall insisted that the CPUSA had originally welcomed the Polish Solidarity movement as a positive step.[15] In fact, in a 1980 interview with the *Washington Post* Hall had criticized the Polish Party leadership for failing to explain adequately to Polish workers what sacrifices were required of them and for having become bureaucratic. He explained the rise of Solidarity as a result of the unwillingness of many workers to endure current sacrifices to achieve future benefits.[16] Hall was far harsher in his assessment of Solidarity given to members of the CPUSA. In a report to the Party he charged that from the union's very beginning, its leaders made unrealistic demands the economy could not meet and that "forces of counterrevolution" had very quickly gained control. "Any objective observer," Hall noted, "and certainly any partisan of socialism, could see that martial law was a necessary emergency step" to prevent the country's destabilization. "The fact that many Polish people, including workers, were misled, does not in any way change what the real stakes were." Hall used the same moral double-bookkeeping the Party always employs to judge communist regimes; there is a clear difference between martial law "to preserve and secure a socialist, working-class society" and martial law used by capitalists on behalf of "exploitation, racism and oppression."[17]

Few American policies or allies receive the benefit of similar evaluations. Since the Party regards the belief that the Soviet Union is a threat to American interests as a fabrication, it is hard to see what American policies short of unilateral disarmament and abandonment of all allies would find much favor. In the mid-1970s the Party did enthusiastically support detente but it understood the concept quite differently from most Americans. To the CPUSA detente was "a special form of the class struggle, not its negation, not its abandonment."[18] It had been forced on the United States because of this country's deteriorating position; it represented "a further shift in the balance of world forces against imperialism."[19] Opponents of detente, then, were regarded as particularly dangerous because they opposed this altered balance of power; they included defense contractors, Zionists, reactionary union leaders and right-wing Social Democrats.[20] When the CPUSA urges a return to detente, it is in effect arguing for American recognition of its decreasing influence in the world.

There is no issue to which the CPUSA has been more attentive in recent years than peace. Since its founding the Soviet Union has feared Western intervention and local communist parties have accorded defense of the Soviet Union their highest priority. Since they believe that the Soviet

Union is a peace-loving nation with no illegitimate demands on any other country as a matter of faith, communists have insisted that it poses no threat to any other peace-loving nation. Blaming the western nations for the post-World War II tension in Europe and for colonialism and imperialism, communists have insisted that the main obstacle to peace lies in the West and, particularly, in the United States.

The CPUSA, like other communist parties, has always made a distinction between its work for peace and pacifism. Communists have insisted that they support certain kinds of wars. During the 1930s, the American League Against War and Fascism, a major Party front, made clear its opposition only to imperialist wars and its endorsement of the class war and the war against Nazism. More recently, Arthur Zipser, a Party spokesman, noted that the CPUSA supported just wars—those of liberation, revolutionary wars, wars against fascism and wars "designed to achieve and preserve socialism."[21] It opposes, in short, wars fought by the United States (except for World War II) and it supports wars fought by the Soviet Union, such as those in Czechoslavakia in 1968, Hungary in 1956 or Afghanistan in recent years.

Consistent with this worldview, the CPUSA places virtually all blame for world tensions and the arms race on the United States. The main political resolution at its 1979 convention asserted that "the primary cause of the insane arms race is US imperialism" which seeks "to stop and throw back the world revolutionary process by military means."[22] Henry Winston insisted that views of the USSR as a superpower that challenges America's true interests are "monstrous lies."[23] Another Party leader, Jim West, chided the peace movement for failing to realize that "there can be no successful fight to drastically cut military spending without debunking and burying the big lie of 'Soviet menace.'"[24]

As is readily apparent, the Party does not shrink from openly defending Soviet interests. Bruce Kimmel, its representative on one peace coalition, charged that it was the "Reagan administration, not the Soviet Union (which) threatens the survival of humanity." By "struggling for peace," communists are working in the interests of the Soviet Union as well as those of the American people.[25]

The Party's position on peace at any given moment, then, can be inferred from the particular needs of Soviet foreign policy. In the last several years, the Party has given major emphasis to opposing the installation of Pershing and cruise missiles in Europe and to denouncing and deriding the Reagan administration for its Strategic Defense Initiative. In contrast to those in the peace movement who also criticize the Soviet Union, the CPUSA regards the Soviets as blameless victims of rapacious America.

Much of the Party's work in the field of peace is conducted under the auspices of the United States Peace Council (USPC). Founded in 1978, it did not become active until the following year. Since then, it has initiated a flurry of activities and has been indefatigable in supporting Soviet peace initiatives and defending Soviet positions in the peace movement.

The USPC is the American branch of the World Peace Council, one of the largest and most active of Soviet front groups. Michael Myerson, the USPC's executive director, once denied that his group was an affiliate of the WPC. In an angry "Open Letter" to the American peace movement attacking those who had "red-baited" the USPC, he emphatically and specifically denied any formal connection between the two. On the other hand, some of the USPC's flyers note that the USPC is "associated" with the WPC. Moreover, at the USPC's founding conference in 1979, Myerson told a reporter from the *Daily World* that there had been great pressure on the USPC not to affiliate with the WPC. The story noted that the group "is affiliated with the World Peace Council and is the first national peace organization in this country to do so."[26] At its Fourth National Conference in 1985 the USPC passed a resolution expressing pride in being "part of the great movement for world peace and social justice" represented by the WPC.[27]

The World Peace Council traces its origin to a 1949 meeting in Paris; it took its present name in 1950. At first headquartered in France, the WPC was expelled by the government in 1951 and migrated first to Prague and then Vienna. Austria banned it in 1957. Its offices have been in Helsinki since 1968.

Organized on a national basis with affiliates in some 135 countries, the WPC has an intricate organizational structure. It is headed by a Council of some sixteen hundred people that meets every three years, usually at the same time as its mass congresses or assemblies. A Presidential Committee, elected by the Council, runs the WPC in the interim. It, in turn, chooses a Secretariat, or executive body, with some 146 members. Several Americans sit on these bodies. Four—Carleton Goodlet, Saundra Graham, James Jackson and Frank Rosen—were recent members of the Presidential Committee. Goodlet is a black newspaper publisher long associated with Party causes, Graham is vice-mayor of Cambridge, Massachusetts, Jackson is a leading black communist and Rosen is a regional president of the United Electrical Workers. Until his death, Abe Feinglass, a labor leader also long associated with Party causes, was one of twenty-six vice-presidents. Karen Talbott, formerly a writer for the *People's World*, the CP's West Coast newspaper, was until recently a member of the Secretariat. She was replaced by Rob Prince, formerly active in the Colorado Communist Party. The Reverend Ralph Abernathy, former head of the Southern Christian Leadership Conference, is one of a handful of Presidents of Honor.

The WPC includes both communists and non-communists among its leaders. The very essence of a front group is that it be broader than a Party organization. Nonetheless, the WPC faithfully and consistently supports Soviet policies.

The State Department contends that the WPC is controlled by the Central Committee of the CPSU via its International Department run by Boris Ponomarev. An International Social Organizations sector of that department is under the supervision of Vitaly Shaposhnikov, who also happens to be a member of the WPC's Presidential Committee. While the WPC claims to be financed by individuals and national peace committees, most of its money appears to come from the Soviet Union. When the organization made a bid for an upgrading of its status as a consulting non-governmental organization with the United Nations Economic and Social Council in 1981, it was forced to withdraw after Western nations demanded a full audit of its finances. The UN group concluded that the WPC received large-scale support from Soviet-bloc governments. The Soviet Peace Fund, an ostensibly non-governmental source of WPC funds, is financed by "donations" of a day's wages by Soviet workers.[28]

In one important sense, controversy over how the Soviet Union controls the WPC or from where it gets its money is beside the point. There is no better proof of its fidelity to the Soviet cause than the positions it has taken over the years. Whether the Soviet Union pulls the strings, making the WPC a puppet, or whether WPC leaders simply mimic Soviet policies is largely irrelevant. The organization's avowed goals are ending the arms race, eliminating colonialism and discrimination, noninterference of nations in the internal affairs of other nations, peaceful coexistence and other worthy aims. In practice, it has defended the Soviet invasions of Hungary, Czechoslavakia and Afghanistan, Soviet placement of missiles in Cuba, and Soviet military and diplomatic policies around the globe. It attacks NATO but not the Warsaw Pact. Even so harsh a critic of American policies as E.P. Thompson of Great Britain has attacked the WPC's strategy of "opposing NATO militarism only."[29]

In 1975 the president of the WPC, Romesh Chandra, who has served on the Central Committee of the pro-Moscow Indian Communist Party, explained the WPC's policies by noting that the USSR supported peace and "the World Peace Council in its turn positively reacts to all Soviet initiatives in international affairs."[30] Late in 1984 one of the WPC's organs, *Peace Courier,* explained that there was no arms race but an "arms chase, with the United States pursuing increasingly dangerous plans for nuclear superiority" and the Soviets trying only to catch up.[31] Despite protests by some Western European communists, the WPC has never condemned human rights violations in orthodox communist countries; it has not hesitated to denounce Northern Ireland, Chile, South Africa, El Salvador and, especially, Israel, for their alleged or real offenses against human rights.

The extent to which the WPC is in thrall to the Soviet view of the world is also obvious from its gyrations over the years. After the Cominform expelled Yugoslavia in 1949 the WPC expelled its Yugoslav representatives. After the Sino-Soviet split, the WPC attacked China—by 1979 Chandra was complaining that "the NATO powers and their Chinese allies are carrying out new aggression and intervention" against the peoples of the world.[32] Although Andrei Sakharov sent a letter to the WPC forum on disarmament in 1976 with the request that it be read to the delegates, it was ignored. When non-communists raised questions about Soviet human-rights violations in 1977, the official reports of the conference did not even mention that the questions had been raised. Two months after the Soviet invasion of Afghanistan, the WPC issued a statement supporting the invasion.[33]

In recent years the WPC has directed much of its effort to fighting American military and strategic policy. It mounted a major campaign aganist the neutron bomb and took credit for helping to halt its production. It fervently opposed the installation of Pershing and cruise missiles in Europe and has also supported a freeze on production and deployment of nuclear weapons, adoption of the no-first-use doctrine on nuclear weapons and creation of nuclear-free zones.

Despite its unabashedly pro-Soviet views the WPC has managed to generate some support in the United States. Some prominent Americans have lent their respectability to its activities. For example, the Reverend Joseph Lowery, head of the Southern Christian Leadership Conference, spoke at the WPC's World Assembly for Peace and Life, Against Nuclear War, held in 1983 in Prague. The gathering was a propaganda exercise on behalf of the Soviet bloc. Charter 77 dissidents were banned, young Czechs trying to rally in support of them were arrested and television crews from the West attempting to film interviews with dissidents were roughed up by police. Among the 175 American delegates were a number of open communists and representatives from such Party fronts as the Women for Racial and Economic Equality (WREE) and the National Council of American-Soviet Friendship. But also present were Maggie Kuhn, head of the Grey Panthers (a member of the steering committee), Dwight Bowman, of the American Federation of Government Employees, Robert Chrisman, editor of the *Black Scholar*, David Brower, of Friends of the Earth, and two city council members from Detroit.

The World Peace Council has also been able to induce or entice a number of congressmen to some of its activities in the United States. Its most successful venture came in 1978 when the WPC held a "Dialogue on

Disarmament and Detente" in Washington D.C. Not only was a National Committee to host the WPC delegation able to enlist such labor leaders as William Winpisinger, president of the International Association of Machinists, and Charles Hayes and Abe Feinglass of the Amalgamated Meat Cutters (among others), but it also included Congressman Ron Dellums who told participants that they "give us courage and inspiration in our fight for disarmament and against the neutron bomb." Among the other members of Congress participating were Dymally (California), and Fauntroy (Washington, DC).[34]

Another WPC offshoot, the International Liason Forum, which shared the same president and secretary (Chandra and Talbot), sponsored the Third Vienna Dialogue for Disarmament and Detente in January 1985. The participants endorsed a wide range of proposals, most of them condemning the United States and its allies for various offenses against world peace, supporting Soviet-backed liberation movements, and discussing tactics for influencing Western governments and public opinion. The American delegation included five people holding posts in the Rainbow Coalition, including the Reverend Jesse Jackson and Jack O'Dell, a former high-ranking official in the CPUSA. Other members of the delegation included Joan Willoughby, chief of staff for Congressman Crockett, Reverend Richard McSorley of Pax Christi, Lyle Wing, co-chair of the National Executive Committee, Nuclear Weapons Freeze Campaign, Jean Carey Bond, editor of *Freedomways,* John Black, vice-president of the Hospital and Health Workers Union, and Karen Jefferson, co-chair of the Southern Africa Support Project. Jackson's speech to this communist-controlled gathering attacked "our adversaries who profit from war, racism and the deprivations of colonialism." While intensely critical of American policies, the text of his remarks does not indicate any criticism of the Soviet Union or its policies, in keeping with the thrust of the entire gathering.[35]

The essence of a front organization, or course, is that its members include non-communists. The rationale is that a group made up only of devoted communists and their close allies would lack credibility and effectiveness; its motives would be suspect. By lending their names and reputations to an organization, respectable people make the organization look respectable. However minor a part the WPC did play in the peace movement, some prominent Americans were rather undiscriminating about the company they kept and the causes they endorsed—assuming that few of them do accept the view that the Soviet Union is blameless and the United States entirely responsible for the arms race, that the Soviet Union has the right to invade other countries and the United States does not or that Soviet apologists masquerading as peace advocates do not harm the peace movement.

The activities of the WPC's offspring, the USPC, provide further confirmation of the point. The leadership of the USPC is firmly in communist hands. The executive director since its founding in 1979 has been Michael Myerson, a member of the Central Committee of the CPUSA.[36]

A key figure in the USPC until her death in the crash of a Cuban Airlines flight from Havana to Nicaragua in January 1985 was Sandy Pollack. In addition to serving as Solidarity Coordinator and Treasurer for the USPC, Pollack was a member of the Party's National Council and served on its International and Peace and Solidarity Commissions. Nor did she limit her activities to the USPC. She was active in movements on behalf of Nicaragua, El Salvador, Grenada, Puerto Rican independence and Chile. An indefatigable organizer, Pollack had been a full-time staff member for the June 12, 1982 nuclear freeze demonstration in New York, organizer of the American delegation to the WPC's 1982 World Assembly for Peace in Prague and, at the time of her death, was helping to organize the April 20, 1985 march in Washington. Thirty-six years old, from a radical family, she had been a member of SDS before joining the Young Workers Liberation League, the Party's youth arm. She joined the CPUSA in 1968, visited Cuba for the first time in 1969 and later served on the National Committee of the Venceremos Brigade. She was also a co-founder of the Tri-Continental News Service which distributed Cuban and revolutionary Latin American writing in the United States. Pollack's contacts and influence in the peace movement were evident at a memorial service held for her at the Riverside Church. A thousand people attended. Among the speakers were Party leaders Henry Winston and Helen Winter; Myerson; Gus Newport of Berkeley, a leader of the USPC; and Leslie Cagan, a leader of Mobilization for Survival. Congressman Rob Dellums sent a condolence message lauding her "legacy of commitment and courage." Reverend William Sloane Coffin noted that "Sandy may not have believed in God but God sure believed in Sandy."[37]

One of the vice-chairs of USPC, Rob Prince, has been the Communist Party's district organizer in Colorado. Several Party members also serve on the Executive Board. Most USPC officials, however, are not publicly identified as communists. The co-chairs have included Sandra Graham, a state representative in Massachusetts; Gus Newport, former mayor of Berkeley; Frank Rosen, an officer in the United Electrical Workers; Sara Staggs, executive director of the Chicago Peace Council; and Mark Solomon, a history professor at Simmons College. By 1983 there were fifty functioning chapters and another twenty to twenty-five germinating.[38]

Myerson insisted at its Third National Conference that the USPC "is not a pro-Soviet organization" and that there are differing "views of how Soviet society conducts itself" within the organization. Some people in the leadership, he insisted, are even procapitalist. What allegedly unites the USPC is that its members know that the Soviets want peace. According to Myerson, the group is labeled pro-Soviet only because some Americans have the delusion that both sides are equally responsible for the arms race. He certainly cannot be slandered by being labeled pro-Soviet. For the executive director of the USPC, there are only "so-called human rights violations in socialist countries." He denigrates Soviet dissidents as a handful of malcontents "who have since left for lifetime lecture posts in Israel and the United States."[39]

It is not surprising that members of the CPUSA would find such an organization a congenial home. It is astonishing that many others would lend their names to it. And yet, the history of the USPC is replete with distinguished and prominent names.

The USPC emerged after a WPC delegation visited the United States in 1977. Local groups were organized in various communities to welcome the delegation and they, along with already existing Peace Councils in Chicago and Los Angeles, formed the core of the new group. By 1978 the USPC held a meeting in New York at which Romesh Chandra spoke. Pauline Rosen was identified as the group's spokesperson.[40] The founding conference was held in November 1979 in Philadelphia. The list of sponsors ranged from such tried and true communists as Carl Bloice, Angela Davis, Charlene Mitchell and Tony Monteiro and people long associated with Party causes like Anne Braden, Harry Bridges, and Vinnie Burrows to such politicians as Congressmen John Conyers and Ron Dellums, and Mayor Gus Newport of Berkeley.

Four hundred people attended the first conference, 40 percent of them from national minority groups. Representative John Conyers told the gathering that "from you I can see the future of America." Michael Myerson defined the major threat to peace as the military-industrial complex in the United States: "The biggest lie of our time is the myth of the 'Soviet threat.'" Among the workshop leaders and participants were Terry Provance of the American Friends Service Committee, Miriam Friedlander of the New York City Council, William Hogan of Clergy and Laity Concerned, James Jackson, Frank Chapman, Tony Monteiro, and Rob Prince.

The founding gathering adopted a host of resolutions, many of which are staples of other peace groups. The USPC called for independence for Puerto Rico, support for Cuba and Nicaragua, isolation of Chile, opposition to Pershing missile deployment in Europe, normalization of relations and aid to Vietnam, Laos, and Kampuchea, support for Salt 2, a just peace in the Middle East, support for the transfer amendment that would shift military spending to domestic uses, and a focus on the role of transnational corporations in South Africa.[41]

These general positions only suggest the bare outlines of the USPC view of the world, however. The Middle East resolution denounced the Camp David agreement as "a military pact imposed on the peoples of the Middle East by US imperialism." It condemned Zionism and antisemitism as racist. While a resolution attacked nuclear power plants, it carefully added that the danger was limited to "the present conditions of private ownership." The resolutions on Indochina denounced America and China and called for an educational campaign to acquaint Americans with the achievements of the Vietnamese regime. The USPC also supported government reparations to Vietnam.[42] The Council's position on Vietnam can also be gauged by the ads it ran in several newspapers in the summer of 1979 in response to singer Joan Baez's criticism of that country's repression of its citizens. One, signed by Wilfred Burchett, called charges of human rights violations "baseless." Another claimed that "Vietnam now enjoys human rights as it has never known in history."[43]

The founding conference did not limit itself to a concern over foreign and military issues. It endorsed USPC affiliation with the National Alliance Against Racist and Political Repression, called for outlawing of the Ku Klux Klan, freeing of the Wilmington 10 and implementation of the Full Employment Act, and opposed revision of the federal criminal code. There is another connection between the USPC and the NAARPR; Frank Chapman, executive director of the latter group, sits on the executive board of the USPC while Michael Myerson, executive director of the USPC, sits on the board of the NAARPR.

In addition to passing resolutions the USPC has issued pamphlets and brochures on a variety of issues. One, by Kathy Kelly, urges the peace movement to put Ireland on its agenda and insists that the crisis and repression in Northern Ireland "can be fully understood only in the larger context of NATO planning for a new world war."[44] Another pamphlet, by Rob Prince, attacking the Camp David agreement and the Saudi arms deal, alleges that the latter was pushed through by a cabal of the Rockefeller interests, Trilateralists, and the oil and gas lobby. Still another pamphlet, this one calling for sanctions against South Africa, was written by Ron Tyson, a staff writer for the *Daily World*. A pamphlet condemned the Grenada invasion as racist, sexist and chauvinistic. Still another one, by Dr. Conn Hallinan, associate editor of the *People's World,* concluded that there was strong evidence to suggest that KAL flight 007, shot down by the Soviet Union, was part of an espionage operation by the United States, which bore responsibility for the resulting loss of life.

The USPC has also sponsored various demonstrations and ad hoc committees to protest various aspects of American foreign policy or to support revolutionary groups. A delegate from the USPC attended the World Conference in Solidarity with the Arab People of Palestine held in Lisbon in November 1979 and signed a communique denouncing Camp David. The USPC sponsored the Emergency Committee Against the Invasion of Lebanon and endorsed the Coalition against the Sharon Visit in 1983. The USPC was also a sponsor of the November 12 (1983) Coalition to protest American policy in El Salvador and the invasion of Grenada. Documents captured in El Salvador indicate that Sandy Pollack met with Farid Handal, brother of the general secretary of the Salvadoran Communist Party, during his visit here in 1980 and helped set up the Committee in Solidarity with the People of El Salvador to support the guerillas.

Most of the USPC's notoriety, however, has been due to its activities on behalf of the nuclear freeze issue. The high point of the freeze campaign was a massive demonstration in New York on June 12, 1982 sponsored by a coalition of numerous groups including the CPUSA and the USPC. President Reagan soon charged that the freeze movement included communists and singled out the USPC for its malign influence. Testifying before the House Select Committee on Intelligence, Edward O'Malley of the FBI charged that while neither the Party nor the Council was critical to the success of the demonstration, they had both been active participants.

The response of the USPC to the charges was to admit most of the facts but to deny their implications. Myerson acknowledged that the USPC included known communists in its leadership and was tied to the World Peace Council. Both factors, he agreed, caused some in the peace movement to keep his group at arm's length. Neither one, he insisted, made the Council a tool of Soviet interests. The Council welcomed communists as "legitimate peace activists." They were "as honest, hard-working, thoughtful and dedicated to the cause of peace as anyone else" in the USPC. Non-communist members resented the charge that they had been "duped." Moreover, Myerson charged, such claims were racist. The USPC was unique among peace groups since it included large numbers of blacks and Puerto Ricans; to accuse them of being dupes was to suggest they did not have minds of their own.[45]

Afghanistan provides a very nice example of the independence followed by the USPC. The same organization that condemned the American invasion of Grenada and the Israeli invasion of Lebanon on the grounds that they violated international law and outraged universally-held moral principles was unable to reach a consensus on the Soviet invasion of Afghanistan.[46] When it did issue a statement it condemned not the invasion but the American response to it. The same people "who brought us the Cold War, the Korean War, the Vietnam War" were building a new crisis and preparing for war to divert attention from real domestic crisis. The Council accused American officials of using the "Big Lie" to distort what was happening in Afghanistan and to advance President Carter's reelection hopes. Not once in the statement was the word invasion used; the USPC could only bring itself to refer to "the events" in Afghanistan. "However one might feel about the Afghanistan events, they must not be used to escalate war preparations and threats against other nations."[47]

The USPC is a pawn of the Soviet Union but an important vehicle for communist influence in the peace movement. It is an organization whose key position is held by a high-ranking communist. It blames the United States alone for the world's problems and defends virtually all Soviet policies. When the Soviet Union does something so outrageous that even non-communist members of the organization cannot stomach it, the crisis is averted by blaming America for responding. As for those non-communists who are members and leaders of the USPC, it is fair to say that if they are not aware of what the organization stands for they have only themselves to blame. The Council does not hide its views or its biases; it flaunts them. Those who work in the leadership of the USPC are not dupes. One has to assume that they either agree with the USPC's policies or exhibit considerable irresponsibility in lending their names and reputations to an organization with which they disagree.

Notes

1. *Daily World,* March 4, 1976.
2. *Daily World,* July 3, 1975.
3. Gus Hall, "The Role of Theory in the Struggle for World Communist Unity," *Political Affairs,* September 1977.
4. Gus Hall, "Marxism-Leninism in the World Struggle Against Opportunism," *Political Affairs,* April 1982.
5. *Daily World,* September 21, 1974.
6. *Daily World,* March 5, 1974.
7. *Wall Street Journal,* October 29, 1976.
8. *Daily World,* February 2, 1977.
9. Victor Perlo, "US-Soviet Economic Competition—The Last Decade," *Political Affairs,* June 1984.
10. *Daily World,* June 2, 1979.
11. *Daily World,* June 25, 1976.
12. Ibid.
13. *Daily World,* January 28, 1977.
14. Gus Hall, "What Really Happened in Afghanistan?" *Political Affairs,* March 1980.
15. *New York Times,* November 2, 1984.
16. *Washington Post,* September 11, 1980.
17. Hall, "Marxism-Leninism in the World Struggle Against Opportunism," op. cit.
18. *Daily World,* June 27, 1975.
19. *Daily World,* April 6, 27, 1974; Gus Hall, "The Struggle for Detente," *Political Affairs,* July 1974.

36   The Communist Party of the United States

20. Gus Hall, "Detente and its Enemies," *Political Affairs,* March 1974.
21. Arthur Zipser, "Communists on the Peace Front," *Political Affairs,* August-September 1979.
22. "Draft Main Political Resolution [II]," *Political Affairs,* June 1979.
23. Henry Winston, "For A People's Peace Crusade," *Political Affairs,* December 1979.
24. Jim West, "Peace Must Be Won," *Political Affairs,* April 1979.
25. *Wall Street Journal,* January 14, 1983.
26. Michael Myerson, "The New Red Scare: An Open Letter," US Peace Council, 1982; *Daily World,* November 13, 1979.
27. *Daily World,* November 14, 1985.
28. See "World Peace Council: Instrument of Soviet Foreign Policy," *Foreign Affairs Note,* US Department of State, April 1982.
29. *Guardian* (London), February 23, 1981.
30. *New Times* (Moscow), July 1975.
31. *Peace Courier,* October 1984.
32. *30th Anniversary of World Peace Movement,* World Peace Council, Prague, 1979.
33. "World Peace Council," *op. cit.*
34. O'Malley testimony, *Soviet Active Measures:* Hearings Before the House Permanent Select Committee on Intelligence, July 1982.
35. Third Vienna Dialogue–International Conference for Disarmament and Detente, Speeches and Reports.
36. Michael Myerson, *These Are the Good Old Days,* (New York: Grossman Publishers, 1970).
37. *Daily World,* January 22, 1985, February 6, 1985.
38. *Daily World,* September 29, 1983.
39. *Daily World,* November 17, 1983.
40. *Daily World,* January 25, 1978.
41. *Daily World,* November 13, 1979.
42. United States Peace Council Founding Conference Program Resolutions, 1979.
43. *Washington Post,* June 27, 1979; *Rocky Mountain News,* July 15, 1979.
44. *Daily World,* March 14, 1985.
45. *Daily World,* November 25, 1982.
46. Ibid.
47. *Daily World,* February 5, 1980.

3

Party Targets

Youth

Since its inception the CPUSA has had an associated youth organization to help it appeal to younger workers and students. Over the past sixty years, it has gone by various names including the Young Workers League, Labor Youth League and Young Communist League. During the 1960s it was known as the W.E.B. DuBois Clubs, after the noted black intellectual who joined the CPUSA when he was 90 years old. The DuBois Clubs were quite small and achieved their greatest renown when then Vice President Nixon charged that the CPUSA had cunningly sought to confuse Americans into thinking that they were connected to the Boys Clubs of America.

In 1970 the Party set up the Young Workers Liberation League (YWLL). It never achieved much success despite its less stringent ideological requirements. Estimates of its membership in the mid-1970s ranged from 3000 to 4000 with high turnover and low dues-payments by members.[1]

As part of an effort to become more visible and open, the Party decided to replace the YWLL with an openly communist group. After a lengthy build-up and extensive publicity in the *Daily World*, the Young Communist League was founded at a convention in Cleveland in May 1983. Four hundred delegates were present. One-quarter were between 25 and 30 years of age, 60 percent were under 25 and 6 percent were under 14 (the remainder were presumably over 30). More than half were workers, one-fifth were unemployed and the others were students, mostly in college. Forty-four percent were white, 56 percent "racially and nationally oppressed." The delegates came from 80 cities across the country.[2]

The convention emphasized the usual litany of communist positions but with a particular focus on the problems of young people. It passed resolutions calling for extending unemployment compensation to first-time job seekers, government provision of food, housing and medical care to youth, government takeover of industries to provide jobs, opposition to draft registration, cuts in the military budget and preventing the overthrow of the Sandinista regime.[3]

As befits a youth group, the YCL tries to present a less serious image than its adult counterpart. It sponsors dances, bowling parties and TV parties for football games. It also engages in more traditional political organizing. Among its activities have been campaigning for Mel King, a major candidate for mayor of Boston, mobilizing marchers for Washington peace demonstrations, registering voters, and endorsing the Hall-Davis presidential ticket in the 1984 election.

The YCL is an affiliate of the World Federation of Democratic Youth (WFDY), the Soviet Union's major front group among young people. The WFDY was founded in 1945. By 1950 most of its non-communist affiliates had quit. The French government soon expelled the organization and it relocated in Budapest. One of the WFDY's major projects is a World Festival of Youth and Students, held every several years. The festivals have invariably endorsed communist positions on a variety of issues. At the eleventh festival, held in Havana in 1978 there were some twenty-five thousand participants. When some of the delegates from Britain and Italy tried to discuss human rights violations in socialist countries, they were unable to do so. The one setback for the Soviet Union was that the festival refused to condemn China. Many of the same groups that sponsor the festival, including the International Union of Students, International Youth and Student Movement of the United Nations, World Student Christian Federation, Continental Organization of Latin American Students, All-Africa Students Union and the WFDY co-sponsored a Prague meeting on disarmament in April 1979 that did condemn Chinese aggresion against Vietnam, the Israeli-Egyptian peace treaty and the neutron bomb.[4]

The theme of the Havana Festival was "anti-imperialist solidarity, peace and friendship." The twelfth festival, held in Moscow in the summer of 1985 and hosted by the Young Communist League, was directed towards building unity among the "forces of peace, democracy, national liberation and social progress." The YCL was the initiator of the festival in the United States. James Steele, then the YCL's national chair, praised the Soviet Union's peace efforts and saw the Moscow location as a symbol of its commitment and demonstration that the young people of the world understand "the grave danger imposed by the Reaganite warmongers."[5]

The YCL took the lead in setting up a National Preparatory Committee to form a US delegation. Steele stepped down from his position as YCL head in April 1985 to work full-time for the Festival, prior to entering the CPUSA's national leadership. He congratulated his YCL comrades for building a united front supporting the Festival and exulted that tens of thousands "are being mobilized in a united youth and student front of the struggle for peace, against the militarist course of the Reagan administration."[6] In addition to Steele, who served as co-chair of the American delegation, other leading members of the YCL such as Elena Mora and Bill Dennison held key positions on the Preparatory Committee. Seth Godfrey, national coordinator for the NPC, had previously been associated with the New York Council for American-Soviet Friendship. The newly installed head of the YCL, John Bachtell, boasted in May 1985 that "through the Festival movement the prestige of the YCL has leaped to new heights."[7]

The NPC was able to garner an impressive number of non-communists to endorse the Festival, including Congressmen John Conyers, Ron Dellums, George Crockett, and Gus Hawkins. A number of mayors issued proclamations on behalf of the Festival. The Massachusetts State House of Representatives endorsed it.[8] Eighteen members of Congress sent a letter of greetings to the International Preparatory Committee applauding the Festival. Signers included Mervyn Dymally and Walter Fauntroy. Even one governor sent a letter commending the members of the American delegation as they left for Moscow.[9]

The festival movement illustrates quite well the mechanics of a communist front. The brochure prepared by the organizers never mentioned the Young Communist League. The YCL was listed as one of some eighty endorsers on a separate sheet. The political coloration of the WFDY or the International Union of Students was unknown to most people. In the guise of bringing together thousands of young people to make friends and demonstrate against nuclear war, the organizers also enlisted scores of non-communists to endorse a Soviet propaganda circus in Moscow, complete with a tribunal at which the United States and Israel were accused of crimes against the Arab peoples. A number of endorsers repudiated their support upon learning of what they had endorsed. Others denied that their declarations implied support of the Festival. It also appeared as though the NPC had used the names of some prominent people without their permission.[10]

The leader of the YCL is John Bachtell. Elena Mora is administrative secretary, and Joe Sims, Bill Dennison and Keta Miranda are vice-chairs. The YCL publishes a monthly paper, *Dynamic.*

Blacks

Just as the forces the Party wishes to cooperate with in the unions remain committed to the Democratic Party, so too does the group which it perceives as the most progressive in the United States—blacks. The Party's 1982 program defined Afro-Americans as a "national minority subject to national, racial and class oppression." Since the black population is regarded as overwhelmingly working class, the Party believes that "the struggle against racism and national oppression is inextricably intertwined with the class struggle."[11]

The Party's effort to build an all-people's front against the Reagan administration has met with greater success in the black community than elsewhere. Blacks certainly have been far less supportive of the administration than most other groups in the United States. Because of their special situation, moreover, communists see blacks as particularly open to critiques of American capitalism. In any case the CPUSA has strongly supported the candidacies of such black Democratic politicians as Jesse Jackson, Harold Washington, and Mel King. The latter's campaign for mayor of Boston was enthusiastically endorsed. Washington's election as mayor of Chicago and the coalition that made it possible were called the "leading edge of the all-people's front."[12] Jackson's presidential candidacy attracted considerable communist enthusiasm and support. In all these cases, the Party saw examples of black-white unity in building people's coalitions.

Charlene Mitchell, head of the Party's Afro-American Commission, urged communists to "reaffirm our determination to be part" of such mass black organizations as the NAACP, Operation Push, the Urban League, SCLC and the National Council of Negro Women. She pointed out that the Party "should be experiencing a tremendous growth" among blacks. Not only are they disproportionately affected by economic crisis but more positively, they are supposedly less affected by anti-Sovietism and anti-communism.[13] George Meyers analyzed the Coalition of Black Trade Unionists as "basically a center organization with Left participation." He insisted that "it needs more of a left face."[14]

Several communist fronts have been able to attract a considerable number of black politicians and civil rights leaders to cooperate with them, most notably the US Peace Council, the National Alliance against Racist and Political Repression, and the National Preparatory Committee for the World Youth Festival. Among them are Gus Newport, former mayor of Berkeley, Representatives John Conyers, Ron Dellums, and George Crockett, and Joseph Lowrey. One of the black organizations that the CPUSA has especially praised is the Congressional Black Caucus. One communist writer exulted that it played "the most progressive role and is most independent of the Democratic Party leadership."[15]

The Party's position on racial issues is not calculated to win support from moderates. It supports not merely affirmative action but job quotas, insisting that control over access to the job market needs to be taken out of private hands, that "all hiring (should be) through government hiring offices."[16] James Jackson, one of the Party's most powerful figures, has argued that "opposition to affirmative action is race discrimination, is racism."[17] Since the Party has also officially called for laws making racist practices a crime, it is at least arguable that the CPUSA believes that anyone who opposes job quotas should be imprisoned.[18] The CPUSA has also argued that blacks should be assured of proportional representation in all elective and appointive governmental positions.[19]

Much of the Party's work among blacks in recent years has been carried out under the auspices of the National Alliance Against Racist and Political Repression (NAARPR), which has been one of its most active and successful auxiliaries since it was founded in 1972. Its origins lie in the National Committee to Free Angela Davis and All Political Prisoners. Davis, a prominent young black communist, had been jailed in 1971 in California. She was charged with murder and kidnapping after an effort to free George Jackson, a black militant with whom she was in love, failed and resulted in several deaths. A gun belonging to Davis was used in the escape attempt.

Davis was acquitted of all charges in July 1972. The Communist Party had built a major campaign around her case and soon transformed her defense committee into the NAARPR, which held its first conference in May 1973. The new group was conceived as a united front with communists cooperating with other radicals to offer "organized systematized resistance to counter-organized, systematized repression." In pursuit of that goal, Charlene Mitchell, one of the Alliance's leaders and the CPUSA's 1968 Presidential candidate, travelled to the Pine Ridge Indian Reservation to meet with Clyde Bellecourt of the American Indian Movement during the confrontation with the government there. Bellecourt became a vice-chair of the Alliance.[20]

Beginning at its second convention in 1974 the Alliance focused its attention on North Carolina, which it regarded as the state with the "most comprehensive wave of repression" in the nation. It sponsored a July 4th march in Raleigh which the Southern Regional Organizer of the CPUSA urged Party members to make "a top priority."[21] Somewhere between five thousand and ten thousand people were present to hear Ralph Abernathy of the Southern Christian Leadership Conference call for abolition of the death penalty and Angela Davis appeal for "a new popular front of the political left."[22]

By the middle of 1974 the Alliance claimed to have twenty-five chapters in twenty-one states and to be affiliated with forty national organizations and one hundred local and regional groups.[23] During preparations for the Raleigh rally it built new chapters in Virginia, Kentucky, and New Jersey.[24] For the next several years it continued to focus much of its attention on

North Carolina, however, particularly on the case of the Wilmington 10, a group of blacks and one white convicted of firebombing a store during a racial riot in the North Carolina port city.

In May 1974 a thousand Alliance members and supporters demonstrated at the Justice Department in support of the Wilmington 10. Its fourth national conference in 1977 focused on the case. One of the main speakers was Ben Chavis, one of those convicted, and by then a leading official in the Alliance. Chavis called it "the only national, multiracial and multinational organization in the country geared to fighting repression." Its activities on behalf of the Wilmington 10 continued into 1978 when the NAARPR organized a march on the White Hose on their behalf. When the last of the Wilmington 10 was eventually freed, the Alliance took credit for the accomplishment.[25]

The Alliance has had its hand in numerous other causes. It carried on a vigorous campaign to defeat reform of the federal criminal code, maintaining that the revision would endanger civil liberties. It has sponsored demonstrations and rallies on behalf of illegal immigrant workers. It has held a Harlem rally to protest police brutality. And, it has been a cosponser of a host of rallies and marches in Washington in opposition to Reagan administration policies.

The CPUSA has given the Alliance its full support and backing from the organization's beginnings. It has also firmly controlled it. The *Daily World* called the NAARPR "an essential organization" and praised it for its "solid achievements (and) ... fighting ability."[26] The Party itself is a member organization of the Alliance.[27] The executive secretary for many years was Charlene Mitchell, one of the Party's key leaders. The co-chairs in the early days were Davis, a member of the CPUSA Central Committee, Carl Braden, long identified with Party causes in the South, and Bert Corona, whose communist ties went back to at least the early 1950s.

One of the Alliance's major achievements has been its ability to enlist prominent non-communists to participate in its activities. At the NAARPR's Tenth Anniversary Conference in 1983 Congressman Charles Hayes served as chair and John Conyers was the major speaker. Guests included Mel King and Gus Newport.

The Alliance's focus on repression is not limited just to the United States. Needless to say, however, it does not extend to the Soviet Union or any other socialist countries. Angela Davis brushed aside arguments that the Soviet Union maltreated Jews, claiming that the "media exaggerates the reports of Jewish oppression in order to divert" attention from American repression of its minorities.[28] Davis "won't pretend that there are no problems in socialist countries" but has contended that repression is inevitable in the United States and that whatever errors are made in Russia get distorted. On these grounds she refused to condemn Soviet repression.[29]

The Alliance has given attention to repression in some countries, however, most notably Israel. In 1974 Davis and the NAARPR protested the "jailing and torture of Arabs in areas occupied by Israel" and declared their support for the PLO.[30] Two years later Davis accompanied Tawfiq Zayyad, the communist mayor of Nazareth, to a press conference in San Francisco, hailed his election as a victory for "progressive forces all over the world" and pledged Alliance aid to Palestinean prisoners.[31] An Alliance delegate attended an Emergency Conference of International Solidarity with the Palestine Resistance held in Athens in December 1976.[32]

The Alliance's vision of America is one of an almost fully realized police state. In a joint article Alliance executive director Frank Chapman and Michael Myerson, executive director of the US Peace Council, denounced various plans for fighting crime and charged that under the guise of doing so, the government was "laying the basis for a potential police state." They charged that "undemocratic institutions, the monopoly corporations, rule our lives" while the American right, including corporations, was "planning more repression, arming the police more heavily and giving them a license to kill."[33]

At its 1985 conference the Alliance identified three priorities for the next year. They were to publicize the Johny Imani Harris case and the issue of the death penalty, to repel attacks on black elected officials and voting rights and to provide support to the Phelps Dodge strikers. One of the speakers, New York City Councilman Wendell Foster, angrily denounced Jews who opposed racial quotas and warned: "just give me what is mine and if you don't you better get out of the way because I'm gonna take it."[34] The Alliance and the Peace Council organized celebrations of the birthday of imprisoned South African leader Nelson Mandela in July 1985 in twenty cities.

The co-chairs of the NAARPR are Angela Davis, Henry Foner, a union official, and Lennox Hinds, a leader of the National Conference of Black Lawyers. Frank Chapman, who became the Alliance's executive director after Charlene Mitchell stepped down, has an interesting history. In 1961 he was convicted of first-degree murder and armed robbery in Missouri and was sentenced to a term of life plus 50 years in prison. Paroled in 1976, he went to work for the American Friends Service Committee as its St. Louis field secretary. He was also active in Mobilization for Survival. He joined the Alliance staff in 1980. In 1982 he received a commutation of his sentence.

Jews

The Communist Party's work among American Jews has not fared very well in recent years. During the 1930s and 1940s Jews were overrepresented in the CPUSA compared to their proportion of the population, largely bcause of the hostility of both Jews and communists to fascism. Even then, only a tiny fraction of American Jews were communists. As evidence mounted of antisemitism in the Soviet Union and as the USSR became the center of hostility to Israel and Zionism, most Jews in the Party quit.

In the early 1970s the Party lost its control of a Yiddish-language newspaper that it had first founded in 1922. The *Freiheit,* the oldest communist periodical in America, was run by Paul Novick, one of its original editors. The CPUSA expelled him in 1972 for not being strongly enough anti-Zionist. When Novick and several other Jewish former communists wrote an open letter to Soviet authorities protesting against Soviet antisemitism, they were denounced, first by a Soviet journal, and then by the CPUSA, which charged that the *Freiheit* was in the "open service" of American imperialism.[35] Although the *Daily World* called upon loyal communist readers of the paper to replace Novick as editor, the Party's influence on the six thousand subscribers was so minimal that Novick remained in charge.

The CPUSA's position on issues of concern to the Jewish community is so extreme that whatever minor influence it once had has largely vannished. Since the essence of Party doctrine is that the Soviet Union is a virtual paradise for all its citizens, and particularly Jews, the CPUSA has defended and apologized for Soviet mistreatment of Jews. In 1973 Hyman Lumer, a key Party leader, admitted that there were no Jewish schools in Russia but insisted that "this is not because they are banned; on the contrary it is because Soviet Jews themselves do not want such schools." Lumer also sounded a frequent communist refrain; only a handful of Jews wanted to emigrate (he put the number at around twenty thousand in 1973).[36] In 1974 Party leaders reported that Leonid Brezhnev himself had assured them that few Jews still wanted to leave and that many who had left now wanted to return.[37] Gus Hall confessed that he had privately believed that the Soviet Union should allow more emigration, but the Party refused to criticize the Soviet position publicly.[38] Hall angrily charged that accusations of Soviet antisemitism were a "big lie." His ringing defense of Soviet policies came at a dinner celebrating the 50th anniversary of the founding of Birobidjain, a Soviet "homeland" for Jews in Siberia that has attracted only a few thousand Soviet Jews.[39] When several "progressive" politicians protested against Soviet antisemitism outside the Russian UN mission in New York in June 1985, the Party newspaper charged that they had allowed American right-wingers to use them by raising false charges of Soviet antisemitism.

Aside from its support for Soviet oppression of Jews, the CPUSA has also parrotted the Soviet line on Israel and Zionism. In 1948 when the USSR supported the establishment of the Jewish state, so too did the

CPUSA. Today, both are implacable opponents of Israel. Years before the United Nations condemned Zionism as racism, Hyman Lumer, the Party's chief theoretician on the Jewish question was denouncing "the reactionary racist character of Zionism itself."[40] Party leader Henry Winston called Zionism the "partner-in-crime" of imperialism in 1979.[41] Another communist explained that it was "a deadly enemy of the best interests of the Jewish people . . . an enemy of peace, freedom and progress everywhere . . . its poisonous influence on the Jewish masses (must be) abolished."[42]

As hostile as the CPUSA is to Zionism, it is just as vicious about the state of Israel. Party speakers and writers frequently compare Israel to Nazi Germany. Herbert Aptheker, the Party's most prominent intellectual, called the Israeli invasion of Lebanon a "blitzkrieg" and the government's justifications comparable to the "Big Lie technique of the Nazis." He charged that Menachem Begin wanted to find "local Quislings" to supplant the PLO and found that Ariel Sharon's speeches "remind one of Hitler." The Phalangist massacre of Palestineans at Sabra and Shatilla were "Jewish-organized and controlled pogroms."[43] Gus Hall insisted that defending the Begin government "defends unjust and criminal aggression in the name of the Jewish people."[44]

The CPUSA fully supports the Soviet-endorsed road to peace in the Middle East: full Israeli withdrawl from the territories conquered in 1967, a Geneva peace conference including the USSR, and creation of a Palestinian state under the aegis of the PLO. The Party has attacked the Camp David peace treaty as an imperialist maneuver and an obstacle to real peace. When one speaker at a New York May Day rally in 1979 praised the treaty, a communist organizer took the microphone to deny that the sponsors shared that sentiment.[45] While the Party has in the past criticized the PLO for calling for the elimination of Israel, it also believes that the PLO has implicitly accepted a two-state solution to the conflict and it rarely finds fault with its policies. Herbert Aptheker has called Yasir Arafat "one of the most remarkable of all leaders of national liberation struggles."[46] The featured speaker at the 8th Anniversary Dinner of *Jewish Affairs*, published by the CPUSA's Jewish Commission, was Zehdi Terzi, the PLO's United Nations representative. He praised the Soviet Union, called the dinner guests "comrades" and was hailed as "our comrade" by Aptheker.[47] While the Party has condemned Arab terrorist raids as Maoist or Trotskyite errors, it has been far more critical of Israeli reprisals or rescue missions, labelling them examples of "state terrorism."[48]

Gus Hall has acknowledged that the Party's position on Zionism is not popular in the Jewish community.[49] The CPUSA believes, however, that most American Jews, while emotionally attached to Israel, are not consciously Zionist. At the Party's 23rd convention "note was taken of the progressive role of New Jewish Agenda," a new American group critical of Israeli policies, as one sign of a change in attitude in the Jewish community.[50]

The CPUSA has also created several front groups to seek support in the Jewish community. Late in 1983 *Jewish Affairs* published an open letter from Soviet Jews to American Jews. The writers denied the presence of antisemitism in the USSR, defended Russia's position on Israel and called for the support of the Soviet position on detente and nuclear weapons.[51] An ad hoc group, Jewish Americans for World Peace (JAWP), soon emerged to publicize the open letter. Its sponsors included a number of prominent communists and Soviet apologists, including Aptheker, Archie Brown, Lester Cole, Dr. Irving Crain, William Mandel, Lewis Moroze, Norman Markowitz and Samuel Neuberger. JAWP took out a full-page ad in a Chicago Jewish newspaper, leading to the formation of a Chicago Peace Yes Committee. It also sponsored a 1984 visit to America by Aaron Vergalis, editor of *Sovietische Heimland,* a Yiddish newspaper published in Russia. Established Jewish organizations shunned Vergalis, a member of the Soviet Anti-Zionist Committee, and he cut short his visit just before a planned press conference.[52]

An older, more established organization is the Committee for a Just Peace in the Middle East which supports the same goals as the CPUSA. It has reprinted articles by Meir Vilner, a leader of the Israeli Communist Party, and Hyman Lumer. The latter's article defended the UN resolution equating Zionism with racism and declared it an ideology hostile to the interests of Jews: in fact, Zionism was declared the "worst enemy" of the Jewish people, separating them from their real allies, workers and national liberation forces.[53]

The Committee has also sponsored a variety of petitions, ads and talks by groups hostile to Israel and American support for Israeli policies. It was, for example, a sponsor of the Coalition for Justice and Peace in the Middle East which urged an end to US arms sales in the area, recognition of the PLO, and Israeli and Palestinean states living in secure and recognized borders. Among the other sponsors were a variety of ministers and such avowed critics of the state of Israel as Abdeen Jabara of the Palestine Human Right Campaign, Daniel Berrigan (who has called Israel a criminal Jewish community), Arthur Kinoy, David Dellinger, Eqbal Ahmed, Randall Robinson of Transafrica, the National Lawyers Guild, Womens International League for Peace and Freedom and Mobilization for Survival, among other groups.[54] The Committee has also sponsored a talk on the Middle East with the PLO's UN representative and Mark Solomon, co-chair of the US Peace Council, another Party front group.

The CPUSA has insisted that American Jews should align themselves with the working class and anti-monopoly movement. It strongly defended Jesse Jackson during the 1984 presidential campaign, claiming that he had forthrightly apologized for his unfortunate language about Jews and that the matter should be closed. The "abusive" attacks on Jackson were, it was claimed, part of an effort by reactionary ruling circles— the real anti-semites in America— to disrupt the unity of the anti-Reagan coalition.

The Party has reserved some of its harshest invective for those Jews whom it perceives as the staunchest enemies of communism and Jewish support for the left. Herbert Aptheker has directed the coarsest attacks. In a speech to Party faithful, he labelled *"Commentary* Jews" as betrayers of the Jewish prophets and called opponents of affirmative action "pen prostitutes," declaring: "It's enough to make you throw up," before describing Albert Shanker, Nathan Glazer and other opponents of quotas, as "liars, hypocrites, demagogues, vermin."[55]

Lewis Moroze heads the Party's Jewish Commission. Herbert Aptheker is editor and Moroze is managing editor of *Jewish Affairs,* which was begun in 1970 and is published bi-monthly. The magazine holds an annual dinner in New York which attracts five hundred to eight hundred people, some of them non-Jewish communist luminaries.

Women

The Party's most important auxiliary for work among women is Women for Racial and Economic Equality (WREE). It was formed in the mid-1970s to help the Party deal with an embarrassing division in its own ranks over the Equal Rights Amendment. The CPUSA had long opposed the ERA on the grounds that it would not solve the problem of sex-discrimination and would actually take away laws protecting women. That position generated dissent within the Party. In March 1974 a CPUSA conference on work among women urged formation of a party periodical that would help publicize a Women's Bill of Rights as an alternative to the ERA.[56]

WREE and its journal *WREE View* called for an end to the arms race, a guaranteed annual income, equal pay for comparable work, affirmative action, a "cultuure free from racist and sexist images of women," federally-funded child care, national health care and full reproductive freedom in lieu of the ERA. During the fall of 1976 the organization also raised money for a program called "Penicillin for Vietnam." Both the CPUSA and WREE finally came out in support of the ERA in 1978 but urged that it be made clear that it would not lead to a reduction in the benefits women already earned.

WREE held a national organizing conference in March 1976 and identified two major goals; reuniting blacks and women in a political coalition and emphasizing the need for women to fight US imperialism. Its national coordinator at the time was Sondra Patrinos, whose prior position had been Communist Party organizer for Eastern Pennsylvania. Another of its organizers, Norma Spector, visited Vietnam in the spring of 1976 as part of a delegation from the Soviet-backed Women's International Democratic Federation; WREE became its American affiliate. WREE's founding conference was in Chicago in March 1977. Among those signing the call to the event were Anne Braden, a leader of the Party-dominated Southern Organizing Committee; Margaret Burroughs; Angela Davis, a leader of the Party-dominated National Alliance Against Racist and Political Repression; actress Ruby Dee; Sandra Graham, vice-mayor of Cambridge, Massachusetts and a board member of the US Peace Council; Brenda Eichelberger; Barbara Gale, vice-president of Local 1199, Drug and Hospital Workers Union; and Patrinos. Five hundred thirty delegates attended; they identified the source of female inequality as "corporate monopoly."[57]

Among the recent activities WREE has sponsored or been involved with are voter registration drives in Harlem, the August 1983 March for Jobs, Freedom and Peace in Washington, and the Women's Coalition to Stop US Intervention in Central America and the Caribbean.[58] In 1983 it sponsored an American tour by the president of the General Union of Palestinian Women.[59] It has also been active in organizing protests against South Africa, at one of which Cecilia McCall, chair of its Peace and Solidarity Committee, was arrested.[60]

WREE claimed to have over three thousand women members with chapters in ten cities in 1983. The bulk of its membership appears to be from the East Coast and California. Cheryl Allen Craig was president in 1983, Pearl Granat and Watteen Trudy were vice-presidents and Vinnie Burrows, the United Nations representative for the WIDF, was international secretary. The National Council of eight members included Dorothy Burnham, Alva Buxenbaum (chair of the CPUSA Women's Commission), Sondra Patrinos and Duba Weinstein, all long identified with Party causes. Norma Spector edits the *WREE View.*

Other Party Auxiliaries

The National Coalition to Fight Inflation and Unemployment was formed in 1975. Elizabeth Merkelson was its executive secretary. Gus Hall indicated that the CPUSA was active in the new group which sponsored a march to Washington in April 1976 that drew five thousand participants. The following year it drew up a People's Economic Agenda to deal with youth unemployment. It has not received much attention in the Party press in recent years.[61]

The National Anti-Imperialist Movement in Solidarity with African Liberation has been active in garnering support for the African National Congress in South Africa and, prior to their independence, insurgent black groups in Zimbabwe and Mozambique. Anthony Monteiro, a member of the Party's Central Committee, is executive secretary. In recent years, the group has been pushing to obtain one million signatures on petitions calling for mandatory sanctions against the South African regime.

The National Congress of Unemployed Organizations was founded in Chicago in July 1983. Arnold Bechetti, one of the CPUSA's leaders, boasted that "with others we were a major factor in founding" the group. Scott Marshall, one of the leaders of the group and the secretary of the Party's Labor Commission, noted that "many, if not most" of the unemployed groups represented at the founding conference "are led by communists and others of the Left."[62]

American Friends of Revolutionary Iran is an organization dominated by communists and devoted to support of the Tudeh Party in Iran. Tudeh, with close links to the Soviet Union, originally gave its enthusiastic support to the Khomeini regime, as did the CPUSA. One *Daily World* columnist, Tom Foley, even noticed that the Ayatollah was a feminist; his stand on women was "egalitarian, humane and democratic." After the regime turned on the Tudeh Party and executed a number of its members, American Friends of Revolutionary Iran turned on the regime. Its supporters include John Abt, Stanley Faulkner, Ishmael Flory (CP leader in Illinois), Charlene Mitchell and Jack Kling (CP leader in Illinois).[63]

The oldest communist front group in the United States is the National Council of American-Soviet Friendship whose roots go back to the American Friends of Soviet Russia, created in the early 1920s. The Council has been a consistent apologist for the Soviet Union ever since, minimizing or justifying every Soviet action, ranging from forced collectivization to the Stalinist purges and terror. For many years its leading lights included such people as Jessica Smith and Corliss Lamont. The current chair is Richard Morford, a Protestant cleargyman who has been active in communist front groups since World War II and served as executive secretary of the Council after the war.[64] The current executive director is the Reverend Allen Thomson.

The Council publicizes the argument that the Soviet people are peace loving and prosperous. It consistently defends Soviet peace initiatives and participates in rallies and demonstrations attacking American military and diplomatic policies. For example, it sponsored a rally for Peace, Disarmament and Social Progress in May 1982 in New York. The main speaker was

Representative Parren Mitchell; other participants included Anne Braden, Ossie Davis, and Ernest DeMaio.[65] The FBI has claimed in congressional testimony that the National Council of American-Soviet Friendship receives funding and directives from the Soviet Union.[66]

There are also a host of other organizations that serve Party interests. The American Institute of Marxist Studies, for example, until recently put out bibliographies on current and past events, paying particular attention to material produced by the Communist Parties of the world.

The Marxist Educational Press, headquartered in Minneapolis, publishes occasional books and papers and also sponsors regular symposia organized around specific topics. Many of the participants and papers reflect the communist view of the world. For example, along with the Departments of Philosophy and Religion of Northern Iowa University, it sponsored a Conference on Marxism and Religion in October 1984. The goal was to promote a dialogue between the religious and secular left. One of the major speakers was communist theoretician Herbert Aptheker who insisted that Marx's denigration of religion as the opiate of the people should not be taken out of context; Aptheker noted that Marx also saw religion as the genuine "sigh of the oppressed." Among the wide variety of speakers and panelists were the Reverend Gilbert Dawes, a Cedar Rapids Methodist minister who argued that religious activists and Marxists were "in the same bed," and Tim Teager, the district organizer of the Party's Iowa-Nebraska District. One panel called for recognition by the religious of Marxist class analysis and an appreciation by the non-religious of religion as part of the culture of the oppressed. It urged that a distinction be made between religious groups that push for "ultraright" goals and those that are theologically conservative. According to the *Daily World*, "the struggle against racism, antisemitism and anti-communism was described as central in combatting the religious right."[67]

Publications

One of the marks of the CPUSA's predominance on the radical left in the United States is the number of newspapers and journals it churns out. No radical group would be taken seriously or take itself seriously if it failed to publish its views. The Party has innumerable outlets, both general and specialized, through which to spread its message.

Daily

People's Daily World— published five days a week, edited by Barry Cohen, a merger of the *Daily World* and *People's World*

Weekly

Voz del Pueblo— Spanish language, edited by Galo Conde
Tyomies-Eteenpain— Finnish language, published in Superior, Wisconsin

Monthly

Economic Notes— published by the Labor Research Association, edited by Gregory Tarpanian
Labor Today— published by Trade Unionists for Action and Democracy
Political Affairs— edited by Mike Zagarell
Dynamic— published by the Young Communist League, edited by James Steele

Bi-Monthly

Jewish Affairs— edited by Lewis Moroze
New World Review— edited by Marilyn Bechtel

Quarterly

WREE View— published by Women for Racial and Economic Equality, edited by Norma Spector
AIS-EIRI— published for Irish-Americans

Notes

1. Walter and Miriam Schneir, "The Socialist Workers: Square Target of the FBI," *Nation*, September 25, 1976.
2. *Daily World*, May 5, 1983.
3. Ibid.
4. *New York Times,* August 7, 1978; *International Union of Students News Service,* June 12, 1979.
5. *Dynamic*, Jan-Feb 1984.
6. *Daily World*, April 20, 1985.
7. *Daily World*, May 10, 1985.
8. Harvey Klehr and Ronald Radosh, "Redfest '85," *The New Republic,* August 12-19, 1985.
9. *Daily World*, July 26, 1985.
10. Klehr and Radosh, "Redfest '85."
11. "For Freedom and Equality: End Racism," *Political Affairs,* February 1982.
12. Ted Pearson, "Chicago: Class Struggle in the Electoral Arena," *Political Affairs,* November 1983.

13. *Black Liberation Journal*, December 1983.
14. Ibid.
15. Ibid.
16. J.C. Webb, "Weber, Sears and the Fight for Affirmative Action," and Central Committee, CPUSA, "The Afro-American Struggle," *Political Affairs,* June 1979.
17. *Black Liberation Journal,* December 1983.
18. *Daily World*, September 26, 1984.
19. "For Freedom and Equality: End Racism," *Political Affairs,* February 1982.
20. *Daily World*, September 28, 1973.
21. *Daily World*, June 15, 1974.
22. *New York Times*, July 5, 1974.
23. *New York Times*, July 2, 1974.
24. *Daily World*, July 18, 1974.
25. *Daily World*, November 1, 1977.
26. *Daily World*, October 15, 1975.
27. *Daily World*, June 15, 1974.
28. *Omaha World-Herald,* May 2, 1975.
29. Orde Coombs, "Angela Davis Keeps the Faith," *New York,* April 17, 1978.
30. *People's World*, August 17, 1974.
31. *San Francisco Chronicle*, October 15, 1976.
32. *People's World*, February 12, 1977.
33. *Daily World*, May 5, 1983.
34. *Daily World*, May 21, 1985; "Maggot Time," *National Review,* August 9, 1985.
35. "Memorandum to Soviet Officials on the Soviet Jewish Situation," *Jewish Currents,* December 1976; *Daily World*, May 12, 1977; *Morning Freiheit,* June 26, 1977.
36. Hyman Lumer, *Zionism* (New York: International Publishers, 1973), pp. 120, 130.
37. *Daily World*, May 9, 1974.
38. *Wall Street Journal,* October 29, 1976.
39. *Jewish Affairs,* 1984 Supplement.
40. Lumer, *Zionism,* p. 72.
41. Henry Winston, "For A People's Peace Crusade," *Political Affairs*, December 1979.
42. Jack Kling, "Some Thoughts on Zionism," *Political Affairs,* September 1981.
43. Herbert Aptheker, "Israel, Lebanon and the Quest for Peace," *Political Affairs,* October 1982.
44. Communist Party press release, June 28, 1982.
45. *Guardian,* May 16, 1979.
46. Aptheker, "Israel, Lebanon and the Quest for Peace," op. cit.
47. *Daily World*, January 29, 1980.
48. *Daily World*, May 14, 1974, July 7, 1976.
49. *Wall Street Journal*, October 29, 1976.
50. Kling, "Some Thoughts on Zionism," op. cit; *Jewish Affairs*, November-December 1983.
51. *Jewish Affairs,* November-December 1983.
52. *Jewish Week,* June 22, 1984.
53. *Daily World*, November 29, 1975.
54. Daniel Berrigan, The Middle East: Sane Conduct," *Liberation,* February 1974;

Committee for a Just Peace in the Middle East Press Release dated November 6, 1980.

55. *Jewish Affairs,* March 1980.
56. *Daily World,* March 7, 1974, June 14, 1974.
57. *Daily World,* March 17, 1976; *Congressional Record,* June 16, 1977, p. 19579.
58. *WREE View,* September-October 1983.
59. *Daily World,* March 30, 1983.
60. *Daily World,* March 13, 1985.
61. *Daily World,* April 6, 1976, January 20, 1977; Gus Hall, "Build a People's Front Against the Economic Crisis," *Political Affairs,* April 1975.
62. Arnold Bechetti, "Communists Are Working-Class Activists," *Political Affairs,* December 1983; Scott Marshall, "Industrial Concentration and Work Among the Unemployed," *Political Affairs,* November 1983.
63. *Daily World,* April 6, 1979.
64. See Ralph Roy, *Communism and the Churches,* (New York: Harcourt, Brace and World), 1960.
65. *New York Voice,* April 17, 1982.
66. Testimony of William Webster, Hearings of the Subcommittee on Security and Terrorism of the Committee on the Judiciary of the US Senate, February 2, 1983, p. 72.
67. *Daily World,* October 30, 1984.

Part 2

Radical Sects and Splinter Groups

Introduction

Communist splinter groups have existed almost as long as the Communist Party itself. The CPUSA, like its counterparts around the world, has traditionally been intolerant of internal dissent. Additionally, dissident communists have frequently been convinced that they alone were in possession of the truth about the laws of society and revolution and have hastened to set up parties with the correct line. Many of these groups have a short half-life; they form, fulminate and founder within a few years. Others, however, have proved more resilient.

Trotskyism has been the most enduring communist splinter movement. Created by Leon Trotsky, one of the architects of the Russian Revolution and later one of its most prominent victims, the Trotskyist movement has endured, but not always prospered, since the 1920s. From the beginning Trotskyists have attacked the Soviet Union as a deformed worker's state and called for a political revolution to overthrow its bureaucratic elite. They have also persistently supported the idea of a permanent revolution, by which they mean that revolutionary movements in underdeveloped countries must fight for socialist, not merely nationalist goals. These positions led Trotskyists to attack communist parties from the left, deriding them from their conservatism and willingness to cooperate with "bourgeois" parties and to compromise revolutionary demands.

Over the years, the Trotskyist movement has suffered innumerable splits. Many of the small groups that have emerged over obscure issues have had brief lives; a few, however have survived and, while hardly prospering, merit brief attention in this section. Several organizations, originally committed to Trotskyism, have abandoned its tenets but remain wedded to Marxism-Leninism.

The 1970s saw the emergence of a host of communist groups professing allegiance to the doctrines of Mao-Tse-tung. Maoism was particularly appealing to many New Leftists searching for a more disciplined brand of politics as the early anarchism and freewheeling style of Students for a Democratic Society gave way to Marxism-Leninism in the late 1960s. Mao's China, embarking on a Cultural Revolution to root out bureaucratic elites, experts, and other manifestations of "conservatism," even within the

Communist Party, was a far more attractive model than the more staid Soviet Union. Maoist views, including support for armed revolutionary movements throughout the world, denunciation of both superpowers, and the belief that the Soviet Union had embraced capitalist values, were grafted onto traditional Marxist–Leninist organizational principles and served as an ideological guide for a variety of small parties.

Most of the host of small Maoist groups disappeared in the course of the decade. Others amalgamated into two Maoist parties—the Revolutionary Communist Party and the Communist Party (Marxist–Leninist)—only the former of which still survives. Still other once–Maoist groups abandoned the doctrine after political changes in China and alterations in its foreign policy tarnished its revolutionary image in the West. In some cases they have returned to a more pro–Soviet position.

In addition to the Communist Party and Trotskyist and Maoist groups, there are a number of other radical sects committed to Marxism–Leninism operating in the United States. Some, notably those connected with the Weather Underground, emerged from the collapse of the New Left and support terrorism. Others profess allegiance to such bastions of communist orthodoxy as Albania while still others are at the boundary line between politics and cults. Several of these smaller groups have a shadowy existence.

4

The Trotskyist Sects

Socialist Workers Party

The Socialist Workers Party (SWP), despite its name, is an organization committed to the achievement of a communist system. "We in the Socialist Workers Party, like Trotsky, are communists," Party secretary Jack Barnes proclaimed in 1983. The Party's goal is a workers and farmers government that will abolish capitalism. It will require a revolution and the establishment of "a new state power—a revolutionary dictatorship of the exploited classes," led by a vanguard Party. This goal cannot be achieved by reform or elections or transitional goals, but only by a revolution, since capitalists will not surrender their power without a fight.[1]

The SWP traces its origin to 1928 when James Cannon, one of the leaders of the Communist Party of the United States, was converted to the cause of Leon Trotsky while in the Soviet Union to attend a Communist International meeting. Returning home, Cannon quietly began to recruit allies within the CPUSA; discovered, the heretics were expelled. At first, the small band of Trotskyists hoped to be readmitted to the movement they had just left and concentrated on recruiting from it. In the mid-1930s the Trotskyists began their efforts to work in a wider radical milieu. They merged with A.J. Muste's American Workers Party in 1934 to form the Workers Party. By 1936, in response to directives from Trotsky, his followers dissolved that group and entered the Socialist Party, the better to capture it for Trotskyism. They were expelled in 1937 (and created the Socialist Workers Party) but not before they had converted most of the Socialist youth group to their cause.

Over the years, however, the SWP has probably lost far more members from splits than it has gained through amalgamations. Forty percent of the thousand–member Socialist Workers Party was expelled or quit in 1940, including Max Shachtman and James Burnham, and promptly formed the

Workers Party. Another series of splits, beginning in the early 1950s and continuing for twenty years, centered around the Party's relationship and disagreements with the Fourth International, a worldwide organization of Trotskyist parties, which had been founded in 1938.

Technically, the SWP was not a member of the Fourth International because of restrictive American legislation passed in 1940. Still, it played a major role in its deliberations and provided in-kind support in lieu of paying dues. The SWP had taken a major role in rebuilding the Fourth International after World War II. In the early 1950s, however, the International's European leadership advocated a policy called "entrism." They urged Trotskyists to dissolve their organizations and join communist or socialist parties, whichever was stronger in a given country, working within them as a secret faction. A group in the SWP, led by Bert Cochran, and comprising one-fourth of the membership, was expelled for supporting entrism. After discovering that the Fourth International had provided secret help to the Cochran forces, the SWP broke away from it from 1953 to 1963.

When the SWP rejoined the Fourth International in the early 1960s, it angered some of its members and provoked another split. One group, led by James Robertson, formed the Spartacist League. Another, led by Tim Wohlforth, set up the American Committee for the Fourth International, which evolved into the Workers League. The SWP's relationship with the Fourth International did not remain friendly for very long. It once again found itself at odds with the International's majority in the mid-1970s when that majority favored a policy of support for Latin American terrorism while the SWP opposed the policy on tactical grounds. One hundred SWP members were expelled in 1974 for supporting the Internationalist Tendency, as the pro-terrorist faction was known.

The latest series of splits in the SWP has again drawn it into conflict with the Fourth International. Much of the dispute revolves around the decision of the Party leadership to jettison some of the traditional theoretical positions of the Trotskyist movement, including the concept of permanent revolution. Party leader Jack Barnes has also, however, clearly indicated his disenchantment with the Fourth International and its isolation in the world revolutionary movement. In a speech in 1981 he charged that "a substantial number of organizations that label themselves Trotskyist are hopeless, irredeemable sectarians" and estimated that 70–90 percent fell into that category. To avoid remaining in sectarian isolation, Barnes believes that the SWP must link itself with successful revolutionary forces. He argued that the most significant world developments of the past period have been the revolutionary events in Central America where the most important thinking about revolutionary strategy was taking place. In

Cuba, Nicaragua, Grenada and El Salvador the groundwork was being laid "for a new, mass communist international" that would reinvigorate the world radical movement. The Trotskyists had the opportunity "to be recognized as legitimate components of the worldwide communist movement that must be built." To gain acceptance from Cuba, however, would require the SWP to shed some of its Trotskyist baggage of the past.[2] The Fourth International has been critical of the SWP's new line and has demanded that it readmit those members expelled for opposing it, so far to no avail.

The SWP's membership began to shrink after World War II. By the late 1950s it had no national industrial union fractions and only several local ones. Membership was just a few hundred. The Party began a recovery in the early 1960s and garnered recruits as a result of its work on behalf of the Cuban Revolution and its support of black nationalists like Malcolm X. The Young Socialist Alliance, founded in 1960, achieved considerable success recruiting on college campuses in the early part of the decade.[3]

SWP membership continued to increase during the 1960s. The Party played a major role in the anti–Vietnam activism of the decade and controlled the National Peace Action Coalition, one of the two largest umbrella anti–war groups. It continued to enjoy some success in the early 1970s; its presidential ticket in 1976 received ninety–one thousand votes. In the second half of the decade, however, the SWP began to run into trouble. With the end of the war, one of its prime sources of recruitment began to dry up. Conscious of its largely student, middle–class composition, the Party leadership decided that it was necessary to "proletarianize" to avoid becoming an organization of "aging cadres based largely among relatively highly paid white collar workers and public employees." In 1978 the National Committee approved a turn to industry and party members were encouraged to obtain industrial jobs.[4]

Membership began to drop. The decline accelerated in the early 1980s as the SWP reversed long–standing policies and abandoned some of the central tenets of Trotskyism. The SWP had twenty–five hundred members in the late 1960s and early 1970s. The Party's trajectory since then has been largely downhill. Hundreds of members resigned; hundreds more were expelled in a series of purges. Membership dropped to thirteen hundred fifty in 1981. By the spring of 1985 it was below a thousand and still dropping, with more than a hundred people expelled in 1984. The Party was 40 percent smaller than it had been in the late 1970s. Party leaders seemed unfazed, explaining that the Party may have been smaller but was stronger since its members fully supported its policies. The SWP's vote in presidential elections has been dropping with its membership; it was forty–six thousand in 1980 and less than twenty–five thousand in 1984.[5]

The SWP's internal difficulties are also related to its conflicts with the

United States government. For the last decade the Party has been pursuing a lawsuit against the United States government, seeking damages for the FBI's counterintelligence operation against the SWP, an operation that went on for years and involved extensive use of government surveillance, informers and harassment of Party members. One Party leader, Ed Heisler, was expelled after it was revealed that he had been an FBI informer.

During the lawsuit, one Party member named Alan Gelfand was expelled from the SWP after he violated Party discipline and personally intervened in the case. Gelfand soon brought suit in federal district court asking that he be readmitted to the Party. He alleged that its leadership was composed of government agents; by expelling him they had violated his First Amendment rights. Gelfand was financed by the Workers League, a dissident Trotskyist sect that believes the SWP to be a tool of American and Soviet agents. Although his suit was dismissed after one week of testimony in 1981, it cost the SWP considerable time, money and effort.

The SWP created the Political Rights Defense Fund (PRDF) in 1973 to provide aid for its lawsuit. The PRDF has also handled a number of other SWP cases, including the Gelfand trial. Recently, its major effort has been devoted to preventing the deportation of an SWP member, Hector Marroquin, to Mexico. It has been able to enlist a number of prominent non-Trotskyists in support of its efforts, ranging from people identified with Communist Party front groups like Ben Chavis and Anne Braden to Victor Reuther and Ed Asner. One of its Brooklyn rallies in 1981 against the Immigration and Naturalization Service was cosponsored by the New York Mobilization for Survival, Palestine Solidarity Committee, Legal Services Staff Association of United Auto Workers District 65 and the president of an Amalgamated Clothing and Textile Workers Union local. Holbrook Mahn is national coordinator and John Studer is executive director.[6]

Jack Barnes is the national secretary of the Socialist Workers Party. Mary-Alice Waters, Malik Miah and Barry Sheppard are national chairs. Craig Gannon is national organizational secretary. Other important members of the Political Committee are Larry Siegle, Doug Jenness and Steve Clark. Almost all the members of the Political Committee are full-time Party functionaries. One of the oddities of the Party leadership is that approximately one dozen are graduates of Carleton College, including Barnes, Waters and Siegle. The *Militant* is published weekly; it is edited by Doug Jenness and Margaret Jayko. *Perspectiva Mundial* is a biweekly Spanish-language newspaper edited by Martin Koppel. Steve Clark edits *New International*, the SWP's theoretical journal. *Intercontinental Press*, published twice a month by the SWP for the Fourth International for many years, recently closed down, "merging its resources" with the *Militant* and *New International*. Pathfinder Press is the SWP's publishing wing.

The Young Socialist Alliance is the SWP's youth arm. It shares the "same fundamental political orientation" and has traditionally been the prime source for Party recruiting. The YSA's membership plummeted from eleven hundred fifty to five hundred fifty–six in one year, 1976–1977, as a result of the SWP's decision to transfer nearly six hundred members into the adult Party to bolster its membership in preparation for a World Congress of the Fourth International. Organizational weaknesses arising out of this decision have apparently not yet been overcome. Andrea Gonzalez is national chair, Stuart Crone is national organizer and Peter Thierjung is national secretary.[7]

The basic Party unit remains the branch. The branches have the primary responsibility for recruiting new members and integrating them into Party life. They hold weekly public Militant Labor Forums. They are also expected to have weekly plant sales of the *Militant* in order to make contact with workers.

The Party's internal troubles, however, have severely affected its ability to carry out such tasks. The *Militant* has gotten smaller as the national organization's financial troubles have mounted. Its circulation has also dropped, from twenty–two thousand in 1977 to under ten thousand in 1982. Paid subscriptions have fallen from twelve thousand to under five thousand in the same period. Smaller branches have been consolidated and many intermediate Party structures have been dissolved. The size of the Party apparatus has likewise been cut.

The SWP began a turn to industry in 1978, ordering its cadres to get jobs in factories. It now has nine national industrial fractions in unions ranging from the Auto Workers to the Steelworkers and the Mineworkers. Its two newest fractions are in the International Ladies Garment Workers Union and the Amalgamated Clothing and Textile Workers Union, where it believes it can make contact with large numbers of immigrant workers. Party members in the fractions meet regularly at both the local and the national level. They are expected to try to recruit fellow–workers into the SWP, involve them in political action or demonstrations, and help to forge a new, revolutionary union leadership.

The turn to industry has not been as successful as the Party would have liked. While a majority of the Party membership is in industry and 80 percent now have "experience in the industrial unions" far fewer have apparently been able to obtain and hold steady jobs. The Party's national fractions lost many members during the 1981–1982 recession. One of the SWP's splinter groups has, in addition, charged that its practice of constantly reassigning cadres from industry to industry has proved debilitating. Not only are SWP members unable to build up any seniority, making them vulnerable to layoffs, but they have been unable to root themselves in local unions.[8]

The Party also enforces a rigid set of organizational norms on its members. The last several years have seen a host of expulsions. Most have been based on deep political divisions in the SWP but the ostensible justification for many of them has been the violation of one or more of these norms. Organized discussion of the Party's program is prohibited except for a three–month period prior to the Party convention. There is a ban on factions. Members of different "tendencies" have been prohibited from communicating with each other based on provisions in the Party rules guaranteeing the leadership the right to oversee the operation of tendencies. Members of the Party have been ordered not to talk to members of other Trotskyist groups. Members have been expelled for refusing to repudiate the views of other members; others have been expelled for answering questions asked by non–Party members of the SWP's youth arm. Expelled members have been refused admission to Party bookstores and forums and physically ejected from them.

The SWP encourages its members to join and try to influence certain other groups. A Party–approved resolution called for work in the National Black Independent Political Party (NBIPP), National Organization for Women (NOW), Coalition of Black Trade Unionists, and Coalition of Labor Union Women. "Party members join these organizations, and branches and leadership bodies participate in carrying out our political work with these organizations."[9] This policy often causes friction. Five leaders of the San Francisco chapter of NOW resigned in 1981, charging that SWP members were a disruptive force in the chapter and were manipulating it in the interests of the Party. The Trotskyists also allegedly opposed all kinds of lobbying and supported only demonstrations and rallies, in line with the SWP's opposition to reform politics.[10]

The SWP has also supported the National Black Independent Political Party and achieved some influence within it. Recently, however, the SWP has complained that its supporters in the NBIPP are under considerable pressure from forces hostile to an independent, class–struggle orientation.[11] In mid–1984 some in the NBIPP were reportedly pressing to expel all SWP members on the grounds that they had divided loyalties.[12]

For many years, American Trotskyists have been critical of both the United States and the Soviet Union—the former for being a capitalist, imperialist power and the latter for being a degenerated workers' state. The SWP insisted on the need for a socialist revolution in the United States and a political revolution to overthrow the Stalinist bureaucracy. Party leaders have always, however, been more critical of American capitalism. In the last few years, however, the SWP's tone has changed. The Party is still critical of Stalinism and the Soviet Union but now gives the Soviet Union political support. It applauds its support for Cuba, the Sandinistas and other revolutionary forces and insists that American workers "have a direct class interest in defending the Soviet Union and other workers' states against imperialist pressure and threats."[13] The Party denounces those who see the USA and the USSR as equally responsible for world problems. In line with its more positive view of the Soviet Union, the SWP has down-played its traditional support for Soviet dissidents like Andrei Sakharov. While supporting his right to emigrate, it charged that the campaign on his behalf was part of an anti–Soviet big–business offensive and had nothing to do with human rights.[14] The same Party that saw its prophet murdered on orders from Moscow responded to charges of a Soviet plot against the Pope by calling them "anti–communist slanders against Bulgaria and the Soviet Union."[15] In 1980 SWP leaders heartily praised the Polish Solidarity move-ment; in recent years they have had little to say about it but have criticized Lech Walesa and charged that anti–communist western forces have been using Solidarity for their own ends.[16]

The SWP has sought to differentiate between most communist regimes now in power and Stalinism. It has labeled the Pol Pot government Sta-linist, condemning it as a "murderous regime" led by "petty–bourgeois revolutionaries from the cities." The Party has given support to the Viet-namese invasion of Cambodia. Likewise, it has called the group led by Bernard Coard that overthrew the Bishop government in Grenada petty-bourgeois and Stalinist.[17]

The SWP has an affinity for two of the more repressive regimes in the world, largely on the ground that they are the object of attacks by Amer-ican imperialism. It has insisted that Iranian workers and peasants are better off now than they were before the Khomeini revolution; while mildly critical of the "capitalist" and repressive government of the Ayatollah, the Party generally supports the Iranian revolution and insists that it remains progressive. Cindy Jacquith strongly endorsed the Iranian position in the Iran–Iraq war.[18] Similarly, the SWP has been unimpressed by charges that Libya supports terrorism. After a British policewoman was killed by shots fired from Libya's London embassy, the *Militant* charged that Libyan dip-lomats were being held hostage in the building and that British and Amer-ican imperialists "have launched a provocative campaign of lies and threats against Libya."[19]

The SWP sees the hope of the future for revolutionaries in Central America. Cuba, Nicaragua, and Grenada (before the overthrow of the Bishop government) were the first revolutions since the Bolsheviks "to consciously use state power to advance not only the interests of the workers and farmers of their own countries, but the extension of the world socialist revolution against imperialism." All three are identified as revolutionary but non–Stalinist. Of the three, it is Cuba that has most transfixed the SWP. It is cited as "the best sustained example of how to put a revolutionary approach into practice in leading the worker–farmer alliance and advancing socialist construction." The Party press frequently publishes official Cuban documents and speeches and interviews with Cuban leaders.[20]

The SWP does not foresee an immediate revolutionary crisis in the United States. It believes this country is in a preparatory period to a crisis. The events of the last twenty–five years in Central America have marked "the opening of the American socialist revolution" but there is still a long way to go. "The conditions under which it will be possible for our class and its exploited allies to take power in the United States will be more similar to those that led to revolutionary uprisings in Cuba, Nicaragua, and Grenada than those that exist in this country today." While they wait for American conditions to reach those of Grenada or Cuba, Party members have been assured that the process of radicalization is underway, sparked by the ruling class offensive against workers. The key to an American revolution is the leadership of radicalized labor unions that will form the core of an independent labor party based on the class struggle.[21]

The SWP has traditionally opposed cooperation or alliances with bourgeois political parties. It runs its own candidates for public office to provide a socialist perspective to voters and makes an effort to contest such positions as mayor or congressman in most large cities. Few such candidates get a substantial vote. The Party has refused to support such Democratic candidates as Harold Washington or Jesse Jackson. During the latter's presidential bid in 1984 the SWP insisted that he diverted attention from the need to lead the masses away from the two–party system. It strongly criticized other leftist groups that supported Jackson, charging them with retreating from basic socialist positions. Thus, the SWP accuses the Communist Party of class collaboration for cooperating with bourgeois parties. The Trotskyists believe that because blacks as a nationality are more proletarian and exploited, they are more progressive than whites. Jackson's campaign was seen, then, as an obstacle to creating an independent black political movement.[22]

The Party's position on most domestic issues does not differ greatly from that of many other radicals, or indeed, liberals. It supports school desegregation and busing, the right to abortion, and bilingualism. It has offered a rather unique defense of illegal immigration to the United States. The illegals should be supported not only because they have been persecuted but because they are fellow–workers who "bring more troops for the army" of the revolution.[23]

In one area, the SWP has staked out a unique position on the American left. While ritualistically condemning antisemitism, it is hostile to American Jews. The SWP has insisted that it is only anti-Zionist and not antisemitic. While the Party is most certainly anti-Zionist, it has also attacked mainstream Jewish organizations and insisted that it alone has fought for the "real" interests of Jews.[24]

The Political Committee issued a resolution in the summer of 1984 denouncing the myth that Jews and blacks in the United States had common interests. Jews had allegedly drifted rightward in their politics since World War II in response to changes in their class composition. Additionally, their support for Zionism had provided "an added impulse to the adoption by many Jews of right–wing positions against national liberation struggles, backing racial discrimination against peoples of color, and support for US imperialism."[25]

The resolution was in part a response to the furor that had erupted about Jesse Jackson's close relationship with Louis Farrakhan, the Black Muslim Minister who had made a series of antisemitic remarks during the campaign. The SWP defended Farrakhan, denouncing the "ferocious smear campaign" against him. Those Jews who attacked Farrakhan did not speak "in the interests of the fight against antisemitism," which presumably dictated silence or acceptance of his threats against Jews and characterizations of Judaism as a "gutter religion." Steve Clark went so far as to condemn Jackson for making a "groveling apology to the racists" at the Democratic convention and insisted that Farrakhan had merely used an erroneous formulation.[26] After two years of defending Farrakhan, the SWP suddenly condemned his antisemitism in November 1985, linking it to his supposedly reformist political perspective.[27]

The SWP has long supported and identified with black nationalist doctrines that have included strong expressions of hostility towards Jews. The Party vociferously endorsed and applauded Malcolm X; it apparently sees no paradox in also applauding Farrakhan, who cheered Malcolm's assassination. In 1983 the *Militant* published and praised a heretofore unpublished article by Malcolm on Zionism in which he charged that the Zionists had deceived and tricked Africans with "the number one weapon of 20th century imperialism—Zionist Dollarism."[28]

The SWP is also adamantly opposed to Israel's right to exist. The Party refers to Israel as a "colonial settler–state" and insists that its presence is illegitimate. While it admits that Israeli Jews are a nationality, they are not an oppressed, progressive one; their nationalism cannot be expressed in a state. The only solution for Israelis is "to unite with oppressed Palestineans" in the struggle against imperialism and capitalism. SWP spokesmen deny that this policy is hostile to the real interests of Jews; they will be guaranteed full rights in a democratic, secular Palestine.

The Party has sponsored pro–PLO speakers, including the organization's United Nations representative, and praised the abilities and leadership of Yasir Arafat.[29] The SWP and the majority of the Fourth International have been at odds on the PLO. The SWP has fully supported Arafat; the Fourth International has blamed the Palestinian leader for negotiating with the United States to end the seige of Beirut and for seeking a deal with Washington. The SWP also denies that bourgeois forces dominate the PLO, calling it a "revolutionary nationalist organization."[30]

Fourth Internationalist Tendency

The Fourth Internationalist Tendency (FIT) is a small group of Trotskyists expelled from the Socialist Workers Party in the last few years. Eighteen SWP members signed a call for the formation of such a tendency within the SWP in June 1982. They were all soon expelled and joined by others. While the FIT functions outside the SWP, its members regard the parent organization as a revolutionary Party in need of reform and wish to be readmitted. In February 1985 the world congress of the Fourth International demanded that the SWP readmit those expelled but the order has been ignored so far.

The FIT held its first national delegate conference in October 1984. It claimed to be functioning in nine cities. The group is structured in local organizing committees and has a national organizing committee. Steve Bloom, Bill Onasch and Evelyn Sell are the national coordinators. Frank Lovell edits the *Bulletin in Defense of Marxism*, published monthly. Other influential figures in the FIT include George Breitman, a member of the national committee of the SWP for more than forty years and, until his death, George Weissman, a long–time member of the Political Committee. The delegates to the conference averaged seventeen years in the SWP.

The FIT urges "100 percent opposition to the Stalinist caste in Poland" trying to crush Solidarity. It opposes the SWP's "softness" towards the Khomeini regime in Iran. It believes that Castroism is a revolutionary force but suffers from serious mistakes and it regards the decision of the SWP "to adopt the Cuban Communist Party as its model" as a serious error.[31] While the FIT has bitterly protested against its undemocratic purge from the SWP, the SWP's refusal to allow its adherents to attend SWP events and the new policies of the SWP that have "publicly turned the ideological foundations of our movement upside down and inside out," it still endorsed the 1984 SWP presidential ticket and continues to regard it as the only revolutionary party in America.[32] It has recently joined with several other small groups to form an organization called solidarity.

Socialist Action

Socialist Action is a small organization of a few hundred people, virtually all of whom have been expelled from the Socialist Workers Party in the last few years. It held its founding conference in October 1983 and proclaimed itself a "public faction" of the SWP, designed to fight to change that group's policies and to get reinstated in its ranks. It has, however, increasingly come to see itself in competition with the SWP and appears to be more interested now in supplanting than in arguing with it.

Socialist Action stands for traditional Trotskyist positions and argues that the SWP has abandoned them. It supports the idea of permanent revolution, i.e., the idea that it is possible to struggle for directly socialist revolutions in underdeveloped countries. It is harshly critical of repressive socialist and revolutionary regimes, including Iran, the Soviet Union and Poland, insisting that radicals cannot apologize for or excuse their depredations to avoid giving aid to imperialism. It is also critical of the supposed violation of democracy within the SWP and has complained that the Party's abandonment of traditional Trotskyism was carried out without full discussion by the Party membership. Among the leaders of Socialist Action are Jeff Mackler, Nat Weinstein and Lynn Henderson.

The group was an active participant at a Cleveland Emergency National Conference held in September 1984. Hundreds of activists from a variety of organizations met to develop a strategy for opposing American policy in Central America. The Conference played an important role in mobilizing support for the April 20, 1985 demonstrations in the United States against intervention. *Frontline*, a radical newspaper, credited Socialist Action with initiating the gathering and developing its strategy of restricting the range of issues to US intervention in Central America, cooperating with mainstream political forces in the Democratic Party and the labor unions and avoiding too–close identification with the Sandinistas or the Salvadoran rebels. Socialist Action's strategy, followed by the organizers of the April 20th San Francisco demonstration, tried to avoid linking the Central American issue to other causes like that of the Palestinians or to support of communist–led regimes or guerrilla groups.[33]

Socialist Action has several hundred members in a dozen cities in the United States, mostly in the Midwest and the West Coast. It has been recognized as a fraternal group by the Fourth International. It publishes a monthly newspaper, *Socialist Action*, and distributes *International Viewpoint*, an English–language publication of the Fourth International.

North Star Network

The North Star Network (NSN) was formed in 1983. Its principal organizer is Peter Camejo, a long–time leader of the Socialist Workers Party and its candidate for president in 1976. Camejo had been on the SWP's National Committee for twenty years before being expelled from the

SWP in 1982. He apparently had lost faith in traditional Trotskyism and had been critical of the Barnes leadership of the Party for not abandoning it more quickly. He was also unhappy about criticisms the SWP had made of some aspects of Sandinista rule, criticisms that were later rescinded. Camejo has described Jesse Jackson's Rainbow Coalition as a significant development in American life, an assessment considerably more positive than that offered by the SWP.[34]

The North State Network regards itself as a "revolutionary but anti-sectarian" group. It wants to serve as a forum, open to all activists who see the need for revolution and wish to establish a government "by, for and of the people." It does not aspire to be a vanguard party or a pre-party formation and has apparently rejected Leninism. Nonetheless, Camejo remained on the International Executive Committee of the Fourth International as a result of support from the United Secretariat of the International as late as 1983. Moreover, Camejo has been quoted as saying that he still believes that the American left needs a vanguard. While apologizing for his past sectarianism, Camejo has also suggested that his generation's rejection of the Communist Party out of hand needs reevaluation because of the role of the Cuban communists and the Sandinistas. Other leaders of the group include Byron Ackerman and Gene Lantz.[35]

The North Star Network has been particularly active in support work for Central American radical movements. It is part of a Bay Area United Forum on the West Coast in which various radical groups including the Bay Area Socialist Organizing Committee (BASOC), *Guardian* groups, former members of the New American Movement and Workers Power (a group including ex-Trotskyists Milton Zaslow, Myra Tanner Weiss and Carl Boggs which publishes *Against the Current*) cooperate. In the fall of 1984 the North Star Network and BASOC announced a planned fusion. A hundred people attended its founding conference at which one report, on the Rainbow Coalition, was given by Wilson Riles, Jr., a prominent black politician from Oakland.[36]

Spartacist League

The Spartacist League (SL) is a small Trotskyist group with a reputation as one of the most doctrinaire of the Marxist-Leninist sects in the United States. It traces its origins to conflicts within the Socialist Workers Party in the early 1960s. The Revolutionary Tendency in the SWP included what was to become both the Spartacist League and the Workers League. After a split in the Tendency, James Robertson, Shane Mage and Geoffrey White were expelled from the SWP in 1964. Their disagreements with the SWP included the charge that the Party had capitulated to such petty-bourgeois

ideologies as Castroism, had stood on the sidelines of the racial issue and
was resistant to developing Party work among southern workers. The dissidents soon published the first issue of *Spartacist*.

For two years those expelled continued to appeal for reinstatement into
the SWP. They finally decided that the party had become hopelessly reformist. An attempt to unite with Gerry Healy's English–based International
Committee of the Fourth International ended in failure when that
Trotskyist splinter organization opted for the allegiance of the Workers
League. In September 1966 the Spartacist League was founded in Chicago
with about seventy–five members. Even that tiny number was soon whit-
tled down. An internal Party document proudly noted that as a result of
"individual drop–outs, factional losses, and our own purging, we managed
to reduce out membership to around forty by the middle of 1969."[37]

Due to its size the Spartacist League saw itself primarily as a propaganda
group, although even that designation was more hope than fact. In the late
1960s, by its own admission, it was "a sub–propaganda group" whose goal
was to become a "stable propaganda group." With so few members the SL
did not see many opportunities for working in mass movements. In fact, it
decided not to participate in them unless they had an "exemplary
character," meaning that it selected only those where there was an opportunity to focus the League's propaganda line or to provide its cadres with
important experience. The SL consoled itself by arguing that it would
recruit those people who "respond more to our powerful ideas than to our
limited ability to put them into practice." One result of that strategy was
that the SL had a limited appeal to workers. Many of its small number of
recruits were students and it established branches in such college towns as
Ithaca, Austin, and Iowa City in the late 1960s. About 10 percent of the
membership was black but virtually all of them soon quit.[38]

The Spartacist League enjoyed a modest growth in the early 1970s,
largely by a small infusion from the remnants of the New Left, particularly
disillusioned Maoists after President Nixon's trip to China. Current membership figures are not available but it is doubtful if there are more than two
to three hundred members. The League has groups in Boston, Chicago,
Cleveland, Detroit, Los Angeles, New York, Oakland, San Francisco,
Washington, Toronto, Atlanta, Madison, Ann Arbor, and Norfolk, but
several of the branches seem practically dormant. The SL's constitution
provides for an elaborate organizational structure but the reality has never
matched its organizational dreams. In the 1970s it had small groups in a
few unions. These members tried to work through caucuses of Spartacists
and other militants. By and large they avoided direct identification with the
SL and focused on issues of rank and file control of the unions.

One unique feature of the Spartacist League's structure is that it recognizes the right to have party fractions and gives them proportional representation on all leading bodies. However, only those who fulfill the duties of membership, as defined by the leadership, have the right of factional prerogatives.

James Robertson is still the national chairman of the Spartacist League. Noah Wilner and Jan Norden edit the *Workers Vanguard*, a biweekly that claims to have thirty–one hundred subscriptions. In the spring of 1986 the League liquidated the Spartacus Youth League (SYL). The League publishes *Women and Revolution; Spartacist* is published by the International Executive Committee of the International Spartacist Tendency, an organization considerably less grand than its name suggests.

The Spartacist League calls for workers to break with the Democratic Party, which it identifies as the liberal wing of imperialism. The SL exulted that Jesse Jackson's "disgusting antisemitic slur" revealed him to his "fake-left cheerleaders." He was "an unprincipled opportunist and demagogue" whose role was to channel the anti–Reagan feelings of blacks into the Democratic Party. The League was even harsher about Jackson's Jewish critics: "those who rant most about black antisemitism are themselves violent racists who believe the only good Palestinian Arab is a dead one."[39]

Much of the League's public activity centers around demonstrations at which it mobilizes its cadres. It has claimed credit for stopping Klan and Nazi rallies. Its Labor–Black Mobilization attempted to prevent the Ku Klux Klan from marching in Washington DC in 1982. The SL was accused of fomenting violence when a riot broke out; it forced a newspaper to retract the charge. Authorities regard the group warily; it was listed as a potential disrupter of the Democratic Convention in 1984 but denied any intent to cause trouble and even offered to help protect the convention.[40] In 1983 the SL filed a successful lawsuit to compel the FBI to retract the charge that it advocated the violent overthrow of the government. The campaign was carried out by the SL's Partisan Defense Committee.[41]

Whether or not it advocates or causes violence, the SL does not practice tolerance. Nor does it limit its attacks to the KKK and the Nazis. The Spartacus Youth League has participated in disruptions of speeches by a variety of people and its newspaper approvingly noted: "Kirkpatrick at Berkeley, Pastora at Columbia, Weinberger at Harvard: Keep them on the run!"[42]

The Spartacist League's foreign policy positions provide general support for the Soviet Union, which it regards as a deformed workers state that conciliates imperialism. One SL speaker insisted that "We'd better be thankful the Soviets have the bomb because it's given us a little breathing space."[43] One of the Party's slogans is "Down with US/China Anti–Soviet Axis." While not uncritical of Soviet foreign policy (the SL condemned the invasion of Czechoslovakia), its practical suggestions (the Czechs should practice critical fraternization, i.e. seek to convince Soviet soldiers they should be in Vietnan fighting imperialism) suggest the limits of its anti–Sovietism. More recently the SL called Solidarity a "Polish company union for the CIA and bankers" and labelled it counterrevolutionary. The SL also supported the Soviet invasion of Afghanistan. One slogan went: "Hail Red Army! Extend Social Gains of the October Revolution to Afghan Peoples."[44] It has also called on the Soviet Union to "Try the Traitors Sakharov!"[45]

The SL remains committed to the Trotskyist concept of permanent revolution. It rejects the Maoist model of peasant–based guerrilla warfare and believes in the decisive role of the working class in any revolutionary movement. Thus, it does not support what it considers bourgeois nationalist revolutions. Its position on the Iranian revolution was "Down with the Shah! Down with the Mullahs! For Workers Revolution in Iran!" The League supports neither side in the Iran–Iraq war. Instead, it urges workers on both sides to turn their guns on their ruling classes.[46] On Central America, the SL has defended the Sandinista revolution but complained that it is too conciliatory to the Catholic Church and the Nicaraguan middle class. It demands that the Soviet Union and Cuba supply Nicaragua "all necessary military aid."[47]

The Spartacists' position on the Middle East issue follows the same general lines. They are critical of the PLO for its nationalism, charging that it retards class struggle and cooperates with imperialism. By making an agreement with the United States to have the Marines oversee his evacuation from Beirut, Yasir Arafat allegedly furthered the goals of a Pax Americana and contributed to the Sabra and Shatillah massacre. At the same time, while critical of the PLO's nationalism, the SL is harshly opposed to Israel. "We defend the Palestinians and Lebanese Muslims against Begin's genocidal campaign, and recognize that every casualty inflicted by the PLO fighters against the Israeli war machine, every Israeli soldier sent home in a bodybag, hastens the day when the Zionist fortress can be overthrown from within," went one statement. The SL calls for a socialist federation that would include the West Bank, Israel and Jordan. This binational state would resemble Yugoslavia in its structure.[48]

Workers League

The Workers League (WL) is a small Trotskyist sect. Its most notable characteristic is its vociferous campaign against the Socialist Workers Party on the grounds that the latter is controlled by a band of American intelligence agents, recruited by a one-time Soviet agent who connived in the assassination of Leon Trotsky.

The origins of this bizarre sect lie in the intricacies of Trotskyist politics. When the SWP began to consider rejoining the Fourth International early in the 1960s, two dissident factions emerged. One, led by James Robertson, evolved into the Spartacist League. The other became the Workers League.

The guiding spirit of the WL was Tim Wohlforth. Originally a leader of the youth group of the Independent Socialist League, led by Max Shachtman, Wohlforth was opposed to Shachtman's decision to disband it and join the Socialist Party in 1958. Instead, he joined the Socialist Workers Party. In 1963 Wohlforth was removed from the SWP's Political Committee due to his increasing opposition to its policies. He particularly opposed its support for Castro and its approval when the Ceylonese Trotskyists entered a coalition government. He became national secretary of the Workers League when it was formed in 1966 and remained in that position until 1974 when he was suspended for security reasons after the League learned that his long-time companion was related to a former official of the CIA. Wohlforth soon rejoined the SWP but quickly became disaffected from it once again.

The current national secretary of the Workers League is David North. Other Party leaders identified in its press include Barry Grey, Fred Williams, Jean Brust and Ed Winn, the national chair of the group's Trade Union Alliance for a Labor Party. The League's youth organization is Young Socialists; among its leaders are Paul Scherer and Paul Tanner. The WL publishes the *Bulletin*, edited by Martin McLaughlin, twice a week, a Spanish bi-weekly, *Pensa Obrera*, and the YS publishes *Young Socialist* monthly.

When the SWP rejoined the Fourth International, it abandoned the International Committee of the Fourth International, the world Trotskyist organization it had belonged to for a decade. The WL became the American affiliate of this latter group. (The Workers League is not legally affiliated with the International Committee because of restrictive American legislation. The relationship between the two is, however, close.) The International Committee was dominated by the British Workers Revolutionary Party (formerly the Socialist Labor League), led by Gerry Healy. The WRP was a vociferous supporter of the Libyan dictator, Colonel Gaddafi. Its most famous member was undoubtedly the actress Vanessa Redgrave, whose antics on behalf of the Palestinian cause gave the WRP some notoriety. In the past two years the WRP has been torn apart by revelations that Healy sexually exploited female Party members. Several splits have taken place and the Party is but a shadow of its former ghostly self.

Although the WL does not provide any figures, it does not appear to have more than a few hundred members. Party headquarters are in Detroit; there are branches in several other midwestern cities, New York, and a few scattered localities. In 1984 Ed Winn and Helen Halyard, the assistant national secretary of the WL, were the League's ticket for the presidency. They were on the ballot in six states and received about ten thousand votes.

The Workers League believes that the "capitalist system is in its death agony." In response to this crisis, capitalists led by President Reagan are mounting a global counterrevolution to destroy living standards and smash labor, to destroy national liberation movements, enslave semi–colonial countries, and reconquer Russia, China and Eastern Europe. The WL "work[s] for the defeat of US imperialism in every war." It is critical of the Stalinist bureaucracy in the Soviet–bloc countries for "direct collaboration with the imperialist war drive" because it seeks peaceful coexistence with the West. Nonetheless, it regards the USSR as more progressive than the United States. The WL thus condemns the Soviet invasion of Afghanistan and supports the Polish Solidarity movement but decries any American effort to combat the Soviet Union as counterrevolutionary.[49]

Since it believes that the bourgeoisie of colonial countries is incapable of a consistent fight against imperialism, the WL thinks it is imperative that their working classes lead these fights and struggle not just for national rights but also for socialism. Thus, while it supports revolutions in Central America and the Caribbean as blows against American imperialism, it is critical of such "bourgeois nationalists" as Castro, Tomas Borge of the Sandinistas, and Maurice Bishop because they did not lead true proletarian revolutions. In a similar fashion, while denying that they are proletarian revolutions, the WL supports all national liberation movements, including those of the PLO and the guerrillas in El Salvador.

The League has harshly attacked Syria and other Arab countries as "bourgeois nationalists" and supported the PLO against "the reactionary conspiracies of imperialism, Zionism, Stalinism and the national bourgeoisie."[50] Some of the League's kindests words are reserved for Libya, to whom it sent "warmest revolutionary greetings" in 1981. Some of its harshest rhetoric is reserved for Israel; the League charged that the invasion of Lebanon was "genocidal" and typical of Zionist crimes.[51] It calls for the destruction of Zionism and the creation of a democratic secular state in Palestine.

The WL's domestic views are predicated on its belief that "Wall Street's policies of mass starvation and war are leading it to prepare the most brutal dictatorship ever seen inside the United States." It denounces and condemns reformism of any variety. In the 1984 elections the League denounced the Democratic Party as anti–labor and Jesse Jackson for giving aid to it. The WL participated in the elections to gain support for a break with the two–party system and to agitate for a labor party built on the unions. Such a party, however, will have to "break with the trade union bureaucrats' cowardly and treacherous policy of collaboration with imperialist oppression abroad and corporate tyranny at home" and drive current labor leaders out of the labor movement. Its demands were appropriately millenial, ranging from nationalizing all banks and basic industry without compensation to their owners, confiscation of all wealth of billionaires and speculators, and free medical care to abolition of the military budget, cancellation of NATO, disbanding of the FBI, CIA and Pentagon and restoration of all cuts in social services. The campaign centered, however, on a call "for the convening of a Congress of Labor Party, committed to fight for a socialist program."[52]

The Workers League does not believe that socialism can be achieved through the ballot box. It advocates the formation of Labor Party committees in factories and neighborhoods. Where layoffs or shutdowns are threatened, these committees should fight for union occupation of the factories and their nationalization under workers' control. In fact, the League's bark seems far more ferocious than its bite. It does not appear to be much more than a propaganda organization and its activities largely confined to support for strikers.[53]

The Workers League has spent the last decade on a campaign to demonstrate that the SWP, the largest Trotskyist party in the United States, is a tool of the FBI. Its investigation of Trotsky's assassination in 1940, in collaboration with the International Committee, has focused on charges that members of Trotsky's entourage betrayed him at the behest of the KGB and that Joseph Hansen, for many years a leading SWP figure, was a "GPU–turned–FBI agent." According to this argument, the FBI, with Hansen's assistance, gained control of the SWP, corrupted its policies, and used it to spy on and disrupt the American labor movement and national liberation movements abroad.

The murder of a Workers League leader, Tom Henehan, in New York in 1977, has added grist to the WL's conspiracy mill. Henehan was shot at a WL dance; the two killers were later convicted of murder. The League, however, has insinuated that his murder was ordered by the SWP in retaliation for the disclosures of its government ties. In a typical example of the overheated rhetoric characteristic of the WL, one pamphlet claimed that "Comrade Tom will now serve as an inspiration to millions all over the world who are fighting to destroy capitalism."[54]

Workers World Party

The Workers World Party (WWP) is a small but active Marxist–Leninist sect. Its primary focus has been on organizing protest meetings and demonstrations on a variety of issues connected to racism and imperialism. Many of these protests have attracted large numbers of other radical groups in temporary united fronts.

The WWP was founded in 1959 by a group of dissidents from the Socialist Workers Party, led by Sam Marcy and Vincent Copeland, and concentrated among Buffalo steelworkers. Some of its founders had been close to the Cochran faction of the SWP, expelled in 1953 for advocating "entrism," a tactic whereby Trotskyists were urged to disband their parties and enter communist or socialist parties in order to subvert them from within. The WWP soon abandoned its early Trotskyism and rarely made any reference to it. In the late 1960s it briefly admired Mao–Tse-tung but it has generally become a strongly pro–Soviet party.

The party's youth wing, Youth Against War and Fascism, was founded in 1962 with just fifty members and soon earned a reputation as the most militant and provocative force in the anti–war movement. YAWF organized the first demonstration against American policy in Vietnam in August 1962. As protests against the war escalated, its members could be found carrying National Liberation Front flags at demonstrations. YAWF was the only group to join the Weatherman organization in Chicago during the Days of Rage in 1969 to participate in pitched battles with the police.

The WWP reached its peak membership with a few hundred members at the end of the 1960s. With the decline of the anti–war movement in the early 1970s it set up groups called the Centers for United Labor Action as part of an effort to gain support from the working class. Members were encouraged to get blue-collar jobs and work in labor unions. These efforts were not entirely successful and the Party's major focus remained on the issues of alleged racism and imperialism. It characteristically sought to build united front collaborations, including other Marxist–Leninist parties, around specific grievances. In 1974, for example, the WWP took the lead in building an Emergency Committee Against Racism in Boston that turned out twenty–five thousand demonstrators during the height of the busing controversy in that city. In both 1967 and 1973 it mobilized demonstrators against Israel, arguing that Vietnam and the Middle East were two fronts in the imperialist war.

By the early 1980s the party had groups in some seventeen cities with approximately three to four hundred members, although one source recently claimed that it had some twelve hundred members, half of them in New York.[55] Most members do appear to be concentrated in the East and the Midwest. Despite these small figures the WWP seems to have an influence on the radical left out of proportion to its size. It sponsors several very active front groups that themselves organize demonstrations and it also organizes marches and protests that bring together a wide variety of radical groups. In addition to Copeland and Marcy, who serves as Party chairman, other leaders include Deidre Griswold, a founding member who was the Party's presidential candidate in 1980 and also serves as the editor of *Workers World*, Tom Soto, Laurie Fierstein, and Fred Goldstein. Published weekly, *Workers World* had an estimated circulation of twenty thousand in 1980. On the ballot in thirteen states in 1980, the WWP got some thirteen thousand votes; in 1984 its presidential candidate, Larry Holmes, received fifteen thousand.

For years the WWP was scornful of electoral politics, insisting that socialism would emerge not from "the rigged election process but through the class struggle."[56] The election of 1980 was its first venture into the political arena. In an even sharper departure from tradition, the WWP supported two black Democrats in municipal races—Harold Washington's campaign for mayor of Chicago and Mel King's candidacy for mayor of Boston—as ways of combatting racism. In 1984 the Party strongly supported Jesse Jackson for president and announced that if he had won the nomination it would not have put up its own candidates. Sam Marcy argued that the Jackson campaign was a powerful symbol against racism as well as a movement against national oppression. Objectively, then, it was a campaign against the capitalist establishment. The Party refused to support Mondale; its candidates Larry Holmes and Gloria La Riva ran on a program of "Jobs, Equality, Socialism, Not War."[57]

Elections, however, are not the WWP's primary interest; nor does support for candidates such as Washington, King or Jackson fully capture its real enthusiasms. The Party admires and defends many of the most repressive regimes in the world, including the Soviet Union, Vietnam, Libya, Cuba, North Korea and Mozambique. While it believes the Soviet Union to be a flawed but important model for socialists, the WWP "defends all the socialist countries unconditionally against imperialism and internal reaction, notwithstanding any differences it may have with the policies of the leader."[58]

Whatever policy differences the WWP has with the Soviet Union, they are not on foreign policy issues. Deidre Griswold defended Soviet intervention in Afghanistan, asserting that Russian aid was no different than "Cuban aid to Angola, Cuban–Soviet aid to Ethiopia, and Soviet and Chinese aid to Vietnam during the war."[59] Robert Dobrow, managing editor of *Workers World*, has argued that whatever problems Cuba has have been caused by the American trade embargo and efforts to overturn the government. Those who want to and have left the island are supposedly a tiny fraction of the population that has been deceived by propaganda about conditions in the United States.[60]

The Party is critical of the Polish Solidarity movement, charging that it is a tool of bankers, the Catholic Church and other reactionary forces to defeat Polish socialism. Andy Stapp, one of the leaders of the American Servicemen's Union during the Vietnam era, dismissed charges that the Polish Communist regime used antisemitism as a tool. He argued that only reactionaries and anti–communists used such tactics.[61]

In contrast to its steadfast support for the foreign policies of communist regimes, the WWP is adamantly opposed to American foreign policy. It fervently supports the Sandinista government in Nicaragua and the rebels in El Salvador. It calls not merely for cutting the American military budget but for "dismantling the Pentagon and the CIA." Larry Holmes supported the right of Puerto Ricans to liberate themselves from American imperialism by armed struggle.[62]

The WWP frequently denounces and protests against American support for Israel and American policy in the Middle East. A party spokesman at one demonstration against the Camp David peace accords charged that they were designed to "insure the continued theft of Mideast oil by the giant US oil monopolies."[63] Delegates from the WWP and the YAWF have attended international conferences in solidarity with the Palestinians and *Workers World* gives strong support to the PLO. The party believes that the "Zionist settler–state" or "the Pentagon's garrison state" is racist and imperialist, has provided no benefit for Jews, has no right to exist, and should be replaced by a democratic, secular state.

On domestic issues, the WWP concentrates on campaigns against alleged racism and discrimination. Gay rights is a major theme and party leaders believe that persecution of homosexuals began only after the development of private property and the patriarchal family. When Jerry Falwell appeared at Town Hall in New York, two of the WWP's front groups protested, disrupting his talk. One spokesman claimed that fascists did not deserve free speech. Another claimed that Falwell's opposition to homosexuals gave a green light to bigots and attacked his "audacity to speak in New York."[64] The WWP also champions the cause of the disabled more than other radical groups; it often announces special facilities at its rallies for them and offers signed interpretation of chants for the hearing-impaired.

While the WWP supports affirmative action with quotas to deal with American racism, its primary focus in this area has been to combat manifestations of racism and offer militant support for attacks on "racists." The Party participated in the coalition formed after the 1979 Greensboro shoot–out to counter the Ku Klux Klan. In 1981 it organized a Martin Luther King Day Memorial Rally Coalition in Buffalo to counter a tiny Nazi demonstration. A party flyer called for a thousand counter–demonstrators with guns. After black riots in Miami Griswold and Holmes argued that such rebellions were both inevitable and justified and they supported blacks' "right to defend themselves against police repression and racist armed vigilante groups by any means necessary."[65] Nor was this an isolated defense of street violence. Speaking at a rally in Washington, DC during an anti–Klan demonstration that had led to violence and looting, Griswold indicated her "solidarity with the Black Youth who were battling police in the surrounding street."[66]

The Party is not as hostile to other manifestations of racism, however. Although it frequently attacks antisemitism and argues that opposition to Zionism is distinct from it, the WWP limits its hostility to white anti-semites. Sam Marcy insisted that for Jesse Jackson to disassociate himself from Black Muslim minister Louis Farrakhan would "constitute a capitulation to the forces of racism and blatant political reaction." According to Marcy even Farrakhan's comments on Hitler had to be understood in historical context. Some oppressed people admired the Nazi leader because he fought against their masters; not because they agreed with his racial doctrines. Racial slurs uttered by the oppressed had to be evaluated differently than those uttered by oppressors. In any case, Marcy argued, those most critical of Farrakhan, American capitalists and Jews, themselves had done little to stop Hitler. Marcy has also argued that like Farrakhan, medieval antisemite targeted Jews "not primarily because they were Jewish, but because the Jews at that time for the most part served as bankers, administrators, supervisors and tax collectors for the lords" who exploited peasants. Another party leader, Monica Moorehead, did admit that Farrakhan's reference to Judaism as a "dirty religion" was incorrect and thought it could be construed as antisemitic.[67]

Youth Against War and Fascism has a National Anti–Draft Network that organizes against registration in schools and communities: it has twenty-five chapters around the country. Among its leaders are Carmen Round-tree, Albert Ramos, Heidi Silver, and Jaime Veve. Active in organizing an anti–draft demonstration in Washington in March 1980, the Network argues that the draft, racism, sexism and homophobia are all tools used by the ruling class to divide the workers.[68]

Many of the activities of the Workers World Party are carried on under the auspices of its several front groups. The most important are the All-Peoples Congress (APC), the People's Anti–War Mobilization (PAM) and the November 29 Coalition. The first two have the most direct links to the WWP. Monica Moorehead and Gwendolyn Rogers are national coordinators of the APC, and Larry Holmes is national organizer. Moorehead and Holmes are prominent WWP figures. Other APC leaders include Steven Kirschbaum, Vera Brown and Bill Roundtree. The coordinator of the PAM is Tom Soto, another WWP cadre. Moreover, it was the PAM that sponsored the first All–Peoples Congress in the fall of 1981. The two organizations appear to be almost interchangeable, sharing offices and telephones in many cities. In some places, such as Houston, Chicago and Detroit, the PAM shares offices with the WWP. The APC seems to focus mostly on domestic issues while the PAM concentrates its energies on foreign policy questions.

The first APC in Detroit in the fall of 1981 drew some one thousand people. It claims to be a coalition of 120 organizations; most of its constituent units appear to be small, ad hoc local groups. Its primary focus has been on combatting the supposed evils of Reaganism and it publishes the All-Peoples Congress Bulletin, a monthly publication. Some of its local groups, of which it claims fifty, have been involved in fighting plant closings and fuel hikes. The Jersey City, New Jersey group was active in the Jesse Jackson presidential campaign. The Detroit group filed a lawsuit, quickly dismissed, to compel the Administration to release surplus food to Mississippi; the Detroit City Council passed a resolution, offered by Council President Erma Henderson, endorsing the lawsuit. The Atlanta APC has initiated a campaign against slumlords.

The All-Peoples Congress also organized marches and speeches to "Roll Back Reaganism" during the National Days of Resistance from April 24 to May 2, 1982. The group claimed to have turned out twelve thousand demonstrators in Washington, fourteen hundred in San Francisco, five hundred in Miami and thousands in other cities around the themes of jobs, housing, social services and getting America out of Africa, El Salvador and the Middle East.

The All-Peoples Congress's biggest splash, however, took place on November 27, 1982 in Washington, when an anti-Klan rally it had sponsored degenerated into a violent melee. When a group of Klansmen announced plans to march in the capital, the APC announced its own plans to respond. Among those endorsing its rally were Congressmen Conyers and Dellums. While several other groups planned anti-Klan activities, the APC insisted that it would not allow the Klansmen to march. Somewhere between three and five thousand demonstrators converged on the city, many brought by the APC which offered free bus rides. Some fifteen hundred of the demonstrators first attended a rally organized by the November 29 Coalition, another group with close ties to the WWP. The Coalition had moved its own planned demonstration in support of the Palestinian cause up two days and shifted it from New York to Washington. The APC sheperded its foot-soldiers to the November 29th rally before the anti-Klan rally; they then marched to the latter meeting led by a man in battle fatigues carrying a PLO flag. Chanting slogans such as "Reagan and the Klan work hand-in-hand," the demonstrators turned violent after police tried to keep them away from the handful of Klansmen. Store windows were smashed, bricks and bottles heaved, cars overturned and some looting took place. Police lobbed tear gas and arrested nearly forty people; twelve policemen were injured. The APC blamed the police for the violence, but it and the WWP also boasted that they had stopped the Klan march. Reverend Walter Fauntroy, the District's representative in Congress, praised the APC's orderly, disciplined rally, and blamed the troubles on members of the Spartacist Youth League, another Marxist–Leninist sect.[69]

The November 29 Coalition, renamed the November 29 Committee for Palestine in 1983, and, more recently, the Palestine Solidarity Committee, was formed in 1981 to gain American support for the PLO. Its name came from the day designated by the United Nations as an annual "International Day of Solidarity with the Palestinean People." Closely allied with the Popular Front for the Liberation of Palestine, headed by Dr. George Habash, the Coalition also has close ties to the Workers World Party. It has held meetings at the People's Anti–War Mobilization offices, and in some cities, had the same mailing address and telephone. All–Peoples Congress leaders Larry Holmes and Monica Moorehead were major speakers at the Coalition's Washington demonstration in November 1982—a demonstration that was moved to coordinate with the APC anti–Klan rally. Its meetings and demonstrations have been heavily and favorably reported in the *Workers World*. Its officers include Steve Goldfield, publications director, Jeanne Butterfield, national chair, and Ginny Krause, national director. One hundred delegates attended its 1987 convention. Leaders noted that the group saw itself as a force in the broad peace and anti–intervention movement focusing on Palestine.[70]

Each group provides support for each other's demonstrations. The People's Anti–War Mobilization sponsored a rally against the Sabra and Shattila Massacre in New York in September 1982. In addition to speeches from leaders of the APC, Valerie Van Isler of the November 29 coalition spoke.[71] Even before the Coalition came into existence, the Palestine Congress of North America thanked the PAM for letting Samih Farsoun, its chairman, speak at a PAM demonstration, "the first time the Palestine issue was raised at a sizable American demonstration," according to the PCNA. Moreover, the PCNA has a representative on the board of the PAM.[72]

The Coalition's first public activity took place in 1981; it claimed that its rallies attracted five thousand people in New York, one thousand in San Francisco, seven hundred in Los Angeles and more in other cities. It was relatively inactive thereafter until the Israeli invasion of Lebanon. In response, it sponsored a series of teach–ins during the summer of 1982 that attracted some three thousand people. It held a "March on Washington" on September 11, 1982 to oppose the "US–Israeli invasion of Lebanon," that drew two thousand people. Endorsed by a variety of organizations aligned with the PLO, the demonstration had a steering committee that included representatives from the WWP, PAM, SWP, National Black United Front, Palestine Council of North America, Mobilization for Survival, Committee in Solidarity with the People of El Salvador, Committee for a Democratic Palestine, Farabundo Marti Solidarity Committee, *Guardian*, Jews Against the Massacre in Lebanon, Supporters of the Lebanese National Movement and the US Anti–Imperialist League. It was endorsed by individuals such as Daniel and Philip Berrigan, David Dellinger, and William Kunstler. Among the speakers was Ben Chavis, a prominent leader of the CPUSA's front, the National Alliance against Racist and Political Repression. Chavis spoke, however, in his capacity as an official of the National Black Independent Political Party.

For the 1983 international day of solidarity, the Coalition held another series of teach–ins around the country. In addition to several PLO representatives, Israeli Trotskyists and anti–Zionists, speakers included Noam Chomsky and the US Peace Council's Mark Solomon. At the largest meeting, in New York, 150 people heard Chomsky, Solomon, a PLO representative, Fred Dube, of the African National Congress and Rabbi Elmer Berger, among others, denounce Israel and Zionism. The most vituperative comments came from black author John Henrik Clark, who suggested that the Palestinian problem started two thousand years ago and was related to European exploitation of the non–European world. Clark complained that Jews had participated in the greatest holocaust in history—the murder of black Africans. The teach–in coincided with an effort to transform the November 29 Coalition into a more activist membership organization from a coalition of groups.[73]

The relationships between the November 29 Coalition and other pro–Palestinian support groups are complex and their base of support in the non–Arab radical community in America differs. The November 29 Coalition emphasizes four major points: opposition to US intervention in the Middle East, opposition to all US aid to Israel, support for the PLO as the sole legitimate representative of Palestinean interests and their right of self–determination and to return to Palestine, and opposition to the role of Israel in the region and the Third World. The National Emergency Committee on Lebanon, founded in 1982, included a representative from the PAM but it is closer ideologically to the Communist Party and limited its public calls to demands for Israeli withdrawl from Lebanon and no American aid to Israel. Thus, WWP leaders like Tom Soto participate in the more moderate National Emergency Committee while exercising major influence in the more maximilist November 29 Coalition. The former group held a rally in New York on July 10, 1982 that attracted five thousand people. Leaflets handed out at the rally listed the Mobilization for Survival and the People's Anti-War Mobilization as contacts for more information.

Most of the WWP's non-Mideast rallies and demonstrations take place under the auspices of the People's Anti-War Mobilization, whose stated goal is to build a "truly united, massive national resistance to combat Reaganism." On May 3, 1981 it sponsored a march on the Pentagon to protest American policies in El Salvador and cuts in domestic programs. The march had the support of CISPES. Larry Holmes was master of ceremonies and the speakers included Bella Abzug, a Maryknoll nun, and Paul O'Dwyer. Twenty-five thousand people were on hand.[74]

PAM has been far less successful at rallying its troops for other demonstrations. It sponsored a counter-inaugural to protest against President Reagan in 1985, but was only able to muster between three and five hundred people. Likewise, a demonstration against the President when he came to New York to speak at the United Nations drew only one hundred people. These episodes suggest that it is only when it provides a focus for individuals and groups upset at particular American policies that PAM can produce large numbers of demonstrators.[75] One such episode took place in July 1983 when seventy-five hundred demonstrators assembled near the Vietnam Veterans Memorial in Washington to "Stop the US War Against Central America and the Caribbean." The protest was sponsored by the Ad Hoc Committee for a July 2 Emergency Coalition which happened to have the same offices and telephones as PAM and the APC. The rally coordinator was Tom Soto.[76]

PAM has recently begun to focus its attention on Southern Africa. It formed a "US Out of Southern Africa Network" to "expose and disrupt political, military and economic links" with South Africa. At one of its gatherings in Chicago, speakers included Camelia Odeh of the November 29 Coalition, Danny Davis, a Chicago alderman, and Monica Moorehead of the APC.[77]

The WWP publishes *Workers World* every week. The PAM publishes the *People's Anti-War Mobilizer*. The APC publishes the *All-People's Congress Bulletin*. The November 29 Committee for Palestine publishes *Palestine Focus*.

Notes

1. Jack Barnes, "Their Trotsky and Ours," *New International*, Fall 1983.
2. Ibid.
3. Not even the Party's brief association with Lee Harvey Oswald, the assassin of President Kennedy, proved harmful. Oswald had been active in the Fair Play for

Cuba Committee, an SWP front group, and had tried to join the Party. He had been turned down only because there was no branch in Dallas and at-large members were not allowed.

4. "The Revolutionary Perspective and Leninist Continuity in the United States," *New International*, Spring 1985.
5. Ibid.
6. *Militant*, June 5, 1981.
7. "The Revolutionary Perspective."
8. Ibid; *Socialist Action*, December 1983.
9. "The Revolutionary Perspective."
10. *San Francisco Chronicle*, August 26, 1981.
11. "The Revolutionary Perspective;" *Militant*, April 6, 1984.
12. *Bulletin in Defense of Marxism*, May 1984.
13. "The Revolutionary Perspective."
14. *Militant*, July 20, 1984.
15. *Militant*, November 9, 1984.
16. *New York Times*, September 18, 1980.
17. "The Revolutionary Perspective."
18. *Militant*, April 8, 1983; *Intercontinental Press*, May 14, 1984.
19. *Militant*, May 4, 1984.
20. Barnes, "Their Trotsky and Ours,"; Fidel Castro, "The Cuban Countryside, Then and Now," and "Farm Cooperatives in Cuba," *New International* Spring 1985.
21. Barnes, "Their Trotsky and Ours."
22. *Militant*, February 17, 1984.
23. "The Revolutionary Perspective."
24. Peter Seidman, *Socialists and the Fight Against Anti-Semitism* (New York: Pathfinder Press, 1973).
25. SWP Information Bulletin, No. 4, 1984.
26. "The Revolutionary Perspective"; *Intercontinental Press*, October 15, 1984.
27. *Militant*, November 22, 1985.
28. *Militant*, February 25, 1983.
29. Seidman, *Socialists and the Fight Against Anti-semitism; Militant*, September 3, 1982.
30. Barnes, "Their Trotsky and Ours"; "The Revolutionary Perspective."
31. *Bulletin in Defense of Marxism*, February 1984.
32. *Bulletin in Defense of Marxism*, January 1984.
33. *Frontline*, May 13, 1985.
34. *Intercontinental Press*, December 24, 1984.
35. *Intercontinental Press*, December 24, 1984, November 28, 1983; *Guardian*, January 11, 1984.
36. *Guardian*, January 23, 1985.
37. *Marxist Bulletin #9*.
38. Ibid.
39. *Workers Vanguard*, March 30, 1984.
40. *Workers Vanguard*, July 6, 1984.
41. *Workers Vanguard*, March 8, 1985.
42. *Young Spartacus*, November 1983.
43. *Workers Vanguard*, December 16, 1983.
44. *Marxist Bulletin #9; Young Spartacus*, November 1983.

45. *Workers Vanguard*, November 15, 1985.
46. *Spartacist*, Autumn, 1983.
47. *Young Spartacus*, November 1983.
48. *Spartacist*, Autumn 1983.
49. *Mobilize Labor Against Reagan: Perspectives of the Workers League* (Detroit: Labor Publications, 1982).
50. *Bulletin*, June 28, 1983.
51. *Bulletin*, September 30, 1982; *Mobilize Labor Against Reagan.*
52. *Mobilize Labor Against Reagan; Bulletin*, January 13, 1984.
53. *Mobilize Labor Against Reagan.*
54. *The Assassination of Tom Henehan: The Investigation Must Continue*, (Detroit: Labor Publications, 1981).
55. George Vickers, "What's Left?: A Guide to the Sectarian Left," *Nation*, May 17, 1980.
56. *Workers World*, April 4, 1980.
57. *Workers World*, February 2, 1984.
58. *Workers World*, April 4, 1980.
59. Ibid.
60. *New York Times*, June 4, 1980.
61. *Workers World*, March 20, 1981.
62. *Workers World*, April 4, 1980.
63. *Workers World*, April 18, 1980.
64. *Workers World*, December 13, 1984; *New York Tribune*, December 12, 1984.
65. *Journal and Guide*, May 28, 1980.
66. *Workers World*, December 3, 1982.
67. *Workers World*, July 12, 1984.
68. *Workers World*, March 14, 1980.
69. *Workers World*, November 12, 1982, December 3, 1982, December 13, 1982; *Washington Times*, November 30, 1982.
70. *Frontline*, September 16, 1985, November 23, 1987.
71. *Workers World*, October 1, 1982.
72. *Workers World*, May 29, 1981, June 5, 1981.
73. *Jewish Week-American Examiner*, December 9, 1983.
74. *New York Times*, May 3, 1981; *Washington Post*, May 4, 1981.
75. *Washington Post*, January 22, 1985.
76. Police estimated there were only 3000–5000 demonstrators; organizers claimed 20,000.
77. *Workers World*, February 28, 1985.

5

The Maoist Sects

Progressive Labor Party

The Progressive Labor Party (PLP) is a small Marxist-Leninist sect that has undergone a number of transformations in its twenty-five year history. Founded as a split-off from the Communist Party of the United States, it was the earliest Maoist Party in this country. In the late 1960s, it exercised a significant role in the Students for A Democratic Socitey (SDS). In the 1970s and 1980s, after its break with Maoism, it defended an unreconstructed Stalinism and was involved in a number of violent and disruptive clashes with authorities.

Several small groups of communists in Buffalo and New York City who opposed the CPUSA's "moderation" in 1959 marked the beginning of PLP. Desirous of a more open communist presence in America, hostile to the Party's belief that the fight for democracy and against monopoly took precedence over the fight of socialism, and critical of the Party leadership's "revisionism," these people were expelled from the CPUSA in 1961. Early in 1962 they began to publish *Progressive Labor.*

In its early years, the Progressive Labor Movement, as it was known, was noted for its flamboyance. It sponsored two illegal trips to Cuba in 1963 and 1964. After one of the trips, Philip Abbot Luce, one of the group's leaders, openly defied the House Un-American Activities Committee, shunning the Communist Party's usual tactic of invoking the Fifth Amendment and boldly proclaiming his revolutionary belief, he left PL for a career as an ultraconservative.

The Progressive Labor Party was formed in 1965 at a convention attended by two hundred people. The new party claimed fifteen hundred members. Few of them were workers; most came from student and middle-class backgrounds. Milt Rosen was chosen Party leader; other major figures were Bill Epton and Mort Scheer. Epton, who was accused and convicted of inciting violence in the Harlem riots of 1964 was expelled from PLP in 1970 in a dispute over black nationalism. PL insisted that all nationalism was reactionary; it opposed the Black Panthers and attacked the National Liberation Front in Vietnam for selling out the Vietnamese Revolution by negotiating with the United States.

After 1965 the PLP disavowed bohemianism and the freewheeling style of its past in an effort to make itself more attractive to workers. It dissolved the May 2nd Movement, its youth group which had been the first student group to oppose the draft, and ordered its members to join SDS. As SDS grew apace in the late 1960s, so too did PLP. Its "old-left" style contrasted sharply with the cultural radicalism of many in SDS, but its Leninist discipline and coherent doctrine enabled it to recruit numerous students. Within SDS, the PLP argued for a worker-student alliance. It sought to send its student recruits into factories on vacations or after their graduation. As PLP gained greater influence in SDS, its opponents, including Mark Rudd, Bernadine Dohrn, Bob Avakian, Mike Klonsky and others, also embraced Marxism-Leninism. At SDS's tumultuous 1969 convention, when it appeared that PLP might win control of the organization, a split took place, leading to its splintering into the Weathermen, the Revolutionary Youth Movement and the PLP-controlled SDS.

PLP's victory in retaining control of the SDS name proved rather hollow; the organization quickly became a shell. In the early 1970s the Party focused on selling its newspaper, *Challenge,* at plant gates. As a result of considerable effort, it pushed circulation to around ninety-thousand in 1970. In 1972 its Workers Action Movement launched a campaign to win thirty hours work for forty hours pay and soon thereafter, PLP began to focus on direct action at the workplace. None of these tactics provided much benefit; party membership shrank rather drastically during the 1970s and virtually disappeared outside a few metropolitan areas.

PLP was also stung by changes taking place in China. In 1971 it charged that its former idol was headed down the same revisionist path earlier trod by the Soviet Union, losing its identification with an existing socialist regime. In the mid-1970s, PLP concluded that its previous activities had been too reformist and it had to reemphasize the need for revolution. That decision led it to become even more shrill and extreme.

It currently has some thirty offices in nineteen states. In the last few years it particularly concentrated on work in the Delano, California area. During the summer of 1984 eighty Party members spent a month there and boosted sales of *Challenge* to five hundred a week. The Party's major front group, the International Committee Against Racism (InCAR) also formed an Anti-Racist Farmworkers Union. Another concentration area is Bushwick in New York.[1]

Although Party leaders are not publicly identified, Milt Rosen apparently is still the major figure in PLP. Party membership is also a closely held secret but it is unlikely to be more than two hundred or so. One Party document urged members to build a base among their friends, with a long-term goal of moving such acquaintances closer to the PLP. Each PLP member was urged to have a base of fifty to seventy-five people and to develop a plan, at regular Party meetings, to move them closer to the organization. Among the organizations PLP members were urged to join to build their base were sports clubs, tenant group, PTA's, and churches.[2]

PLP publishes *Challenge-Desafio,* a bilingual weekly newspaper. A French edition, *Le Defi* is published in New York; an Arab edition, *Al Tahaddi,* in Detroit. The Party also produces a monthly, *Progressive Labor.* InCAR publishes *Arrows.*

Much of the Progressive Labor Party's public presence comes through the International Committee Against Racism. According to a Party statement "InCAR is a radical organization led by the Party which the Party builds in order to advance the struggle for communism."[3] It was founded in 1973 and its leaders included Dr. Robert Kinlock, Toby Schwartz, and Finley Campbell, a former professor. In 1978 InCAR had about fifteen hundred members. One Midwest regional conference in 1980 drew three hundred participants and the group claimed that two thousand people participated in its 1984 convention.

The PLP and InCAR have been active in a variety of demonstrations in the past several years. They have frequently challenged Ku Klux Klan and Nazi rallies with counter-demonstrations of their own, organized around the theme of smashing and destroying their opponents, not simply protesting against them. They have used rocks, bottles, and bricks, forced their way into radio stations and trashed movie theaters as part of their anti-racist crusade.

In 1980, for example, InCAR activists wrecked a San Francisco movie house showing "Birth of a Nation."[4] The following year, responding to a Nazi protest against an Israeli independence day rally, PLP and InCAR demonstrators, chanting "Death to the Nazis," barricaded them in the basement of a civic center and bitterly protested that "Zionists" had prevented them from attacking the Nazis.[5] In 1982 PLP and InCAR members broke through police lines and attacked Klansmen in Hannibal, Missouri.[6] One hundred seventy-five attacked Klansmen in Rockville, Maryland on the grounds that it was necessary to "squash these rodents physically."[7] When the Klan and Nazis held a white pride rally in Arlington, Virginia, they were "met by a hail of rocks and bottles" from the PLP and InCAR. One injured a policeman; *Challenge* exalted over his injury and criticized the All-Peoples Congress, a Workers World Party front group, for trying to stop the violence.[8] At the largest such counter-demonstration, PLP and InCAR mobilized a thousand people in Boston to demonstrate against the Klan.

Another tactic employed by the two groups is to disrupt the speeches and classes of people whom it accuses of racism or fascism. PLP carried out an extensive campaign against the discipline of sociobiology and the view that intelligence is linked to heredity. It "led many direct attacks upon the public addresses of Jensen [a prominent scholar of heritability] and his gaggle of apologists."[9] The PLP's newspaper proudly reported that "we shouted down fascist Falwell at Harvard."[10] PLP members disrupted a Northwestern University class taught by Arthur Butz, who has argued that the Holocaust never took place. They threatened to disrupt a speech at San Diego State University by Louis Farrakhan that was later canceled. Several physicians belonging to InCAR hit Mayor Koch of New York with eggs at a speech.

The PLP and InCAR thus do not limit their disruptions to just alleged Nazis. After one series of rallies calling for the firing of a Wayne State professor who had been Nazi war criminal Klaus Barbie's superior when Barbie worked for American intelligence after World War II, PLP insisted that there was no difference between Nazis and liberals; "the Nazis could not survive without the liberals." As a collaborator, the professor deserved "the same fate as the collaborators who were caught before him."[11] In 1985, Barbara Foley, a faculty member at Northwestern University and a member of InCAR, helped lead a demonstration that prevented contra leader Adolfo Calero from speaking on campus. She was quoted as saying that "he has no right to speak here tonight and we are not going to let him."[12]

Perhaps because it sees no difference between Nazis and liberals, PLP uses the word fascist rather loosely to characterize the most disparate groups and individuals. Solidarity is a "mass fascist movement," while the Polish government it opposes is a "fascist pro-Soviet regime."[13]
The Khomeini regime's "Islamic fundamentalism is an ideal front for fascism and imperialism." Afghan rebels "are in fact anti-worker fascists." Lebanese Phalangists are "a Christian fascist group." Meir Kahane is a fascist. Menachem Begin and Yitzhak Shamir are "more openly fascist" than their Labor Zionist opponents. Mayor Harold Washington of Chicago is a black social fascist.

PLP's characteristic style is pithy, simplistic and vulgar. One headline several years ago explained "ALL Presidential Candidates Stink."[14] Jesse Jackson is "another lackey of racist rulers" who shares the same politics as Richard Nixon. Louis Farrakhan is a "punk" too stupid to realize that Hitler hated blacks as well as Jews.[15] By defending capitalism, union leaders "are ready to defend fascism, which the bosses are moving towards to save their system."[16]

PLP is quite open and blunt about its ambitions. The bosses, who control all political parties in America except the PLP, will never give up power peacefully; workers must "organize a violent revolution." After seizing power they need to build a red army to defend themselves. It will be possible, the Party believes, to institute communist economic relations immediately following the seizure of power. This would mean abolition of the wage system and realization of the dictum of to each according to his need. Providing to each according to his work would discriminate against sections of the working class.

The new government would of necessity be repressive: "we want a system that corrects or punishes capitalist behavior." It would not be democratic: "would we let religious nuts vote . . . [people] who are clearly wrong and thinking in a dangerous way?" The revolution would be led by the PLP, a Party following the dictates of communist centralism and led by a central leadership: "the Party's duty is to make sure no policies are put into effect which go against the interests of the working class, no matter what kind of pseudo-democratic procedures were used to arrive at those policies." The dictatorship of the proletariat may last for two hundred years or for a million. While no one can know how long will be necessary, a lengthy period will be required to cleanse the earth of bourgeois habits.[17]

The Progressive Labor Party does not see anything worth defending in the communist world. Thus, it does not shrink from the prospects of nuclear war. It sees one as inevitable. Such a conflict would destroy the capitalist world but "it could be the beginning of a communist world."[18]

PLP's views on the Middle East are of a piece with its other positions. It denounces nationalists like Arafat who allegedly want their own country and own workers to exploit. It denounces the Israeli capitalists who use "intense racism" against Arabs and Sephardic Jews to perpetuate their rule and make "alliances with fascist butchers" like South Africa, the Shah of Iran, Somoza, and Mobutu. It attacks Syrian leader Assad's "fascist repression." It scorns communist parties in the Mideast for making too many concessions to nationalism. The PLP has argued that one of the Soviet Union's errors was to recognize the Zionist state of Israel since "all Zionists are exploiters who are lined up with imperialism." The only road to peace in the region is genuinely communist revolutions.[19]

Although PLP had often linked Zionism to Nazism, it became even more vitriolic after the invasion of Lebanon. One headline read; "Reagan, Begin: Nazi Mass Murderers." An article charged that Israel "went one up on the Hitlerites" since the former did their massacres in the open.[20]

The PLP was allied briefly with a revolutionary Israeli group called the Red Front in the early 1970s. InCAR has published a letter of support from one of the Front's leaders, Dan Vered, who was convicted of spying for Syria.[21]

Revolutionary Communist Party

The Revolutionary Communist Party (RCP) is one of the few survivors of the New Left inspired Maoist movement of the 1970s. Still loyal to its Maoist roots, it frequently engages in disruptive and provocative behavior. The Party has been unable, however, to grow in the last several years and both its behavior and its rhetoric have become more feverish.

The RCP's origins date to 1969 and the founding of the Bay Area Revolutionary Union (BARU) by a coalition of disillusioned Progressive Labor supporters and independent leftists, many of them veterans of Students for a Democratic Society. One of its founders, an ex-Berkeley student named Bob Avakian, soon became a major figure in SDS as it split apart. BARU changed its name to the Revolutionary Union in 1970. That year another founder, Bruce Franklin, a Stanford English professor, led a split-off that resulted in the formation of Venceremos, a group advocating armed guerrilla violence.

The Revolutionary Union was only one of a number of largely local Maoist groups that sprang up around the country in the early 1970s after the demise of SDS. In 1973 the independent Maoist newspaper, *The Guardian,* sponsored a New York symposium on uniting the various groups and building a new communist party. Twelve hundred people attended. That was the last gasp of unity, however. By 1973 rivalries and disagreements among the Maoist groups were rife. In particular, the Revolutionary Union was at odds with the October League, another Maoist group centered in Atlanta. Disagreements with the *Guardian* led to RU members being kicked off the newspaper in 1973.

By the end of 1973 the Revolutionary Union had some six to eight hundred members, branches in twenty-five cities, and was the largest of the Maoist groups. It very quickly faced severe pressures. The group decided to focus its activities on labor union and strike support. In an effort to penetrate the white working class, it adopted conservative cultural policies, opposing the Equal Rights Amendment and expressing hostility to homosexuals. It also opposed special demands on behalf of blacks. In 1974 the RU created the Committee for Decent Education, which was active in the Boston school busing controversy, opposing the busing of black students. RU insisted that busing only intensified national hostilities and built anti-white attitudes on the part of blacks. Its alliance with white racists enraged many others on the left and also led to the resignations of most of RU's black membership.

Both the October League and the Revolutionary Union formed full-scale communist parties in the mid-1970s, the former the Communist Party (Marxist-Leninist), CP-ML, and the latter the Revolutionary Communist Party in 1975. In addition to its own student group, the Revolutionary Student Brigade, whose membership peaked at around six hundred in 1978, the RCP also controlled the Vietnam Veterans Against the War and, until the mid-1970s, the US-China People's Friendship Association. It also initiated Unemployed Worker Organizing Committees and, in 1977, the National United Workers Organization, but neither effort produced many concrete results. The RCP's most successful project in this period was a Get the Rich Off Our Backs counter-bicentennial march of some three thousand people in Philadelphia in 1976.

The mid-1970s also provided the new communist movement with its greatest crisis, provoked by the arrest of the Gang of Four, a group of Mao's supporters, in China and the sweeping reorientation in both domestic and foreign policies inaugurated by Deng Xiao Ping. Until the upheaval the RCP, in line with Chinese policy, excoriated both the United States and the Soviet Union as imperialist superpowers. In 1976, for example, it attacked Cuba as a Soviet puppet and refused to support the Soviet and Cuban-backed MPLA in Angola.

During 1977-1978 the RCP was paralyzed. While its rival, the CP-ML, enthusiastically endorsed the Chinese government's actions, thus earning its recognition as the "official" Chinese-approved party, the RCP temporized. Finally, in 1978 the RCP condemned the Deng government, charging that revisionists had taken power in Peking and had opted for expertise, elitism and leniency in art and culture. Avakian attacked the reintroduction of Shakespeare, Beethoven, Chopin, Bach and Rembrandt as examples of decadence.[22] The RCP called the Chinese government "a fascist bourgeois dictatorship" and party members were expelled from the US-China People's Friendship Association, whose chairman, William Hinton, had once been a leading figure in the RCP but who remained loyal to the Chinese government.[23]

The harsh condemnation of China led to a split in the RCP. In 1977 it had perhaps two thousand members. One-third of the Party quit, including Hinton, vice-chairman Mickey Jarvis and Nick Unger. They formed the Revolutionary Workers Headquarters which supported the purge of the leftists in China but played down support for Deng. The RWH and the CPML found it increasingly hard to maintain their radical credentials while supporting Chinese foreign policy, which more and more required recognition of the Soviet Union as the major enemy and endorsed a tacit alliance with the United States. By 1984 both of them had disbanded.

The RCP attempted to demonstrate its revolutionary mettle in 1978 when Deng visited Washington, DC. It mounted loud and violent demonstrations against him. On January 29, 78 RCP'ers were arrested at an unruly rally while Deng was at the White House. More than a dozen were convicted of various felony charges, including Bob Avakian who labelled Deng "a puking dog who deserves worse than death."[24] The Party launched a major campaign protesting the injustice done to the "Mao-tse-tung Defendents." Avakian fled to France to avoid what he claimed was political persecution; one newspaper ad demanding that the French government offer him refugee status was signed by such notables as Julian Bond, Daniel Berrigan and Ben Chavis. Even though the charges against him were eventually dropped Avakian has remained in France, leading the Party from there.

The RCP has remained true to its Maoist heritage. It recently sent greetings to the Gang of Four, including Mao's widow, "who are holding aloft the red banner of proletarian revolution and communism in the face of bitter defeat." The Party claims that China is in the grip of a "reactionary bourgeois dictatorship" and that it is steadfast in defending Marxism-Leninism-Mao-Tse-tung Thought.[25]

The RCP believes that the USSR has restored capitalism and become an imperialist superpower no different than the United States. It condemns both in equally vituperative terms. One Party slogan goes: "The Whole System is Putrid! Down With US-Soviet War Moves!" In one symbolic gesture two RCP members splattered red paint on American and Soviet diplomats at the United Nations, shouting "our flag is red, not red, white and blue; down with Soviet-American war moves."[26]

In 1984 the RCP was one of the initiators of a new Revolutionary Internationalist Movement that united about a dozen or so Maoist organizations from around the world. The most notorious is the infamous Shining Path guerrillas of Peru whose armed struggle is fully supported by the RCP. The RCP's inflated sense of its own importance can be garnered from the report it issued of the announcement of the new revolutionary international's founding: "as the clock ticked midnight, small groups of proletarians . . . waited for copies of the Declaration and studied them into the night in advance of May 1 actions the next day."[27]

The RCP's foreign policy positions are as extreme as its support for the Shining Path terrorists. It finds all revolutionary governments in the world too moderate. After the victory of the Sandinistas, the RCP attacked them for not instituting socialism and for cooperating with the bourgeoisie. Likewise, it supported Robert Mugabe's guerrillas in Zimbabwe until they agreed to participate in elections; then they attacked Mugabe as a sell-out. Bob Avakian has even attacked the Soviet Union for fighting World War II on a patriotic, bourgeois, democratic basis.[28]

The RCP does not believe in united fronts with nonproletarian forces; thus it shuns cooperation with feminist or nationalist forces. It tends to employ dramatic and confrontational gestures, often on May Day, when, each year, it mobilizes its members to plaster cities with posters and to engage in relatively small but often disruptive demonstrations. For example, two RCP'ers were convicted of destroying government property after they barricaded themselves into an office at Fort McPherson in Georgia to dramatize plans for a May Day rally. In 1980 some four hundred Party members were arrested in about two months. Among other things, they flew a red flag from the Alamo and put a freshly killed pig's head in the Oakland City Hall. In 1984 120 marched on May Day in San Francisco "many wearing Palestinian Kafiyehs and Sandinista bandanas." The group included "revolutionary youth, including black and Latino proletarian youth, anarchist-leaning punks from Berkeley and San Francisco, and a scattering of revolutionary youth active in political movements."[29]

The RCP's provocations are based on its belief in the theory of the single spark. The Party's strategy is to seize any spark of struggle, try to fan it and spread it. This results in its cadre seeking to find a struggle, jumping into it and trying to expand it. When the struggle ends, the cadre move on, searching for the next spark. The Party also believes in a variation of the anarchist doctrine of propaganda of the deed. It uses shocking actions to gain publicity. Thus, it disrupted George Meany's funeral by putting a May Day manifesto on his coffin and splashed paint on diplomats at the United Nations. During the 1984 Olympics, a number of RCP youth were arrested after a protest march in which they chanted "Red, White and Blue—We Spit On You!"[30] One small group of RCP'ers invaded the cafeteria of a black high school in Washington, DC in 1980, shouting "no work, no school, to hell with the whiteman's rule" and burning an American flag. The students were not impressed and pelted them with garbage, milk and fruit. Six communists were arrested.[31]

The RCP's militancy and extremism mean that it refuses to take part in the political process at all. It was scornful of Jesse Jackson's presidential candidacy, denouncing him as a "goodwill ambassador for US imperialism."[32] The RCP wants nothing to do with American elections: it urged Americans not to vote and proclaimed that "We don't want our fair share. We want to tear the whole system down! Elections are the wrong arena. It's going to come down to revolutionary war!"[33]

The RCP's latest activity has been to focus attention on stopping World War III. On April 29th it has sponsored nationwide No Business As Usual

Day to protest against nuclear weapons and preparations for war. Its focus was quite different than that of the nuclear freeze movement, which the RCP scorns. It has argued that the "freeze campaign takes the national interests of the US as its starting point and this sort of position can only lead to support for imperialist war when the actual thing goes down."[34] Carl Dix, an RCP leader, called for different kinds of "mass political disruptions." Local groups held a variety of events, ranging from "die-ins" to building monuments to the dead of the next war. Generally, turnouts were small, usually no more than two or three dozen people.[35]

The RCP probably has no more than five hundred members nationwide. It has branches in twenty-three cities; they often operate out of Revolution Books bookstores. In addition to Avakian, Party leaders include Carl Dix and Clark Kissinger, a former leader of SDS. The RCP publishes the *Revolutionary Worker* weekly and *Revolution,* a theoretical magazine, quarterly.

US League of Revolutionary Struggle (Marxist-Leninist)

The US League of Revolutionary Struggle (Marxist-Leninist), (LRS), is one of the remnants of the Maoist student movement of the 1970s. With the demise in the early 1980s of the Communist Party (Marxist-Leninist), the LRS is the last basically pro-Chinese radical sect. A decade ago this "new" communist movement had been flourishing. Among the leaders of the LRS are Carl Davidson, formerly a leading member of the CPML and Amiri Baraka, once known as LeRoi Jones, who has had a bizarre and ideologically diverse career ranging from raving anti-semitism and black racism to extreme Maoism.

LRS describes itself as "a multinational Marxist-Leninist organization" with chapters across the country that support black, Chicano, and other struggles in the United States and other countries "against the domination and bullying of the two superpowers, the US and the Soviet Union." It was founded in 1978; many of its activists came from two smaller Maoist groups, the I Wor Kuen and the August 29 Movement. At its second congress in 1984 the LRS decided that the time was not yet right to declare itself a vanguard Communist Party. The League still has hopes of unity with the remnants of the CP-ML and the Revolutionary Workers Headquarters, another defunct Maoist group, but their disintegration in recent years is seen as a major setback for the revolutionary left. The LRS sees itself as "the only intact, functioning anti-revisionist communist organization in the US today." Its policy is "to work cooperatively with all other left groups" ranging from the Communist Party to the Democratic Socialists of America.[36]

Like many Maoist groups, the League for Revolutionary Struggle has faced a real theoretical and practical dilemma ever since the Chinese government moved away from more radical Maoist policies and began to develop closer ties with the United States. Its solution is to note that it supports the Chinese revolution and "respects" Mao but to insist that it makes its own decisions. The LRS denies it is Maoist although it concedes that Mao's writings inspire many of its members. The LRS claims that it does not necessarily endorse everything China does, but it believes China has the right to make its own decisions. Overall, however, it believes that China's foreign policy promotes peace and supports national liberation struggles.

The League opposed the Vietnamese invasion of Cambodia. Pol Pot might have "committed grievous acts against the Kampuchean people" which "tarnished the prestige of world socialism"[37] but the LRS charges that reports on the atrocities committed by his regime are overblown and that he was taking steps to rectify the errors.[38]

The LRS insists that it opposes both American and Soviet aggression—it opposes the Soviet effort to export revolution in Afghanistan. It criticizes the USSR for imperialism and lack of democracy. It also opposes Cuban intervention in Africa and the main issue it sees in Central America is the struggle of the people against US imperialism.

The League was reserved in its enthusiasm for Jesse Jackson's presidential candidacy. Baraka was critical of Jackson and people close to him for wanting "to become big colored muckety-mucks in the Democratic Party." Nonetheless, he believed that "Jackson's campaign pushed the whole electorate to the left." The next step for the Rainbow Coalition is to move in the direction of independent politics. Baraka himself struck a moderate tone, calling for a focus on black voter registration. He also criticized Louis Farrakhan for failing to distinguish between Judaism and Zionism. [39] The LRS urged a vote for Mondale to beat Reagan, since Mondale at least wanted to move to the right more slowly than Reagan.[40]

Despite Baraka's mild censure of Farrakhan and the fact that *Unity* criticized Jackson's "clearly incorrect slur against Jews" and also attacked Farrakhan as a nationalist, *Unity* has strongly attacked critics of African National Congress figure Fred Dube, a teacher at the State University of New York, Stony Brook, under fire for allegedly propagandizing in the classroom against Zionism. Baraka is a member of the Afro-American Studies Department in which Dube taught.[41]

The League for Revolutionary Struggle publishes *Unity*, a bi-monthly in English and Spanish. Its editors are Reese Erlich, William Gallegos and Jean Yonemura. Contributing editors are Amiri Baraka, Carl Davidson, and Mae Ngai. The group also publishes a monthly, *Forward.*

Communist Workers Party

The New Democratic Movement is the latest incarnation of the Communist Workers Party (CWP), one of a host of small Maoist groups that formed during the 1970s, drawing their membership largely from the remnants of the New Left. With a small membership and an extreme program that limited its appeal and effectiveness, it would hardly merit notice if not for one shockingly violent confrontation in Greensboro, North Carolina in 1979 during which five Party members were killed by Ku Klux Klansmen and Nazis. Transformed by that incident from an ineffective extremist group into a media curiosity, the CWP briefly won some attention and enjoyed a brief and small surge in energy. By the mid-1980s it had faded back into obscurity, although it was attempting, with some success, to infiltrate the Democratic Party and obtain government grants.

The CWP was formally organized in late 1979. Many of its leading figures were veterans of the student movement of the 1960s, including the general secretary, Jerry Tung, born in China in 1948 and raised in the United States. Tung initiated the Asian Study Group in 1973. Its roots were in New York's Chinatown and the Asian Studies Program of City College of New York. It evolved into the Workers Viewpoint Organization (WVO) by 1976 as it assimilated various local Marxist-Leninist groups. The formal conversion to the Communist Workers Party occurred at a convention in October 1979 in New York. One-third of its members were of Chinese or Japanese origin and many of its leaders were Asian-Americans. A remarkable number were very highly educated; many were medical doctors. Most came to the CWP from the student movement; others emerged from a black radical group in Greensboro, North Carolina led by Nelson Johnson.

The CWP was never a very large organization. FBI director William Webster suggested in Congressional testimony in the early 1980s that it had two thousand members nationwide, with five hundred of them in New York, but most other estimates were much lower. One figure probably closer to the mark was that at its height in the early 1980s, the CPW had somewhere between seven hundred and a thousand members. Most were on the East and West Coasts and in North Carolina.[42] The founding congress, which might have been expected to attract virtually all Party members, had a reported attendance of five to seven hundred people.

Until the Greensboro killings, the WVO/CWP devoted much of its effort to labor organizing. The group believed that the working class was being held back from fulfilling its revolutionary mission by labor "misleaders." To gain contact with workers, a number of Party members were "colonized," i.e., they obtained jobs in industry by lying about their educational backgrounds and set out to discredit established union leaders and to take over local unions. The tactic achieved some temporary success in North Carolina, where Party activists managed to gain office in some textile union locals and in some Cone Mill textile plants. A series of unsuccessful strikes and counterattacks by the unions combined with very little success at recruiting ordinary workers into the WVO/CWP encouraged the Party to try a different tack in 1979.

Beginning in the summer of 1979 Party leaders in North Carolina began to focus on resistance to the Ku Klux Klan as an alternative recruiting tool to labor organizing. Fifty CWP members disrupted a Klan showing of the movie, Birth of A Nation, in the small town of China Grove, North Carolina. Emboldened by their ability to force armed Klansmen to back down and convinced that this gave the Party "credentials and credibility," CWP'ers planned another confrontation with the Klan. One internal Party document called for increased militancy at such a gathering and noted that "a confrontation with the Klan would be best if we can get it."[43]

The CWP held a "Death to the Klan" rally in Greensboro on November 3, 1979. It issued an open letter to Klan and Nazi leaders, calling them cowards and daring them to appear at the rally. A caravan of right-wing extremists did drive to a staging area and opened fire on a group of CWP'ers preparing to march. Five Party leaders were killed; three were doctors, one was a black woman and another was a Cuban-American. Neither a state nor a federal prosecution resulted in any convictions of the assailants despite videotapes of the actual shootings. The defense claimed that they had been provoked by the communists. A civil suit for damages did result in awards against several Nazis and Klansmen and two police officers accused of failing to protect the marchers.

The Greensboro and China Grove incidents were not the only times that the CWP used violent language or violent acts to achieve its ends. Shortly after the killings, a coalition of radical and civil rights groups organized a march in Greensboro to protest against Klan activities. The CWP was expelled from the coalition for refusing to promise not to carry weapons on the march.[44] When the accused Nazis and Klansmen first went on trial for murder, twenty people, including a number of CWP'ers, scuffled with police and four were arrested at the courthouse. Nelson Johnson disrupted a press conference being held by North Carolina governor Jim Hunt in 1980, called him a murderer, and charged that Hunt and President Carter "cooperated in the assassination of the CPW Five" because of the purported role of government informants in the case. A CWP member threw eggs at Hunt and Representative John Anderson during the 1980 presidential campaign.[45]

The Party's most determined assault on mainstream politicians, however, came during the 1980 Democratic convention. On August 12 some fifty CWP supporters demonstrated in Newark, burning efffigies of candidates Carter, Reagan and Anderson. The following day one hundred fifty CWP'ers tried to storm a Democratic fundraising event at the New York Plaza Hotel, injuring six police. That night there were four attempted firebombings; at each site CWP slogans were found. On August 14 two hundred Party members tried to storm Madison Square Garden during President Carter's acceptance speech. Wearing helmets, carrying pick handles and mace, they were repulsed and fifteen were arrested. Inside the convention hall, Dale Sampson, widow of one of the doctors slain in Greensboro, set off firecrackers near the podium; another Party member shouted slogans.[46]

In 1976, as Workers Viewpoint Organization, the group broke up rival communist groups' meetings, throwing chairs on stage and attacking enemies with baseball bats and hammers. Internal Party documents paint a clear picture of a group with few compunctions about the use of violence or weapons. One called for "bold actions including armed self-defense." A Southern Regional Party Bulletin urged members to break the bonds of legality and advised that each member should be "self-sufficient;" it suggested military training and drilling with guns. Anyone inclined to confuse the CWP with a peaceful democratic socialist group would have been stopped short by its six-page membership application which included questions about the extent of the applicant's training with firearms and in the martial arts.[47]

Nor did the party confine such calls to its internal organs. Signe Waller proclaimed that "violent revolution is necessary to change the system."[48] The CWP itself has called "on the American people to unite and overthrow the criminal rule of monopoly capitalism by whatever means necessary." And, its newspaper insisted that "government terror must be countered by the people's armed might, not by choice, but out of necessity to reduce the people's losses. At this point, it will be the duty of the CWP and all revolutionaries to lead the American people in insurrection."[49]

Its heroes included Joseph Stalin and Pol Pot, whose successful revolution in Cambodia, the Party asserted, had been undermined by false CIA propaganda that he had massacred huge numbers of people. By the mid-1980s, however, the CWP came to realize that its apocolyptic style had become counterproductive. The notoriety and support it had won from the Greensboro shootings had largely dissipated. As early as 1981 two CWP leaders suggested that it might be necessary to participate in electoral politics to enable the masses to vote for a candidate "without running substantial risks of direct militant actions."[50]

By 1984 the CWP was an enthusiastic backer of Jessee Jackson's candidacy for president. Jerry Tung claimed that the five murdered Party leaders "were among the forerunners of multinational unity in the South which Jesse Jackson's Rainbow Coalition is now striving to actualize."[51]

This enthusiasm was largely tactical, however. The CWP still regarded Jackson as an "infamous careerist and opportunist." His effort, though, would energize blacks and enable them "to develop into a revolutionary movement." Since American capitalism no longer had the economic resources to deal with their demands, the result would be growing repression. The CWP would reap the benefits. "While Jackson's campaign has had the effect of ploughing the ground (that is, arousing the masses), the choice of crops is up for grabs." The Party did not repudiate other forms of struggle such as armed self-defense or work in unions, but added to them working in electoral arenas.[52]

The CWP did denounce Jackson's slurs against Jews but did not deem them serious enough to cause progressives to abandon him. The publicity given to the episode was seen as part of an effort by some Zionists to label Jackson as an antisemite.[53] Phil Thompson insisted that it was necessary to differentiate between the actions and statements of "racist Zionist leaders (and that of Israel)" and "the majority of Jewish people."[54]

Involvement in the Jackson campaign apparently convinced the CWP that the two-party system offered fertile ground in which radicals could work. Speaking at a workshop during the People's Convention, a radical counterpart to the 1984 Democratic gathering in San Francisco, Jerry Tung, the general secretary of the CWP, argued that radicals should work within the Democratic Party because "we can get funding from the Democrats to sustain our struggles." It was an accurate prediction.[55]

The CWP suspended publication of its newspaper, *Workers Viewpoint,* in the summer of 1984 while reassessing its views. Less than a year later it changed its name to the New Democratic Movement, abandoned its revolutionary rhetoric and called for entering the Democratic Party and the union movement. The documents of the founding convention, however, made clear that the Party was only changing its marketing tactics, not its long-term goal. In addition to reaffirming several Marxist-Leninist organizational norms, the NDM supported the right of blacks, Chicanos, Native Americans, Hawaii and Puerto Rico to self-determination, including secession from the United States. One leader, Frank Chen, urged training members "to become better professional revolutionaries."[56]

A resolution on strategy and tactics called for concentrating cadres and resources in local areas "where we think we can succeed." One of those areas was New York. Jerry Tung boasted that the Party there had been able to establish institutions and engage in electoral work in mutually beneficial ways; he praised "the institutionalization and the work in electoral politics and how they help each other, leveraging each other . . . creating jobs and projects and enhancing our authority and influence as well as making money." Tung also explained that the CWP had been able to buy access to some figures in the Democratic Party: his group had raised $5000 overnight for the Jesse Jackson campaign. He explained: "when you can raise money for political purposes, quickly, . . . when you do it in the right place, in the right atmosphere, and look (dress up) right, and the (Democratic) Party bosses are there, then that money makes them take you seriously."[57]

The New Democratic Movement has maintained a low profile since its founding almost two years ago. Instead, the CWP appears to have used Asian-Americans for Equality (AAFE) as its stalking-horse in the Democratic Party. AAFE has recently obtained more than three million dollars in grants from New York State and city to create a shelter for the homeless on the Lower East Side and to support its own operations. In a very brief period of time it has also become a powerful force in the Village Independent Democrats, a storied Greenwich Village political club, and has even elected one of its leaders to the New York State Democratic Committee.

Concluding the NDM Convention, Tung noted that in dissolving the DWP, "we folded our old banner and called to an end a chapter of our political development. It was very moving and we sang 'The Internationale.' I think it is probably the last time we will sing 'The Internationale' together. But when we achieve cultural hegemony in this country then we can sing it once more, together." The report noted that this remark was met with applause and chants of "NDM! NDM! NDM! LOCAL POWER! LOCAL POWER! LOCAL POWER!"[58]

Line of March

Line of March (LOM) is a small Marxist–Leninist sect headquartered on the West Coast. It publishes *Frontline*, whose editor is Irwin Silber. Silber, also the guiding spirit of LOM, was a long–time member of the CPUSA. During the late 1940s and 1950s he was active in Party cultural activities, particularly centered around the folksong movement. During the 1960s and 1970s he was an influential figure in the *Guardian* and was instrumental in moving that newspaper into the Maoist orbit. Shocked by Chinese opposition to the Angolan Popular Movement for the Liberation of Angola in 1976, and disturbed by Chinese "collaboration with American imperialism" Silber began to distance himself from Maoism. Now, Silber has ditched his Maoism and returned to a position very close to that of the CPUSA. Many Line of March members have joined him in his latest political odyssey: "It is out of the Maoist legacy that our trend has come."[59] While critical of the Communist Party, Silber and the LOM are staunch defenders of the Soviet Union and hope to "reform" the CPUSA. Other important figures in the group are Max Elbaum, Dale Borgeson, Linda Burnham, Bruce Occena, Melinda Paras and Bob Wing.

LOM came into existence in 1980 with the intention of interacting with and guiding the communist movement in the United States. It insisted that a revisionist wing in the American communist movement—the CPUSA—believed that the transition to socialism could take place in a peaceful manner. On the other hand, a left–opportunist wing, Maoism, was trying to cooperate with US imperialism around the banner of anti–Sovietism. The goal of the LOM was to reconstruct a Marxist–Leninist trend from the collapse of the new communist movement—destroyed by its commitment to Maoism.

Silber has charged that Maoists and others who adopt anti–Sovietism are inherently unstable allies in the peace and anti–intervention movements. He calls for rigorous struggle with anti–Sovietism even at the risk of the broad unity of these movements. Anti–Sovietism cannot be Marxist–Leninist since the only force consistently standing for peace and against imperialism in the world is the Soviet Union.

LOM supports Soviet foreign policy with no ifs, ands, or buts. It opposes Solidarity in Poland and complains that the junta is too soft with the Pope. Silber is not worried that most Polish workers supported Solidarity or the Pope against the regime: "Communists do not indulge in the luxury of permitting the subjective sentiments of the workers at any particular moment to determine their own estimate of what objectively serves the interests of the working class," he wrote.[60] LOM also opposes the Afghan "feudalists," supports the Vietnamese invasion of Cambodia and was given to writing lengthy paean to Yuri Andropov's economic reforms.

Frontline compares Israel to Somoza, the Shah, South Africa, and Thieu. It seems to lean to support of the Popular Front for the Liberation of Palestine and the Democratic Front for the Liberation of Palestine in the PLO. The source of the war danger in the Mideast "remains Zionist aggression" which has "genocidal origins." There is a need for the anti–imperialist and solidarity movements to defend Palestinian self–determination and the PLO as the sole legitimate representative of the Palestineans. There can be no coexistence with Zionism—a unified democratic secular state is the only alternative.[61]

Line of March criticizes the CPUSA for overestimating the strength of the American left and the weakness of Ronald Reagan. The CPUSA has strengths—its links to the USSR, its class and race composition and its trade union positions—but it is an "extremely poor vehicle" for leading the working class. Its political program is in error and it sees the working class as a homogeneous grouping, growing more unified. LOM sees splits and divisions within the working class, the major one being racial because of white skin privilege. LOM also objects to the CPUSA's anti–monopoly emphasis. Since the Line of March believes that the trade union movement is pro–imperialist and opportunistic, it argues that Leninists must mount a challenge to unions, not unify with them against monopolies. Nonetheless, LOM maintains that despite the CPUSA's errors, they are less severe than those of the Maoists.[62]

The Line of March supported Jesse Jackson's presidential campaign and claimed that the attacks on him were motivated by a desire to discredit his Mideast positions and support for affirmative action. Jackson had supposedly discomfitted the ruling class because he had penetrated the two–party system as the voice of the underclass. LOM was relatively favorably disposed towards Louis Farrakhan until his "irresponsible" statements showed how "narrow bourgeois nationalism" can be reactionary.[63]

Line of March calls for building the Rainbow Coalition as an independent political force. Linda Burnham and Phil Gardiner, two members of LOM's Black Liberation Commission, nonetheless opposed suggestions that blacks abstain from the 1984 election because Walter Mondale was the Democratic Party's candidate. Since blacks had established a progressive beachhead in the Democratic Party and needed to beat Reagan, the LOM urged support for the Democratic Party.[64] The aim, however, was not to reform or change the Democrats. Radicals were urged to work in the Democratic Party to split it and to split the labor movement in order to build an independent party. The Jackson and Harold Washington campaigns were seen by LOM as the beginning of this fissure in the Democratic Party.[65]

LOM sees a need for a "Leninist party of professional revolutionaries."[66] It began publishing *Frontline* in June 1983 to reach a broader audience of activists. It claims that its adherents are active in the peace and solidarity, anti–racist, labor, women's, and immigrant rights struggles and are united by a belief in the united front against war and racism as the basis for first a progressive and then a revolutionary movement. LOM also played a role in the West Coast Marxist Scholars Conference in April 1984 organized by the Marxist Educational Press. The CPUSA played a leading role in the conference.[67] In 1981 it started the US Anti–Imperialist League to do solidarity work for Central America and Palestine.

In addition to *Frontline* and *Line of March*, a theoretical journal, LOM also publishes *Class Lines*, issued quarterly by its Labor commission. Its journals pay careful attention to developments in the CPUSA. The Communist party, in return, has sharply responded to some of LOM's critiques, indicating that some Party members have probably been influenced by them or that they echo criticisms in the CPUSA of its "moderate" policies.

Notes

1. *Challenge*, March 6, 1985.

2. *Progressive Labor Magazine*, Spring 1982.

3. Ibid.

4. *Variety*, June 18, 1980.

5. *Challenge*, May 20, 1981.

6. *Washington Post*, April 25, 1982.

7. *Challenge*, November 17, 1982.

8. *Challenge*, November 16, 1983.

9. *Progressive Labor*, May 1980.

10. *Challenge*, May 11, 1983.

11. *Challenge*, February 23, 1983.

12. Joseph Epstein, "A Case of Academic Freedom," *Commentary*, September 1986.

13. *Challenge*, March 3, 1982.

14. *Challenge*, March 26, 1980.

15. *Challenge*, May 2, 1984.

16. *Challenge*, January 4, 1984.

17. *Progressive Labor Magazine*, Spring 1982.

18. *Challenge*, March 31, 1982.

19. *Challenge*, February 8, 1984.

20. *Challenge*, September 29, 1982.

21. *Challenge*, September 3, 1980.

22. *Guardian*, March 22, 1978.

23. *Guardian*, September 20, 1978.

24. *Los Angeles Times*, May 2, 1980.

25. *Revolutionary Worker*, May 4, 1984.

26. *Washington Post*, May 1, 1980.

27. *Revolutionary Worker*, May 4, 1984.

28. Bob Avakian, *Conquer the World* (Chicago:RCP Publications, 1981).

29. *Revolutionary Worker*, May 4, 1984; *San Francisco Chronicle*, May 1, 1980.

30. *Los Angeles Herald-Examiner*, August 13, 1984.

31. *Washington Post*, March 15, 1980.

32. *Revolutionary Worker*, June 29, 1984.

33. *Revolutionary Worker*, July 13, 1984.

34. *Revolution*, Winter-Spring 1985.

35. *Revolutionary Worker*, March 8, 1985.

36. *Forward*, January 1985.

37. Ibid.

38. *Unity*, January 25, 1985.

39. Ibid.

40. *Unity*, October 12, 1984.

41. *Unity*, April 20, 1984.

42. Testimony of William Webster, Hearings of the Subcommittee on Security and Terrorism of the Committee on the Judiciary of the US Senate, February 2, 1983; *Charlotte Observer*, August 24, 1980.

43. "Proposed Plan for Klan Campaign; "Southern Regional Bulletin," CWP Documents in my possession.

44. *Miami Herald*, February 3, 1980.

45. *Daily News*, June 17, 1980; *News & Observer*, July 24, 1980, August 12, 1980.

46. *New York Times*, August 15, 1980.

47. "Proposal to Continue the Anti-Klan Campaign;" Southern Regional Bulletin," CWP Documents.

48. *New York Tribune*, June 7, 1983.
49. *Workers Viewpoint*, October 19, 1983.
50. *Guardian*, September 2, 1981.
51. CWP Press Release, 1984.
52. *The 80s*, Fall 1983.
53. *Workers Viewpoint*, March 29-April 4, 1984.
54. Ibid.
55. *Guardian*, July 25, 1984.
56. *New Democratic Movement National Bulletin*, July 1985.
57. Ibid.
58. Ibid.
59. *Line of March*, June 1984.
60. *Frontline*, July 11, 1983.
61. *Frontline*, October 3, 1983, June 27, 1983.
62. *Frontline*, November 28, 1983.
63. *Frontline*, March 30, 1984.
64. *Frontline*, September 17, 1984.
65. *Frontline*, July 9, 1984.
66. *Line of March*, June 1984.
67. *Frontline*, May 14, 1984.

6

Miscellaneous Sects

Weather Underground Organization

The Weather Underground Organization, a product of the disintegration of the New Left and the turn towards radical terrorism on the part of some student radicals of the 1960s, is practically defunct today. Over the years, however, it has spawned a number of above-ground support groups that continue to function and remain involved with terrorist activities.

The Weather Underground Organization (WUO) was an outgrowth of the Weatherman Faction of SDS. Weatherman developed in 1968–1969. Its leaders include Bernadine Dohrn, Bill Ayers, Jeff Jones, Mark Rudd and John Jacobs. A product of the fierce internecine wars in SDS, Weatherman believed that a black revolution in America was imminent and would destroy American imperialism. The task of whites, particularly college students, was to provide black revolutionaries with support. The group rejected class war for racial war. Over the years, it developed into a terrorist organization with close ties to black terrorists.

SDS split irrevocably in 1969 with the Progressive Labour Party controlling one rump, a group of incipient Maoists another and the Weatherman faction a third. Dohrn and several other Weathermen travelled to Cuba for advice shortly afterwards. There they met with a delegation from the Provisional Revolutionary Government of Vietnam which urged them to begin armed struggle. The Weathermen proceeded to organize into affinity groups which engaged in wild bouts of sexual orgies and drug use to break down bourgeois habits; they also trained with weapons.[1]

The Weathermen urged revolutionaries to invade Chicago for demonstrations in "Days of Rage" in October 1969. Their optimistic expectation that ten thousand demonstrators would heed their call proved wildly inflated; they could actually muster only about six hundred, some of them from the YAWF, the youth group of the Workers World Party. A three–day orgy of street fighting, broken windows and three hundred arrests followed as the radicals fought street battles with the police. Afterwards, the Weathermen engaged in brutal self–criticism sessions. A War Council of four hundred people, meeting in Flint, made plans to go underground. They also heard Dohrn praise the Charles Manson gang for their brutal murders and glory in the sadistic means used to kill a pregnant woman.

Dohrn, Jones, Jacobs and Terry Robbins were the directing force of the WUO. One collective, located in New York, and headed by Robbins, had already staged one firebombing when the townhouse they were using as a bomb factory exploded in March 1970. Three people, including Robbins, were killed; two others, including Kathy Boudin, managed to escape. The WUO continued to insist that "revolutionary violence is the only way" and carried out a series of bombings over the next few years, attacking the New York City Police Headquarters, the Presidio Army Base, courthouses in New York and California, and the Capital (the bomb went off in a woman's bathroom; it had been planted by Dohrn and Boudin). Altogether, the WUO took credit for some two dozen bombings in a six–year period. It also arranged the jailbreak of Timothy Leary, the LSD guru, and helped him get to Algeria.

By 1973, with the war in Vietnam winding down and underground life having lost its glamour, the WUO moved in the direction of Marxist orthodoxy and becoming a communist party. Clayton Van Lydegraf became a more influential figure in the leadership. Van Lydegraf had been a leader of the communist underground in the Washington State area in the 1950s. Disgusted by its moderation, he had left the CPUSA and joined the Progressive Labour Movement in the late 1950s. Even PLP had expelled him as an ultra–leftist, however. His hardline Marxism–Leninism and the WUO's extremism produced a nice fit. The first product of this new turn in the WUO was a book, dedicated to such disparate heroes as John Brown and Sirhan Sirhan and distributed by the Prairie Fire Organizing Committee (PFOC).[2]

The Prairie Fire Organizing Committee was the legal arm of the Weather Underground, formed in 1974 as a publishing group for WUO pamphlets, and taking its name from a statement by Mao that "a single spark can start a prairie fire." The first one was entitled *Prairie Fire: The Politics of Revolutionary Anti–Imperialism* and was signed by Bernadine Dohrn, Bill Ayers and Jeff Jones. It announced that "we are communist men and women" and urged its supporters to form an above–ground arm of the WUO. Chapters were soon formed in several cities with perhaps a thousand members. Members of PFOC helped facilitate communication and logistics for WUO members living underground.[3]

The PFOC organized a National Hard Times Conference in Chicago in early 1976 that attracted some two thousand people. The Workers World Party assisted in the organizing and many of those present represented other Marxist–Leninist parties and support groups. Among the PFOC organizers for the event were Russ Neufield, Shelly Miller, Jennifer Dohrn, Julie Nichamin, Arlene Bergman, and Eve Rosahn. Rather than endorsing the WUO as the leadership of the American left, however, the conference denounced it as racist and accused the WUO of betraying its revolutionary ideals.

After the failure of the conference, disagreements began to split the WUO. One faction, led by Bill Ayers and Jeff Jones, argued for inversion, or coming up from underground. Another group, based in California and led by Van Lydegraf, favored more emphasis on cadre development and militancy. The latter group sharply attacked Dohrn, Ayres and Jones for a variety of sins, including male chauvinism and racism. They made a self-confession and then were expelled from the organization they had founded. Ayers and Dohrn surfaced in 1980; Jones was arrested in 1981.

In November 1977 five members of the winning faction, including Van Lydegraf, were arrested and charged with conspiracy to bomb a California state senator's office. They were convicted of lesser charges.

More WUO members began to surface in the last half of the 1970s. Several served brief jail terms or were put on probation. A small core, however, remained underground and developed an alliance with several small, violent black organizations, including the Black Liberation Army, an offshoot of the Black Panther Party, and the Republic of New Africa, an extremist group that advocated an independent black state in part of the southern United States.

The WUO's above–ground support group, the PFOC, underwent a similar metamorphosis, becoming more actively involved in support work for a variety of foreign "liberation" movements. In the mid–1970s it endorsed a variety of pro–Palestinean demonstrations and rallies. The PFOC formed the Material Aid Campaign for ZANU in 1977. It was renamed the Revolution in Africa Action Committee in the early 1980s and began to focus its efforts on support for the FLNC (Congolese National Liberation Front) which was seeking to overthrow the Mobutu regime in the Zaire. The new group continued to share the WUO's commitment to armed struggle, praising bombings carried out in the United States and asserting the need to use armed struggle to defeat US imperialism. Its newsletter, *Revolution in Africa*, justified bombings.

The Revolution in Africa Action Committee remained a small organization, however, One demonstration it co–sponsored with another PFOC front group, the John Brown Anti–Klan Committee, could muster only twenty-five people to march in solidarity with African liberation movements in New York. Even this small demonstration was linked to Israel; one of the demands of the marchers was for an end to Israeli assistance to Mobutu.

Breakthrough, one of the PFOC's political journals, has called for "a resistance that operates on all levels to disrupt the US war machine from within." Although the Vietnam War provided the impetus for many of those in the WUO to begin their protest careers, the newest focus of the PFOC is Central America. It has endorsed demonstrations, protests, and bombings (to show "that U.S. aggression wll be met by determined anti-imperialist struggle"). The PFOC endorsed the bombing of a computer center at the Washington, DC navy yard by the Armed Resistance Unit and noted that "we welcome the growth of armed struggle in the US" since it can "help lead many people to become part of a revolutionary movement which fights the system itself."[4]

The John Brown Anti-Klan Committee (JBAKC), was formed in 1978. It has chapters in thirteen cities and a national office in New York. One spokesperson said the group had fewer than three hundred members nationwide in 1983.[5] Many of them are young white women.

Despite its name the group has involved itself with more than just anti-Klan organizing. It cosponsored a march in 1981 to celebrate the International Day of Solidarity with the Palestinian Revolution along with the May 19th Communist Organization, still another WUO front. The march's slogans included "Victory to the PLO!" and "Zionism is Racism! Defeat White Supremacy!" The JBAKC emphasizes that the state of Israel is illegitimate. It connects the struggle against this "white settler state" to the struggle against two others—South Africa and the United States, where it supports the demand of the Republic of New Africa for an independent black state. "The John Brown Anti-Klan Committee is committed to fighting and defeating organized zionist forces and all forms of organized white supremacy." In 1983 fifteen members picketed the Israeli consulate in Boston to protest Israeli support of the Mobutu government in the Congo, the bete noire of the Revolution in Africa Action Committee.[6]

The JBAKC's major focus, however, is to protest against anti-black racism in the United States. It insists that Ku Klux Klan activity is promoted and encouraged by the FBI, police and legal system because American imperialism is in crisis and needs to prepare for the advent of fascism. In addition to this emphasis, the group's propaganda includes demands to "Free the Land!", the slogan of the Republic of New Africa and "Death to the Klan!" The latter slogan, in fact, is the name of its newsletter.

The John Brown Committee's opposistion to the Klan is not based on a desire to safeguard civil liberties or strengthen American democracy. Its goal is building an anti-Klan movement based on support of the struggle to "free the Black nation." The only way for blacks to win their rights in America, it argues, is for them to win the struggle for self–determination. Not only does it support black secession from the United States, but it adds a call for socialism and independence for all oppressed nations in the United States—Puerto Ricans, Mexicans, and Native Americans.[7]

Another characteristic of JBAKC protests is that they often have involved arrests and/or violent confrontations with the police. It insinuated itself into a demonstration of two thousand people against the Klan in Houston, chanting "Death to the Klan." Houston police arrested several JBAKC members and supporters. Twelve hundred demonstrators, including some from the JBAKC, tried to halt a parade of seventy Klansmen in Austin in 1983. Some hurled rocks; twelve people, including several police, were injured.

Not all, or even most JBAKC events are so well–attended. When a neo–Nazi group received permission to use an Arlington, Virginia high school for a White Pride Day in November 1983, the JBAKC organized a counter–demonstration. Although the Progressive Labour Party and the All Peoples Congress also provided demonstrators, the largest contingent—about twenty people—were from the JBAKC, whose banners attacked the Klan and also called for "Land and Independence for New Afrika—The Black Nation!" Three people were arrested. Other demonstrations, at courthouses or in front of city halls, have resulted in only a dozen or so protesters.

The JBAKC has also campaigned against "killer cops" with slogans urging people to "Stop White Vigilantism! Don't Work with the Police!" Supporting police is regarded as a step in the drive to fascism. Furthermore, police do not stop crime but commit it. "Crime exists because imperialism exists, and the police are major perpetrators of crime."[8]

True to its affinity with the WUO the JBAKC approved of violence and supports it openly. It justified attacks on policemen and supported those who use violence against the authorities. In accord with this reasoning JBAKC members have refused to cooperate with investigations into criminal and terrorist activities. Four members of the JBAKC were subpoenaed by a federal grand jury looking into a series of bombings, including that of the US Capital in November 1983. All refused to cooperate and issued a statement saying that "we recognize these bombings as a legitimate form of resistance to US militarism."[9]

After a number of WUO, May 19th and BLA members were arrested in a bungled armed robbery of a Brinks truck that led to the murder of two policemen and a guard in Nyack, New York in 1981, the JBAKC put out a leaflet supporting the defendants, charging that the government was embarked on "an attempt to destroy the armed clandestine movement and its support networks, both public and private." It accused the government of violating international law by treating revolutionaries as criminals.[10]

The group's leaders are not usually publicly identified but among them are Lisa Roth, a member of the National Steering Committee; Betty Ann Duke and Linda Evans, leaders of the Austin, Texas chapter and both former members of the WUO and active in the May 19th Communist Organization, another WUO spinoff; Howard Emmer, head of the Chicago chapter; Terry Bisson; Julie Nichamin, one-time leader of the WUO and initiator of the Venceremos Brigades which recruited young Americans to travel to Cuba; Julie Nalibov and Christine Rico.[11]

The WUO also created a variety of other front groups, many of which are interrelated and cooperate closely with each other. The John Brown Anti-Klan Committee, for example, has also sponsored meetings and protests with the Women's Committee Against Genocide, the Committee for the Suit Against Government Misconduct, the May 19th Communist Organization, the Moncada Library, and the New Movement in Solidarity with Puerto Rican Independence and Socialism. The Committee for the Suit Against Government Misconduct was formed to press charges against the government for surveillance of WUO sympathizers and relatives.

There was considerable overlap in the membership of these organizations. For example, Judy Clark and Eve Rosahn were actively involved in the Committee for the Suit Against Government Misconduct. Clark was also active in the PFOC and the May 19th Communist Organization. Rosahn, once a member of Columbia SDS, had been a PFOC activist, and was indicted for aiding the May 19th defendants in the Brinks robbery— although the charge was later dropped. Michelle Miller was a leader of the New Movement in Solidarity with Puerto Rican Independence and Socialism, a PFOC organizer, and active in the May 19th group. Miller's roommate, Sylvia Baraldini, was one of the leaders of the May 19th Communist Organization. She and Miller were found guilty of criminal contempt for refusing to testify before a federal grand jury investigating bombings committed by the Puerto Rican terrorist group, the FALN.

By far the most notorious of the WUO offshoots is the May 19th Communist Organization, a small, New York–based terrorist group. A descendant of the New York wing of the PFOC, its name comes from the birth date of Ho Chi Minh and Malcolm X. That date was also the occasion, in 1971, when the Black Liberation Army opened its campaign against the police by wounding two officers guarding the home of a prosecutor in the Panther 21 case. May 19th was formed in 1978, proclaiming that "we are revolutionaries within the white oppressor nation of the US empire, committed to the final defeat of US-led imperialism and to the building of a socialist world . . . In Southern Africa, Puerto Rico, Iran, inside the US, the ultimate weapon to defeat US imperialism is armed struggle and waging people's war."[12]

May 19 saw its role as being to align white revolutionaries with the fight for black self-determination as advocated by the Republic of New Africa. Whites had the responsibility to "fight alongside" black revolutionaries and aid in freeing "Afrikan prisoners of war."[13] Several May 19 members, for example, were part of the Anti-Springbok 5, arrested after a melee at Kennedy Airport protesting the tour of a South African rugby team. An airport guard was partially blinded by acid thrown by a demonstrator.

May 19 was never a very large organization, although it did have a rather unique social composition. A substantial proportion of its membership was white women, many of them committed to lesbianism.[14] Press reports estimated its membership at anywhere from forty to four hundred.[15] Its notoriety did not derive from its small demonstrations, even such violent ones as the Springbok affair. Rather, it came from the role of several members in the attempted holdup of a Brinks armored truck in Nyack, New York in November 1981 that left two policemen and one security guard dead.

The group that carried out the robbery and murders included gunmen from the Black Liberation Army and the May 19 group as well as WUO member Kathy Boudin who had gone underground after a bomb destroyed a Greenwich Village townhouse she and other Weathermen were using to manufacture explosives in 1970. Boudin and David Gilbert received long prison sentences after their convictions in the Brinks case.

Some of Boudin's supporters issued a statement after she pleaded guilty, lauding her idealism. While expressing regret at the loss of life in the Brinks case, they denounced her sentence—twenty years to life in prison—as unduly harsh and criticized the legal system for various repressive measures that violated human rights. Among the signers were Daniel Berrigan, Anne Braden, Noam Chomsky, Arthur Kinoy and Benjamin Spock.[16]

Judith Clark, another leader of the May 19 Communist Organization also was convicted in the Brinks case. Clark had been expelled from the University of Chicago in 1969 and jailed for seven months for participation in the Weathermen's Days of Rage. After 1978 she was a spokesman for the May 19 Communist Organization; she was also a plaintiff in the lawsuit against the government brought by WUO supporters and relatives, and, for good measure, was active in the PFOC. Clark travelled to Beirut in September 1981 as a representative of the May 19 group and met with Bassem Shariff, a leader of the PFLP.[17]

Still another May 19 leader, Sylvia Baraldini was convicted in 1983 on racketeering charges for involvement in a series of robberies, murders and the prison escape of BLA leader Joanne Chesimard. She received a forty-year sentence. A document found on Baraldini when she was arrested suggested the use of new tactics—including targeting US Attorneys or grand jurors "to demoralize these agents of imperialist strategy."[18]

Neither the May 19 Communist Organization nor any of the other WUO fronts were discomfited by the Brinks holdup and the murders. Sylvia Baraldini charged that the arrests in Nyack and the investigations they spawned into the affairs of her group were "acts of terrorism against the Black liberation struggle, its supporters, and the Black community in general." In a press release May 19 denied that it was a terrorist organization and insisted it was under attack because it supported self–determination, the armed struggle of such oppressed nations as American blacks and Puerto Ricans and militant struggle against white supremacy. It charged that Judith Clark was a political prisoner and there was "an alleged Brink's robbery."[19]

The Material Aid Campaign for ZANU–PF called the Nyack robbery an "attempted expropriation," while the JBAKC held a memorial honoring Sam Smith, one of those from the Black Liberation Army killed after the Nyack shoot–out. In November 1981 the May 19 group, the New Movement in solidarity, Moncada Library, Women's Committee Against Genocide, JBAKC, and Committee for the Suit Against Government Misconduct sponsored "A Program of Unity Against Repression: A Call to Resist" in New York along with the Republic of New Africa and the MLN, a support group for the Puerto Rican terrorist group, the FALN. Two hundred seventy-five people attended. That same month May 19, JBAKC, and Women Against Genocide sponsored a program called "Long Live Palestine: An Evening in Solidarity with the Palestinian Revolution." It drew about fifty people. A statement of Clark's was read and a contingent was organized for the demonstration later that month sponsored by the November 29 Coalition, controlled by the WWP and also allied with the PFLP.

It took several more years for other members of May 19 wanted in connection with the Nyack affair to be captured. Timothy Blunk and Susan Rosenberg were arrested near Philadelphia in late 1984 with 740 pounds of explosives and numerous guns. Blunk had been convicted of splashing acid on an officer at the Springbok demonstration. Rosenberg claimed that they were "revolutionary guerrillas and have been captured in the course of building a resistance to this government."[20] They were sentenced to almost sixty years in prison. Their arrest led to the capture in 1985 of Marilyn Buck, supposedly the only white member of the BLA, who had been wounded in the Nyack shoot–out, and Linda Evans. In late May 1985 Dr. Alan Berkman and Elizabeth Duke of the May 19 group were arrested. Berkman had been a fugitive for two years; he was charged with treating Buck's wound. Evans and Duke had been leaders of the Austin chapters of the JBAKC and the May 19 movement.

Despite the documented record of their violence and support for violence, members of the May 19th Communist Organization and the Black Liberation Army were able to count on the support of a number of other people on the left when they refused to testify before grand juries investigating the various bombings and robberies that had taken place. Among those signing ads supporting their grand jury resistance were Ti–Grace Atkinson, Daniel Berrigan, Anne Braden, Emile DiAntonio, Frank Donner, Arthur Kinoy, William Kunstler, and Morton Sobell.

With the successful prosecution of many of the members of the May 19th Communist Organization and the emergence from underground of numerous WUO figures, it is unlikely that more than a handful of these ex–student terrorists are still at large. Other May 19th members and members of other legal support groups like the JBAKC continue, however, to function. And, the May 19th group has issued statements of support for a series of bombings carried out from 1982 to 1984 by the Armed Resistance Unit and the United Freedom Front, two obscure "anti–imperialist" groups. Seven members of the latter group were convicted in 1985 for a variety of bombings in the New York area. One has been convicted of murdering a New Jersey state trooper.

The two black organizations whose members and supporters have been linked to the bungled Brinks robbery emerged from a quite different milieu than the student radicals. The Black Liberation Army (BLA) is a small terrorist group with ties to the Weather Underground Organization. Its members have been implicated in a variety of violent crimes, including murder and armed robbery; many of them are currently in prison.

The BLA developed out of a split in the early 1970s in the Black Panther Party. One faction, loyal to Party founders Huey Newton and Bobby Seale, retained the Panther name. Another group, centered in New York and supportive of Eldridge Cleaver, a fugitive then in Algeria, formed the core of the Black Liberation Army. In contrast to the Newton faction, which had decided to emphasize community organizing, the BLA urged the murder of police officers and robberies to finance revolutionary politics. It viewed its role as being an avenger of police brutality and the builder of an economic base for the black community through expropriations of white money.[21] Cleaver later broke with his former comrades; after returning to the United States he repudiated his past beliefs and became a conservative.

The BLA probably never numbered more than twenty-five to a hundred members. It first achieved notoriety in May 1971 when it took credit for killing two New York policemen sitting in their patrol car in Harlem. In 1973 one of the BLA's leaders, Joanne Chesimard, also known as Assata

Shakur, was involved in a shootout with police on the New Jersey Turn-pike. One BLA member and one policeman were killed; Chesimard was sentenced to life in prison. The organization soon went into decline as other members were killed in gun battles, jailed or became fugitives. Until 1981 the BLA was thought to be defunct.[22]

In 1979 Chesimard escaped from prison in a daring raid that involved BLA members and white radicals associated with the May 19th Commun-ist Organization. Rhapsodized as the "soul" of the BLA, she now lives in Cuba.

The BLA next burst into prominence in 1981 when several members of the group were involved in the botched Brinks holdup in Nyack, New York. One BLA member was killed shortly afterwards by police; several others were tried and convicted of a variety of charges stemming from the Nyack case as well as ther armed robberies and the Chesimard escape. Nathaniel Burns, who also used the name Sekou Odinga, testified that the Brinks robbery was carried out by "a revolutionary armed task force" led by "soldiers of the B.L.A." Arguing that the BLA was at war with American fascism and imperialism, he insisted that the robbery was designed to expropriate funds for the revolution and the killings were justified. Burns was acquitted of charges he had participated in the Brinks affair in a federal trial but was found guilty of another robbery and conspiracy in the Chesimard jailbreak.[23]

A BLA collective that plotted the robbery apparently operated out of an acupuncture clinic in Harlem. The reputed mastermind of the robbery was Mutula Shakur (Gerald Wayne Williams). Two others charged in the Brinks case, Edward Joseph and Cecil Ferguson, had convictions for manslaughter and armed robbery in their pasts. They were both convicted of federal charges as accessories to various crimes and given sentences of twelve and one-half years. Another BLA member, William Johnson, was arrested on a drug charge in Belize and deported to the US in 1982. Johnson was the husband of Republic of New Afrika leader Cynthia Boston. He was later found innocent. Still another BLA soldier, Donald Weems, had escaped prior to the Brinks robbery from a New York prison where he was serving time on an armed robbery charge. Weems and Joseph had both been defendants in the Panther 21 case in the early 1970s, charged with, but not convicted of, conspiracy to commit various crimes.[24] Weems was sentenced to a lengthy prison term for his role in the Nyack killings.

Marilyn Buck, reportedly the only white member of the BLA, provided some of the group's ties to the WUO. Although clear-cut connections are lacking there also appear to be some connections between the BLA and the Republic of New Afrika (RNA). When Sekou Odinga testified in court, his supporters called out "Free the Land," one of the slogans of the RNA. Moreover, Mutula Shakur allegedly had ties to the RNA and, according to his lawyer, William Kunstler, Cecil Ferguson was a member of the RNA.[25] One leading RNA member, Cynthia Boston, was arrested in the aftermath of the Brinks case but charges against her were later dropped. RNA leaders, however, have denied any connection with the Brinks case.[26]

The Republic of New Afrika is a black separatist organization with a history of violent conflicts with law enforcement agencies. It was founded in 1968 in Detroit at a conference attended by two hundred delegates. Two brothers, Milton and Richard Henry, were the leaders. The latter, having changed his name to Imari Obadel, soon gained control of the organization and in 1970 moved it to a farm outside Jackson, Mississippi, which was proclaimed to be the capital of the black nation.

The RNA's program calls for the establishment of an independent black nation in the states of Mississippi, Louisiana, South Carolina, Georgia and Alabama as "reparation for oppression of blacks in America." Its chief slogan is the demand to "Free the Land."[27]

The RNA has always been a small organization. At its height it had perhaps one hundred fifty to two hundred members. In the early 1980s it claimed to be active in twenty states. For a brief period after its founding the president was Robert Williams, in exile in Peking as a fugitive from a kidnapping charge in North Carolina. Williams, a black separatist, re-signed after returning to the United States in 1969. Betty Shabazz, Malcolm X's widow, was a vice–president in the early years. Current leaders include Obadel and Dara Abubakari (Virginia Collins), co–presidents; Chokwe Lumumba, Minister of Justice; and Fulani Sunni Ali (Cynthia Boston), minister of information.

The RNA has been involved in several violent clashes with police. In 1968 more than one hundred members were arrested in Detroit after a policeman was killed in a confrontation with the group. In 1971 nine members were tried and four convicted on murder charges after a Mississippi officer was killed in a raid on the RNA house looking for a fugitive. Richard Henry received a twelve–year sentence and the group's activities were considerably disrupted.

The RNA has also given rhetorical support to violence. In 1970 Henry called for a "second–strike capability" for blacks, an "Underground Army, the black guerrillas in the cities."[28] After the Brinks shoot–out, Lumumba insisted that while the RNA believed only in self–defense and not terrorism, it supported those who were involved in the murders.[29] Yet, Tyrone Risson, an ex–RNA member, testified that the core of the group that committed the Brinks robbery grew out of the Republic of New Afrika. Several of the Brinks defendants insisted that the "expropriation" was designed to raise money to finance a Republic of New Afrika. Sekou Odinga, a BLA militant, described himself as a citizen of the Republic of New Afrika.[30]

The Republic of New Afrika has found its allies in the white community to be largely drawn from the ranks of those close to the Weather Underground Organization. It has co–sponsored a variety of demonstrations and rallies with WUO fronts such as the JBAKC. In the early 1980s two RNA delegates attended a Libyan–sponsored conference.[31]

In May 1983 the RNA, along with the Center for Black Studies at Wayne State University, sponsored the first Black Nation Day Conference. Fifteen hundred people attended; among the announced speakers were Robert Williams, Louis Farrakhan, H. Rap Brown, Kwame Ture (Stokely Carmichael) and the Reverend Herbert Daughtry of the National Black United Front. The gathering's goals included raising the consciousness of the black nation, helping to spark a black independence movement and promoting the unification of black groups.[32]

Several other small groups appear to be related to the Republic of New Afrika. They include the National Committee to Defend New Afrikan Freedom Fighters, chaired by Ahmed Obsfemi, and the New Afrikan Political Organization. The latter group, which emphasizes many of the same themes as the RNA, attempts to organize ex–convicts, whom it calls POW's.

In October 1984 New York police arrested nine blacks described as belonging to the New Afrikan Freedom Fighters or the Revolutionary Communist Military Command, a military arm of the RNA. The nine, many of whom hold advanced degrees and responsible jobs, were accused of plotting armed robberies and the escape of Donald Weems, one of the Brinks defendants. They were acquitted of plotting robberies and jailbreaks but several were convicted of illegal possession of weapons. Defense attorneys claimed the group was only preparing to defend themselves and distribute a newspaper called *Arm the Masses*.[33] The RNA publishes *The New Afrikan*.

African People's Socialist Party

The African People's Socialist Party (APSP) is a small communist sect espousing a brand of black revolutionary politics. It was founded in 1972 in St. Petersburg, Florida by Joseph Waller, who now uses the name of Omali Yeshitali. Once a member of the Student Non–Violent Coordinating Committee, Waller has also been convicted of passing counterfeit money. The APSP moved its headquarters to Oakland, California in the late 1970s after the demise of the Black Panther Party. Its small membership is apparently composed of one–time SNCC activists, ex–Black Panthers and some dropouts from the Republic of New Afrika. It has a handful of chapters, mostly located in the South, Southwest and West Coast. Neil Holmes is international director.

APSP styles its members as "true, genuine communists." Yeshitali has called for the building of "an independent revolutionary social movement under the leadership of the black working class." The Party desires a "Black Revolution which will tear the entire house down, brick by rotten brick."[34] It identifies its ideological heroes as Marcus Garvey, Malcolm X and Kwame Nkrumah.

The APSP defines the struggle in the United States as part of the world–wide African Liberation Movement. Blacks in America are seen as colonial subjects and the group believes that "the destruction of colonialism, led by a conscious black revolutionary socialist party will constitute the critical blow in the struggle for socialism within US borders." The primary responsibility of white workers, whom the Party refers to as North Americans, is to work under the direction of and in solidarity with the subject and colonial peoples of the United States.[35]

The group's platform states that America was founded on genocide. It calls for an end to all taxation of blacks, immediate freedom for all blacks in jail, withdrawal of all police from the black community, the right to build an African People's Liberation Army, reparations from the United States and Europe and an all–African socialist government. According to the APSP all black problems in America, from hunger to housing, are due to colonial domination. It insists on a break with the two–party system and has attacked Jesse Jackson as a tool of the black petty bourgeoisie and white liberals, saying he is used to channel black anger into conventional political directions.[36]

The APSP created the Committee in Solidarity with African Independence (CSAI) as a support group for its activities. Largely white, CSAI's membership includes a number of Weather Underground Organization supporters and sympathizers. Under the direction of chairman Rick Ayers it works in support of black revolution.

Most of the APSP activities seem to center around tenant organizing and community projects. It has sponsored several tribunals on reparations for blacks. At the international level APSP has attempted to build an African Socialist International with few results. In 1984 the group was split when Linda Leaks, Yeshitali's wife, led a feminist revolt. He denounced the rebels as part of an FBI provocation and claimed that they had been influenced by Dykes Against Racism Everywhere, a lesbian organization allegedly controlled by the Workers World party.

The African People's Socialist Party publishes a monthly newspaper, *The Burning Spear*.

All-African People's Revolutionary Party

The All–African People's Revolutionary Party (AAPRP) is a small, communist organization dominated by Kwame Ture, once known as Stokely

Carmichael. It is the most outspokenly antisemitic radical–left group now functioning in the United States.

AAPRP was founded in 1972 by Stokely Carmichael, who had gained notoriety as the fiery chairman of the Student Non–Violent Coordinating Committee in the period when it abandoned its commitment to non-violence and began preaching Black Power. Carmichael was also briefly the prime minister of the Black Panther Party in the late 1960s but quarrelled with Party leaders over his commitment to black nationalism. Carmichael moved to Guinea and became a disciple of Kwame Nkrumah, but retained his American citizenship and has continued to travel back and forth between Africa and America.

The AAPRP describes itself as a small party, based in Africa, that tries to build chapters throughout the African world. It is a "permanent, mass, independent, socialist, revolutionary, Pan–African political party" that fights for the "destruction of capitalism, imperialism, settler colonialism, neo–colonialism, racism, zionism and apartheid." Party pamphlets list some sixty groups across the country and claim chapters in Africa, Europe, Canada, Central and South America as well. The Party focuses its recruiting efforts on black college students, insisting that "African students are the spark of the African Revolution!"[37]

Ture defines AAPRP's ideology as Nkrumahism, a blend of egalitarianism, humanism, individualism, collectivism and dialectical materialism. Its goal is the "total liberation and unification of Africa under an All–African Socialist government" which will enable the African peoples "to bury capitalism."[38]

The Party does not seem to be especially active in the United States. It does sponsor a yearly African Liberation Day in Washington, DC. Up to three thousand people have attended this event, although in 1984 only about seven hundred participated. The AAPRP supported Jesse Jackson's presidential candidacy and one of the Party's leaders, Bob Brown, was a full–time organizer for Jackson. It also supported Harold Washington's mayoral bid in Chicago.[39] The Party also claims to have developed a Guinean project, building a hospital in that country, and organizing seminars and lectures, including hosting Guinea leader Sekou Toure at Howard University.

Prospective Party members are required to undergo a period of political education, participating in a work/study circle that meets once every two weeks for three to five hours. Party rhetoric can be quite explicit about what is necessary to achieve its goals: "everything we gain, we gain through bloodshed," Ture told students at the University of Pittsburgh.[40]

Both Ture and the AAPRP are tainted with antisemitism. The former has a long history of making derogatory and hostile statements towards

Jews. Like virtually all radical groups, the Party is bitterly critical of Zionism, proclaiming that "Zionism and Apartheid Are Racism! They Must Be Destroyed!" It has issued brochures attacking "the illegal, racist Israeli settler regime."

One Party brochure goes much further, however. It calls Zionism "a well–organized and financed, international conspiracy which controls the economic and political life of the United States and Europe, using this stranglehold to steal and colonize the land of Palestinian people." The brochure claims that Zionism is distinct from Judaism and argues that the former exploits "the poor Eastern European Jews who work for slave wages in the factories and farms of Israel." Despite the alleged distinction, the brochure goes on to denounce "Jewish capital" for crimes ranging from financing slavery to the gold mines of South Africa. The international Zionist movement is alleged to control all banks and businesses in black America, "selling us rotten meat in the corner store, dry rotted clothes and charging high rent for slum buildings." Most civil rights groups are "controlled by Zionists and Jews" who also control the entertainment industry and exploit black stars.[41]

Ture has also attended Palestine National Council meetings in Damascus; the AAPRP has sent a delegation to Libya's Green Book Conference in the early 1980s and has attended other anti–Zionist gatherings.[42]

Communist Party USA/Provisional

The Communist Party USA/Provisional (CPUSA/P) is a small, cult–like sect that operates primarily through a front group, the National Labor Federation (NLF), which in turn operates a host of other innocuous–sounding front groups like the Eastern Service Workers Association, Eastern Farm Workers Association, California Homemakers Association, Coalition of Concerned Medical Professionals, and so on. A number of these latter groups operate anti–poverty programs and have received funding and aid from church groups.

Membership in the CPUSA/P is estimated at only about three hundred fifty. Some ex–members claim that the NLF has a military wing, trains its members in guerrilla tactics and speaks of armed revolution. Others insist that the group's fiery rhetoric has little relationship to reality and is mostly talk. Critics contend that it has set various dates for an armed revolution in the United States, while others insist that such inflammatory discussion took place in the past but has largely been abandoned. Whatever its plans, the CPUSA/P has its members live communally, work continuously and give their money to the organization, prompting charges that they are "political Moonies."[43]

The head of the CPUSA/P is a man in his mid–40s now known as Geno Parente, a man with a strange past. In the 1960s Parente ran a left–wing bookstore in San Francisco. His real name is apparently Gerald Doeden. He was allegedly involved with an organization called the National Liberation Front Continental Armed Services Division of the Liberation Army Revolutionary Group Organization (LARGO), which, despite its impressive–sounding name and the dire threats it made of revolution, included perhaps half a dozen people and was regarded by law enforcement officials as kooky.[44]

The CPUSA/P was formed in the 1970s from the remnants of a revolutionary group called Venceremos. The Bay Area Revolutionary Union had split in the early 1970s, with one faction evolving into the Maoist Revolutionary Union and another, led by Bruce Franklin, forming Venceremos and supporting armed revolutionary struggle. Within a few years, Venceremos collapsed with most of its members in jail or disillusioned. What was left apparently formed the core of the CPUSA/P.

Information on the group is scanty. Parente himself denies that the CPUSA/P even exists and calls the charges made against it lies. One of the leaders of one of the Party's fronts admitted that the group was communist but sidestepped the question of its affiliation with the CPUSA/P. There have been charges that the NLF has or had ties to Lyndon LaRouche's National Caucus of Labor Committees, another cult–like group that made a transition from the far left to the far right. Other Party figures include Diane Ramirez, David Shapiro and Sheila Averbach. The National Labor Federation maintains its headquarters in Brooklyn. Its center of strength appears to be on Long Island.

The Party's front groups rely heavily on volunteers. To help it recruit, the NLF successfully infiltrated the Commission on Voluntary Service and Action (CVSA), a religious group that publishes a guidebook listing organizations needing volunteers—a guidebook widely used by churches. The NLF listed some forty of its own fronts. After complaints to CVSA, that group sought to rectify the situation and discovered that the NLF had taken control of the guidebook project and was publishing it on its own.[45]

In 1984 the FBI's Joint Terrorist Task Force raided the CPUSA/P's offices on the basis of information alleging that it was preparing to engage in violence. Although papers were seized, no arrests were made.[46]

New Alliance Party

The New Alliance Party (NAP) is in large measure the handiwork of Fred Newman, a one–time college teacher whose therapeutic theory and practice have inspired several small, cult–like organizations over the past decade. The NAP has been actively involved in New York City politics; in the last year it has intensified efforts to become a more national organization.

Newman was a philosophy instructor at the City College of New York when he first came to notice in the radical community. In 1968 he formed a radical collective called If–Then which boasted that its pamphlets and brochures were the most obscene in New York. If–Then evolved into the Centers for Change, a commune that ran sensitivity groups where Newman also began a therapy clinic. In 1974 Newman and his small band of followers joined Lyndon LaRouche's National Caucus of Labor Committees (NCLC), a bizarre sect making a transformation from the far left to the far right. The NCLC at the time had just completed a campaign of violence and intimidation against other left–wing groups and was concentrating on charges that the Rockefeller interests and the CIA were engaged in a massive brainwashing effort. After a brief stay in the NCLC, Newman and his followers resigned to form the International Workers Party (IWP).[47]

The IWP held its founding conference in September 1974 with some forty-five members and branches in New York and Doylestown, Vermont. It criticized the bankruptcy of the American left and attributed its failings to lack of leadership. To provide that new leadership IWP organizers needed to undergo personal, revolutionary changes in themselves through therapy. The IWP also called for the formation of united fronts with working class organizations and movement groups to lead to "international socialist revolution."[48]

The IWP apparently never grew beyond five hundred to one thousand members. It claimed to have disbanded in 1976—although its internal Party organ was still being published in 1977—and its activists formed the New York City Unemployed and Welfare Council, whose president, Joyce Dattner, was a Newman follower. A host of other Party fronts soon appeared, including the Coalition of Grass Roots Women, New York City Union of Lesbians and Gay Men, Federation of Independent Unions, New Black Alliance and Women's Independent Democratic Organization. In 1979 the Newmanites organized the New Alliance Party.[49]

The New York Institute for Social Therapy and Research, set up in 1978, became the headquarters for Newman's therapy practice; its profits appear to be the major source of funding for the New Alliance Party. Some Party members and supporters have been recruited from patients undergoing therapy at the Institute. Newman's theory holds that each individual is governed by a bourgeois ego that prevents unity with others and encourages self–gratification. The role of the radical therapist is to lead the individual to overthrow the dictatorship of the bourgeois ego and to liberate the proletarian ego by means of a personal revolution.[50]

While there are probably not many more than a hundred hard–core members of Newman's group, several thousand others are on its periphery or involved in one of its front groups. The NAP claims to have thirteen thousand dues–payers and a hundred thousand readers of its weekly newspaper, *National Alliance.*[51] On occasion its candidates for public office have received a substantial vote. Dennis Serrette and Nancy Ross, the NAP's presidential ticket in 1984, were on the ballot in thirty-three states. While Serrette fell a bit short of his stated goal of six million votes, he still received 47,209, more than either the CPUSA or the SWP. On the other hand, when the NAP mounted an attempt to get fifty thousand votes and a line on the ballot for its New York gubernatorial candidate in 1982 it could muster only fifty-five hundred.

The Party's base seems to be on the Upper West Side of New York where it has tried to be active in community politics. It has focused its attacks on Democratic reformers and occasionally supported some traditional Democrats. For several years its co–chair was New York City Councilman Gilberto Gerena–Valentin of the Bronx. A small core of people have been closely associated with Newman for many years and appear to have major roles in the NAP. They include Hazel Daren, Gail Elberg, Ann Green, and Nancy Ross. Newman himself is on the executive board. Jacqueline Salit is editor of *National Alliance.* Emily Carter, a resident of Jackson, Mississippi was the national chairman in 1985 and Linda Curtis was national field organizer.

Carter reported in mid–1985 that the New Alliance Party was negotiating a merger with LaRaza Unida, a Chicano party centered in Colorado. Claiming that the NAP was black–led, she enthused that a union with the Chicano group "will change American and world history." Newman explained that the NAP "supports nationalist politics but not racialist politics" like the Democrats.[52]

The NAP's goal is to build an independent party to counter fascism. It charged in 1984 that there was no difference between Mondale and Reagan. Its platform was similar to that of the CPUSA and the WWP, calling for cuts in national defense, jobs for all, and increased spending on social programs. On foreign policy it supported the Sandinista regime and attacked the Duarte government in El Salvador. Presidential candidate Serrette argued that the Soviet threat had been exaggerated. The Party praised Jesse Jackson's campaign; after the election Nancy Ross, the NAP's coordinator, moved to Washington to head the DC office of the Rainbow Alliance Confederation's lobbying arm. Despite its name and its profession of complete support of Jackson, the organization appears to be another NAP front and to have no connection to Jackson's official Rainbow Alliance.[53]

The New Alliance Party has been plagued by charges of antisemitism for years. On the surface, the charge seems odd since several the NAP's leaders, including Ross, are Jewish. The NAP is very hostile to the state of Israel and supports the PLO but denies strenuously that it is antisemitic. It has, however, cooperated with individuals and groups who are. The most recent example is the admission in the Party's newspaper that the "NAP worked in coalitions with the Nation of Islam," led by Louis Farrakhan. More telling is the charge the NAP makes that "it was the racist white media which inaccurately portrayed Farrakhan as antisemitic." Joyce Dattner, an NAP leader, claimed that Farrakhan was an ally "in the struggle to root out the evils of racism and antisemitism." Fred Newman has denounced Jews as the "stormtroopers of decadent capitalism" against colored people, complained that they had "sold their souls" to the devil—international capitalism—and called on them to liberate themselves "behind the leadership of people of color the world over."[54]

Marxist–Leninist Party of the USA

The Marxist–Leninist Party of the USA (MLP–USA) is a very small communist sect that professes allegiance to the Albanian Communist movement. The group does not provide public information either on its leadership or its size. Party headquarters are in Chicago and there are branches in New York, Seattle, Oakland, Boston and Detroit. The MLP–USA publishes a weekly newspaper, *The Workers' Advocate*, while the Caribbean Progressive Study Group in New York, apparently closely aligned with the Party, publishes *The West Indian Voice*, which supports national liberation for the West Indies. The Boston branch publishes the *Boston Worker*. The Party also puts out *Proletarian Internationalism*, which carries material from fraternal parties around the world. The Detroit branch produces *Struggle*, edited by Tim Hall, which aspires to be a literary journal. Its first issue "calls upon all those who feel the urge to battle the capitalist bloodsuckers through creative literature" to contribute.[55]

The MLP–USA traces its origins to the American Communist Workers Movement (Marxist–Leninist), founded in 1969. In 1973 it became the Central Organization of United States Marxist–Leninists. In January 1980 at a founding conference the party itself was formed. Its first communique indicated its intention to firmly uphold "the People's Socialist Republic of Albania, the bastion of world revolution and the only genuinely socialist country in the world today." In addition to former Albanian Communist leader Enver Hohxa, the Party's other hero is Joseph Stalin—it has proclaimed: "Eternal glory to J.V. Stalin!"[56]

The Party sees "revolutionary ferment ... at work everywhere" and believes that it will lead to the "overthrow of the oppressors through revolutionary violence." It is adamantly hostile to America, charging that the United States' "monopoly capitalist class is a center of fascism and reaction on the world scale." At the same time it fervently denounces the Soviet and Chinese "social–imperialists."[57]

The MLP–USA is allied with several other small pro–Albanian groups around the world, including the Movement of Popular Action/Marxist–Leninist of Nicaragua and the Workers Communist Party in France. It regards orthodox communist parties as revisionist traitors to the working class, denouncing the CPUSA, for example, as a "counter–revolutionary capitalist party." While it supports the Nicaraguan Revolution, the MLP–USA voiced hope that it "may yet go beyond the petty–bourgeois Sand-inistas with their vacillating policy of concessions to the rich."[58]

The Party is also extremely hostile to the state of Israel, charging that "Zionism means, first and foremost, the terrorist extermination of the Palestinians and expansionist wars against the Arab peoples." It even de-nies any real psychological connection between Jews and Israel; in order to justify the settlement of Palestine, the Zionists supposedly "dug up biblical references to the Hebrew tribes that had lived in Palestine three thousand years before." The Party also accuses Zionists of having "demagogically seized" on antisemitic incidents to bolster their own support.[59]

While harshly critical of Israel, the MLP–USA is not happy with those seeking Israel's destruction. It has accused the Democratic Front for the Liberation of Palestine and the Popular Front for the Liberation of Pal-estine of being disguised national–reformists under the "rotten influence of Soviet revisionism and Castroism." It has also attacked the PLO for seeking an accommodation with imperialism and Zionism.[60]

Notes

1. Much of the historical background is taken from Peter Collier and David Horo-witz, "The Untold Story of the Weather Underground," *Rolling Stone*, September 30, 1982.
2. *Prairie Fire: The Politics of Revolutionary Anti-Imperialism*, Communications Co., 1974.
3. *Ibid.*
4. *Breakthrough*, Summer 1984.
5. *Montgomery Journal*, February 10, 1983.
6. *Jewish Times*, July 7, 1983.
7. JBAKC Leaflet, 1983.
8. "Stop Killer Cops," JBAKC Leaflet, (no date).
9. *Washington Post*, January 16, 1985.
10. JBAKC Leaflet, 1981.
11. On Duke and Evans, see *Daily Texan*, Spring 1983.
12. *Principles of Unity of the May 19th Communist Organization* (1978).

13. *Ibid.*
14. Ellen Frankfort, *Kathy Boudin and the Dance of Death*, (New York: Stein & Day, 1983).
15. *Time*, November 9, 1981, *NY Post*, February 1, 1982.
16. *Guardian*, May 16, 1984.
17. May 19th Leaflet, 1981.
18. Eugene Methvin, *Reader's Digest*, December 1984, "Terror Network USA."
19. May 19th Communist Organization press release, dated November 2, 1981.
20. *Philadelphia Inquirer*, December 1, 1984, *New Haven Register*, December 13, 1984.
21. *Newsday*, January 10, 1982.
22. *New York Times*, April 21, 1981.
23. *Newsday*, September 13, 1983.
24. *Newsday*, March 27, 1982, *New York Daily News*, November 18, 1982.
25. *Newsday*, March 27, 1982.
26. *New York Daily News*, November 9, 1981.
27. *New York Daily News*, October 28, 1981.
28. *New Afrikan*, June 29, 1971.
29. *New York Times*, October 31, 1981.
30. *Newsday*, November 27, 1982.
31. *Denver Post*, (no date given).
32. *Detroit News*, March 24, 1983.
33. *Guardian*, October 31, 1984, *New York Times*, August 6, 1985.
34. *The Burning Spear*, October 1984, June 1984.
35. *The Burning Spear*, June 1984.
36. *Ibid.*
37. AAPRP Pamphlet, 1982.
38. *Ibid.*
39. *Guardian*, April 4, 1984.
40. *Pittsburgh Press*, October 8, 1981.
41. AAPRP Educational Brochure No. 1, November 1975.
42. *Denver Post*, (no date given).
43. *Berkshire Eagle*, October 3, 1983, *Boston Globe*, March 1, 1984.
44. *American Legion Firing Line*, May 1970.
45. Jean Lyles, "How the Revolutionaries Conned the Bureaucrats," *Christian Century*, July 20-27, 1983.
46. *Newsday*, February 19, 1984.
47. An excellent history of the NAP is Joe Conason, "Psychopolitics," *Village Voice*, June 1, 1982.
48. *International Worker*, October 3, 1974.
49. Conason, "Psychopolitics."
50. *Ibid.*
51. *News World*, November 1, 1982, *National Alliance*, June 14, 1985.
52. *National Alliance*, June 14, 1985.
53. *New York Times*, October 20, 1984; *National Alliance*, June 21, 1985.
54. *National Alliance*, June 21, 1985; For the charges of anti-Semitism see *Jewish Week*, September 10, 1982, *Village Voice*, April 20, 1982, *Our Town*, August 15, 1982, *New York Alliance*, September 27, 1982.
55. *Struggle*, June 1985.
56. *Communique of the Founding Congress of the Marxist-Leninist Party of the USA*, 1980.

57. *Ibid.*
58. *Ibid.*; *Workers' Advocate*, July 1, 1985.
59. *Zionism is Racism in the Service of Imperialism*, Chicago, 1983.
60. *Ibid.*

Part 3
Radical Groups

Introduction

The influence and impact of the radical left do not stop with the Communist Party or the numerous splinter groups already described. The 1960s saw the emergence of a radical movement called the New Left that often regarded the Soviet Union and traditional communism as hidebound and conservative, lacking in revolutionary vigor and commitment. A small number of those who joined the New Left became terrorists, joining such groups as the Weathermen.

Most New Left organizations, however, disbanded and disappeared in the 1970s. Paradoxically, however, the revolutionary spirit of the New Left survives and even flourishes in a number of groups that focus on opposition to specific issues and policies of the United States government. In this section of the book we shall examine this broader, non–communist radical left mileau, focusing on several of the dozens of organizations that inhabit it.

Without being communist fronts, these organizations have, at the least, friendly relations with the newly invigorated Communist Party. They cooperate with it, participate in united fronts with the Party and its front groups, and welcome Communists into their own ranks.

Traditionally, many mainstream liberal and reform organizations and even some radical groups refused to join in coalitions with the Communist Party, for they regarded American communists as mouthpieces for the Soviet Union and enemies of democratic values. This refusal was reinforced by the Party's historical aptitude for attempting to seize control of the organizations in which its members were active. Stripped of the protective coloration offered by alliances with respectable organizations, the CPUSA had been less able to gain respectability and influence. By cooperating with the CPUSA in some fashion, organizations are doing more than affirming its constitutional right to function in the United States. They are conferring a certain degree of respectability upon it, affirming that they share a variety of its goals, and, most importantly, providing a moral seal of approval.

Just as important as the willingness of these groups to cooperate with the Communist Party on practical matters is their theoretical hostility to anti communism. While sometimes conceding that the Soviet Union or other communist countries may be guilty of causing the arms race or interfering in the affairs of other countries, or abusing human rights, many of these groups insist that America is by far the greater sinner. They may pay lip service to allocating blame to both sides, but their open and passionate emphasis is on the evils of America and the West.

If President Reagan regards the Soviet Union as the "evil empire," most, if not all, of these radical groups regard America, Israel and the West in that light. Seeing America as a racist, imperialist and militarist capitalist power, radicals active in a variety of these movements have forged numerous links and interconnections in the past several years. By joining together, they hope to achieve a greater influence than their individual organizations may wield. They also feel that they have a duty to make the American people see what they perceive to be the connections between the capitalist war machine of the United States and American behavior in the Middle East, Nicaragua, or South Africa. In their view, America is engaged in a worldwide effort to destroy progressive forces. They believe that the entire notion of a Soviet threat is manufactured by the United States as a means of bolstering and maintaining American militarism and imperialism.

One result of the cooperation between various groups has been a series of conferences and projects organized around the theme of "deadly connections." Disappointed that a massive June 12, 1982 anti–nuclear march in New York City had failed to condemn the Israeli incursion into Lebanon then taking place, several people argued that intervention abroad of any kind raised the danger of nuclear war. The link among nuclear war, intervention, and meeting human needs has become a constant theme of the left.

The Deadly Connections theme has also become a stick with which a variety of radical organizations are able to beat Israel. In fact, Israel plays almost as large a role as the United States in this radical demonology. The radical left has become stridently anti–Israel, which it sees as the strongest opponent of communism in the Middle East, and, in fact, as one of the most vital opponents of the Soviet thrust on the international scene. Many of the leading figures in these groups have long denounced Zionism and castigated Israel in the most extreme language.

The organizations in the following section are among the most prominent members of this emerging radical network that has among its most enduring characteristics an unrelenting hostility to the United States, the West, Israel and Zionism, and a passionate commitment to the forces of world liberation, which are identified (with varying degrees of zeal) with the Soviet Union, Vietnam, the Palestine Liberation Organization, the

African National Congress, the Sandinistas and other "liberation" movements. They also share an aversion to anti–communism, agreeing with the Communist Party that it is equivalent to McCarthyism, counterrevolution and reaction and poses a danger to world peace.

7

Committee in Solidarity with
the People of El Salvador

Opposition to American involvement in the affairs of foreign countries has long been a powerful current in political life. Isolationism has had both left– and right–wing connections. There were strong currents of opposition to American involvement in the Spanish–American War, World War I and the frequent American intervention in Latin America throughout this century.

During the Vietnam War a portion of the anti–war movement based its activities, not on opposition to American policies, but on support for the victory of the communist–led National Liberation Front and the North Vietnamese government. Likewise, the opposition to American policies in Central America includes people who support the revolutionary movements and provide assistance to them. The largest and most active of the anti–intervention groups with such ties and views is the Committee in Solidarity with the People of El Salvador (CISPES).

CISPES was founded in 1980 following a trip to the United States that winter by Farid Handal, an activist in the revolutionary movement and the brother of Shafik Handal, head of the El Salvador Communist Party. His mission was to create a support network for the FMLN/FDR, the coalition of political and military forces seeking to overthrow the government. Farid's report on his trip was later seized in a raid on a guerrilla hideout. While in the United States, he met with representatives of the CPUSA Central Committee, including, most importantly, Sandy Pollack, and officials of the Cuban Embassy. Pollack, a top officer in the United States Peace Council, was also a member of the Permanent Bureau of the World Front in Solidarity with the People of El Salvador, headquartered in Mexico. She proposed that a national conference to create a solidarity organization be held; the result was CISPES.[1]

For its part, CISPES has steadfastly denied that it was created by the

FMLN/FDR. Philip Wheaton, one of CISPES's founders, charged that the Handal documents were forgeries and, while conceding that CISPES founders met several times with Handal and that he participated in solidarity meetings, disputed claims that he had any link to the organization.[2] CISPES called charges that it was funded by the FMLN/FDR or is its agent or that it is aiding the enemy "lies."[3]

Whether or not CISPES was formed at the behest of the guerrillas and with the aid of the Communist Party, it has very close ties to the FMLN/FDR and has become an integral part of the radical left in the United States. In its fundraising appeals CISPES proclaims its purpose to be merely to mobilize American public opinion against American intervention in El Salvador and to promote solidarity with the FMLN/FDR which it regards as the only legitimate force in the country and the representative of 80 percent of the population. CISPES, however, has another agenda. It is not a peace group or an anti–war organization.[4]

The focus of CISPES's work is El Salvador. It acts as a propagandist for the revolutionary forces, lobbies Congress and the American people, raises funds and material for the guerrillas, and has prepared to disrupt governmental functions over American policy. Carroll "Carlos" Ishee, husband of the Southeast regional coordinator of CISPES, was killed in August 1983 fighting with the FMLN, after serving in their movement for eighteen months. When news of his death was received at a CISPES national conference, it was named in his honor.[5]

CISPES has proclaimed that its goal and that of other Central American solidarity groups is "to provide direct, concrete support for particular revolutionary movements." One facet of such support is its People to People programs that includes such things as material aid, organizing tours, solidarity brigades and human rights campaigns. It also uses such "grassroots" work as letter–writing campaigns to public officials and government agencies.[6] CISPES has been involved with sanctuary activities in American churches. At one Episcopalian church in New Brunswick, New Jersey, pastored by the Reverend Henry Atkins, a priest and CISPES activist, CISPES monitors stayed with one Salvadoran family at all times.[7] In 1981 CISPES circulated a forged "dissent paper" on American policy in Central America that was used to undermine American support for the regime. Several national columnists later admitted having accepted its veracity; CISPES has apparently never acknowledged responsibility for its role in what the FBI called a disinformation campaign.[8]

By far the most controversial of CISPES's activities is its material aid campaign. A number of local chapters support New El Salvador Today (NEST) that raises money to support the guerrillas. CISPES sees such campaigns as an opportunity to reach out beyond traditional left–wing peace groups to show that the US government is opposing forces more in tune with American values than the Duarte regime. What those values are may be at least partially gleaned from a Vietnam—El Salvador rally that CISPES co-sponsored to celebrate the sixth anniversary of the "liberation of Vietnam from imperialism" and to support the struggle in El Salvador.[9] In any case, the State Department charged in February 1985 that the DC CISPES chapter was raising money to build a shoe factory but was deceiving donors by not emphasizing that the factory would be built in a guerrilla area and the products would go to the guerrillas. CISPES responded that it had not deceived anyone about where the money was going.[10] CISPES has sponsored concerts by Holly Near and Ronnie Gilbert to raise money for medical supplies for the rebels. At its 1985 convention, it pledged to raise $300,000 in medical aid for the next year. At the same time it received a message from Guillermo Ungo, one of the leaders of the FDR, thanking CISPES for its "invaluable contribution."[11]

CISPES has not confined its attention to Central America. Its activities on other issues demonstrate the linkages that have formed among a variety of radical groups and provide further evidence of its own leftist agenda. One of CISPES's targets is the state of Israel. In April 1984 *Alert* "proudly" presented an article by Stuart Schaar on Lebanon. Schaar noted that the Druse and Shiite militias had demonstrated that America and its allies "are vulnerable to carefully staged, well-coordinated attacks" and concluded that "with a will to win, a unified progressive movement armed with portable weapons and backed by popular support still can defeat the American giant and its surrogates."[12]

CISPES has also forged links with the November 29 Committee for Palestine, a group that supports the Popular Front for the Liberation of Palestine and is closely allied with the Workers World party. They cosponsored a rally in Austin Texas in 1983 linking American intervention in the Mideast and the Caribbean to American intervention in Central America.[13] At another co-sponsored meeting in New York the theme was the counterrevolutionary role of Israel in Central America as a Pentagon surrogate. Among the speakers was Eqbal Ahmad, who denounced the "US puppet Israeli garrison state" to the hundred people in attendance.[14] Nor are these the only examples of cooperation between CISPES and the Workers World Party. A May 1981 march on and rally at the Pentagon, organized primarily by the Peoples Anti-War Mobilization and the Workers World Party featured two masters of ceremony. One was WWP leader Larry Holmes; the other was Heidi Tarver, a leader of CISPES.

On October 24, 1984 the November 29 Committee picketed an Israeli Bonds dinner in Chicago. The demonstration was also endorsed by a variety of radical groups, including CISPES, the National Lawyers Guild, National Black United Front, solidarity groups for the Nicaraguan and Guatamalean people and the Peoples Anti–War Mobilization. The leaflet distributed by the protesters linked Israeli's "deepening alliances with right-wing dictatorships around the world" to its "fundamental nature as a colonial–settler state based on the 1948 expulsion of the indigenous Palestinians and racist discrimination against those Palestinians who remain." It expressed confidence that anti–intervention forces in the United States would "begin to understand the essentially reactionary role of Zionism in the world today."[15]

CISPES is far more interested in protest than in traditional political tactics. In part, this bias is a reflection of the group's perception that neither the Democratic nor the Republican parties is enthusiastic about its goal—promoting the victory of the Marxist–dominated FMLN/FDR. While both Republicans and Democrats support the Duarte government, CISPES insists that he is "providing the 'moderate' facade behind which the US can pursue its military intervention."[16] Accusing him of being an American puppet, doing nothing to stop death squads and terror bombing of civilians, it argues that unmasking that facade "has become a task of top priority for all who oppose US intervention."[17]

CISPES did approve of the political views of Jesse Jackson and the Rainbow Coalition. At a national conference in January 1984 CISPES debated its relationship to the Jackson campaign. Although a minority wanted to endorse his candidacy, the conference only called for support of the Rainbow Coalition and work with its staff on American intervention in Central America.[18] As the campaign developed, many CISPES members were active in the Jackson campaign. One of them, Suzanne Ross, a national leader of CISPES and a Rainbow delegate to the Democratic Convention, exulted that "for the first time, there was a group of people inside the convention as radical as those outside," but expressed regret that CISPES had failed to endorse Jackson.[19]

After the convention, CISPES continued its efforts to tie together the various strands of the radical agenda. It endorsed Jackson's call for a struggle against apartheid, noting that he had been a reliable ally on Central America; an editorial in *Alert* endorsed civil disobedience around the issues of South Africa and Central America.[20] The Nuclear Freeze Movement initiated a coalition that included both CISPES and Operation Push; some thirty-five thousand Chicagoans marched in October calling for "Nuclear Freeze Now, Meet Human Needs, No More Vietnams." Jackson was one of the speakers at the rally and called for unity among all progressive forces. CISPES regarded the event as an important step in uniting disarmament and anti–intervention groups with the black community. A similar rally in Boston in September 1984 drew seven thousand marchers; there the call more specifically called for an end to American intervention in Central America and the Mideast.[21] CISPES has also been a participant in a variety of marches on Washington. It took part in the August 27th March of 1983 for Jobs, Peace and Freedom. It was also active in organizing the Spring Mobilization Coalition that planned the April 1985 Actions in Washington, whose four themes were freeze and reverse the arms race, cut military and increase social spending, oppose apartheid and racism and get America out of Central America and the Caribbean.

The ties between CISPES and other radical groups go beyond cosponsoring demonstrations. At its national conference in January 1984 one of the main speakers was Ann Braden, long identified with Communist Party causes in the South and a leader of the Party–dominated Southern Organizing Committee.[22] When CISPES and the National Lawyers Guild formed a Coalition of Conscience to demonstrate outside the Louisville hall where Ronald Reagan and Walter Mondale held one of their Presidential debates in 1984, a disagreement arose with anti–Reagan union members also demonstrating over the former's demands that a Salvadoran refugee and Ann Braden speak to the group.[23] The United States Peace Council, another important Communist Party front group, is represented on the CISPES steering committee. Former Mayor Gus Newport of Berkeley, co–chair of the USPC, made a national speaking tour in the fall of 1985 under the sponsorship of the USPC, NEST, and CISPES to speak about his trip to the "liberted areas" of El Salvador. CISPES also worked very closely with the Mobilization for Survival to organize demonstrations at the Republican Convention in 1984.[24]

CISPES has somewhere between two hundred fifty and three hundred chapters across the country and claims to have ten thousand members. In recent years CISPES has made major efforts to increase its Chicano and Latino membership but most members are still white. CISPES recruits mainly from the political left but has also been successful at attracting support from the religious community. The Louisville chapter, for example, noted that "besides the left in Louisville, the most reliable base for CISPES and anti–interventionist politics has been the progressive religious community." In addition to its coalitions and alliances with extremist political groups, CISPES has built ties to mainstream churches in such organizations as the Central American Solidarity Coalition. CISPES has eight regional offices and a national headquarters in New York.[25] Some of its local affiliates use other names, such as the Latin American and Caribbean Solidarity Association in Miami, and some are affiliated to the National Network in solidarity with the People of Guatamala or the National Network of Solidarity with the People of Nicaragua as well as CISPES.

Despite efforts to unite the three groups, it has proven impossible. Eighty delegates from forty-two chapters of NISGUA, meeting in 1984, worried that Guatamalan concerns would get short shrift in a united organization. CISPES defeated a proposal for unity at its 1985 convention, but voted to set up a coordinating body. NISGUA, whose national coordinator is Jean Welsh, has mounted a boycott of Coca–Cola to protest labor troubles at Coke's bottling plant in Guatamala.[26]

NNSNP, whose national coordinator is Debra Reuben, concentrates on building support for the Sandinista government. When the United States imposed a trade embargo on Nicaragua, for example, NNSNP held an emergency meeting in Washington, called for nationwide protests, and endorsed civil disobedience at the local level. Signers of a Pledge of Resistance took part in the demonstrations on May 7th. Almost half of the sixty-five thousand signers have agreed to commit acts of civil disobedience in response to American policies in Central America. Sixteen hundred people were arrested across the country, including more than five hundred in San Francisco. Thousands more participated in demonstrations. In response to Congressional approval of funding for the contras, more than 35,000 people demonstrated on June 12th, with two thousand arrests.[27]

CISPES also has close ties to the Casa El Salvador Farabundo Marti, an organization of Salvadorans living in the United States, that supports the Marxist guerillas.

While CISPES professes to be concerned about the violation of democracy abroad, its commitment to democratic procedures in the United States is less than exemplary. At a January 1984 national conference it called for "creative harrassment" of supporters of President Reagan's Central American policies.[28] Local chapters have organized disruptions of speeches by "unacceptable" figures. For example, in March the Washington chapter took credit for forcing the conservative Young Americans for Freedom to cancel a program where Roberto D'Aubisson and other ARENA and PCN speakers were scheduled. The Kalamazoo chapter worked with a student group to mobilize two hundred demonstrators to deny a CIA recruiter access to a college campus. *Alert* noted that Henry Kissinger was due to speak in Minneapolis, "where, if he has not already been dissuaded by then from making public appearances, he will be faced with more protests." CISPES was one of the organizations participating in a demonstration against Kissinger in San Francisco that turned into a riot. Gonzalo Santos, a CISPES leader, blamed the police for the violence. CISPES appears to have gone beyond the traditional view of civil disobedience. After twelve members of its National Administrative Committee were arrested in April 1985 for invading the White House grounds to protest the Administration's funding for the Salvadoran government, they issued a statement charging that the American government "has lost the legitimate power to govern in our name and with our support."[29]

In the last few years there have been disagreements within CISPES about the role it should play in American political life. At its first national convention held in May 1985 in Washington, five hundred delegates debated two alternatives. The minority, which included LaVaun Ishee, Southeast regional coordinator; Bob Ostertag, editor of *Alert*; and Gonzola Santos, the Rocky Mountain regional coordinator, saw CISPES as the "solidarity arm of the North American people and movement, not the North American arm of the Salvadoran movement." From this perspective, CISPES would openly help to shape the agenda for the revolutionary left in America. The majority, while not opposed to multi–issue coalitions, wanted to focus on solidarity work on behalf of El Salvador. While rejecting the proposal that CISPES take a greater role in building a radical American movement, the delegates also removed a provision from the group's charter that discouraged people from organized political parties from assuming any leadership positions above the chapter level. The new national officers were Michael Lent, chosen to be national coordinator, Angela Sanbrano and Mary Ann Buckley. Several leaders of the losing faction soon left the organization.[30]

In 1985, CISPES had concentrated its efforts on publicizing the brutal air war it claims the Duarte regime is waging in El Salvador with American support while building its own base through outreach programs to enable it to better influence Congress.

Notes

1. *Soviet Active Measures*: Hearings Before the Permanent Select Committee on Intelligence, House of Representatives, 97th Congress, 2nd Session, July 13, 14, 1982.
2. *New York City Tribune*, May 21, 1985.
3. *Alert*, June 1984.
4. Bill Keller, "Interest Groups Focus on El Salvador Policy," *Congressional Quarterly*, April 24, 1982.
5. *Alert*, March 1984.
6. Ibid.
7. *Alert*, November 1984.
8. *Soviet Active Measures*, op. cit.
9. *New York City Tribune*, May 28, 1985.
10. *Guardian*, February 27, 1985.
11. *Frontline*, June 24, 1985.
12. *Alert*, September 1984, April 1984.
13. *Palestine Focus*, January 1984.

14. *Workers World*, July 12, 1984.
15. November 29 Committee Leaflet, 1984.
16. *Alert*, June 1985.
17. *Alert*, September 1984.
18. *Alert*, March 1984.
19. *Alert*, May 1984, September 1984.
20. *Alert*, November 1984.
21. Ibid.
22. *Alert*, March 1984.
23. *Alert*, November 1984.
24. *Alert*, September 1984.
25. *Alert*, March 1984, June 1984.
26. *Alert*, July–August 1984.
27. *Alert*, June 1985; *Christianity and Crisis*, July 22, 1985.
28. *Alert*, March 1984.
29. Ibid., May 1984.
30. *Frontline*, June 24, 1985; *Alert*, October 1985.

8

Clergy and Laity Concerned

Central American policy is not the only issue that has led to an alliance between the radical left and some segments of the religious community. Partly under the influence of liberation theology, which provides a spiritual justification for radical political activism, and partly as a legacy of the Vietnam protest movement, some ministers and priests have developed ties to the radical American left.

One of the most visible such ministers is the Reverend William Sloane Coffin, until recently chief minister of the Riverside Church in New York, once a prominent figure in the protest movements of the 1960s when he served as chaplain of Yale University. Under Coffin's direction, the Church created a Disarmament Program run by Cora Weiss, another anti–war activist, and fervent supporter of the Vietnamese Communist government. Weiss, an heiress, is married to Peter Weiss, an attorney prominent in the National Lawyers Guild. The Weisses have also played an important role in the Institute for Policy Studies. The Disarmament Program of the Church has been actively involved with the Mobilization for Survival and similar groups.

The most substantial institutional support for radicalism within the religious community is Clergy and Laity Concerned (CALC). CALC was founded in 1965; its original name, Clergy and Laymen Concerned About the Vietnam War, indicated its early focus. Supported by many of the most eminent religious figures in the United States, including Rabbi Abraham Joshua Heschel and Reverend Martin Luther King, Jr., it demonstrated and lobbied against continued American involvement in the war.

By 1970 CALC began to focus more attention on the role of American corporations in US foreign policy. One of its major campaigns centered on the promotion of infant formula in underdeveloped nations. After several years of stagnation following American withdrawal from Vietnam and the Communist victory there, CALC began a new focus in 1981 on building a multiracial movement. It now claims to have more than 50 chapters and nearly 30,000 supporters. Its codirectors are the Reverend John Collins and Sister Blaise Lupo.

Local chapters have considerable autonomy and often are involved in many worthwhile and praiseworthy causes. Most members are no doubt motivated by the highest religious idealism and concern for the helpless, unfortunate or needy.

Although many of CALC's founders and members undoubtedly based their opposition to American policy in Vietnam on moral or political grounds, by the mid–1970s CALC's position began to foucs more on support for the North Vietnamese. One of CALC's founders, Reverend George Webber, has noted that since then, many CALC members have seen their task as "revealing to America its dishonorable role in world affairs." He cited "the distortion of reality and the subsequent failure of foreign policy that results from viewing the world through the lens of anti–communism . . . the covert imperialism of the US economy . . . [and] the militarization of our country."[1]

In 1974 a CALC delegation went to Saigon to investigate South Vietnamese violations of the Paris Peace Agreements. The overthrow of the South Vietnamese government by North Vietnam in violation of the accords brought no such protest. In fact, CALC has consistently minimized or ignored or apologized for Hanoi's aggression and massive violations of human rights. In 1977 the Reverend George Webber, CALC's chair, condemned the United States for blocking normalization of relations with Vietnam. Two years later, Barbara Fuller, a CALC official, justified the Vietnamese invasion of Cambodia and even excused the forced exodus of the boat people. She claimed that the mass dislocation had been caused by the Vietnamese desire to gain control over the country's rice supply and forbid capitalist activities which had been monopolized by the ethnic Chinese. She too called for normalization of relations.[2] Several months later, Fuller blamed the American trade embargo for weakening the Vietnamese economy and helping to create the invasion of Cambodia, the Chinese invasion of Vietnam and the boat people.[3] The organization was critical of Joan Baez for her denunciation of human rights violations in Vietnam.[4]

CALC's fidelity to Vietnamese totalitarianism might be dismissed as a reaction to the American role in the war were it not that it adopts a similar view in other situations. Late in 1979 *CALC Reports* noted that "political and civil rights are meaningful only when economic and cultural rights are recognized." Such an attitude not only has led CALC to denigrate political and civil rights, but it has not prevented the organization from focusing its indignation on capitalist societies while crediting socialist economies with the protection of economic rights. Thus, the same editorial immediately noted that "the greed of multinational corporations for resources and profits results in gross violations of human rights and threatens, ultimately, life on our planet." No comparable worries about the failure of communist societies to provide their people with bread, peace or freedom was voiced.[5] In an article in *CALC Report*, Sidney Lens, one of the founders of Mobilization for Survival, blamed the United States for the cold war and the arms race. According to Lens, America opposes the Soviet Union "because they stand in the way of our building an empire of multinational corporations."[6]

Indeed, CALC is almost exclusively critical of the Western world. CALC's view of the Soviet Union emphasizes "understanding." In one article reprinted in *CALC Report,* William Sloane Coffin suggested that if the Soviets have sinned, so too has the United States: "I believe the world is sustained by a kind of international solidarity of people who are ashamed of what their governments are doing."[7] This attitude requires CALC'ers to believe that individuals in the Soviet Union occupy comparable roles vis a vis their government that Americans do. Karen Collins, formerly an editor of CALC's journal, has admitted that "the fundamental decision–making is more centralized in the Soviet Peace Committee than in the US peace movement" but denies that the former is manipulated by the Soviet government. Even though it doesn't criticize the Soviet government, it is representative of the Soviet people. Collins warns that such unofficial Soviet peace groups as the Group to Establish Trust, fiercely persecuted by the Soviet government, has "been used by anti–Soviet elements in this country to bolster fear of communism."[8]

While CALC apologizes for or minimizes Soviet actions it would bitterly condemn if practiced by the United States, it also urges a moral truce with communism. CALC has called for reconsidering the "validity of 'anti–communism' as the cornerstone of our military policy."[9] It has published an article by Jack O'Dell, an official in Operation Push and former high–ranking member of the CPUSA, in which he claimed that "the injection of this pathology [opposition to communism] into the intellectual blood-stream of American life [since World War II] has taken a heavy toll on the capacity for critical thinking.[10]

CALC gives reflexive support to anti–American third world nations and revolutions. For example, it sponsored a press conference in 1979 for James Cockcroft, a sociologist at Rutgers, who had just returned from Iran and enthused about its new democracy under the Khomeini regime—the liberation of women, free elections, the flexibility in political life and the control the people exercised over the clergy.[11] When the American hostages were seized in Tehran, CALC issued a statement deploring intransigence on both sides—the Iranian demand for the immediate extradition of the Shah and the American demand that the hostages be freed unconditionally.

The only condemnation CALC made was of the United States for implying that blame for the hostage–taking rested solely with the Iranian government.[12] Don Luce, then CALC's International Representative, praised Fidel Castro's role at the 1979 Non–Aligned Conference in Havana and concluded his article with a quotation from Fidel; "our causes triumph because they are just."[13]

Although it did not endorse Jesse Jackson, CALC has been enthusiastic about the concept of his Rainbow Coalition. CALC was represented at the Organizing Committee of the Rainbow Peace Caucus held in New York in October 1984.[14] The lead article in *CALC Report* in September 1984 was on "The Theological Importance of the Presidential Campaign of the Reverend Jesse Louis Jackson."

Its author, Ben Chavis, was one of the Wilmington 10. Chavis is an official of the communist–dominated National Alliance Against Racist and Political Repression. He is also a national representative and a leader of the National Black Independent Political Party. Ordained while in prison, he serves as the director of the United Church of Christ's Commission on Racial Justice. He was identified as the coordinator of Clergy and Laity for the Jackson campaign in 1984.[15]

Chavis has a long history of support for the Palestinian cause and hostility to Israel. "We all know" he explained in 1982, "that the Democratic Party stands with the Zionists. We all know that the Republican Party stands with the Zionists. The National Black Independent Political Party, however, stands with freedom fighters."[16] Chavis has also noted that "the Sandinistas are our heros (sic) and heroines."[17] And, he has made no bones about why he is involved in the anti–war movement: "When we talk about disarmament, we're talking about disarming imperialism."[18]

In his *CALC Report* article, Chavis applauded the Jackson presidential campaign for offering "a unique opportunity to reaffirm the essence of the Christian faith through political praxis." Divine salvation was achieved through "social justice, world peace and electoral politics." Chavis asked if "a nation like the USA that is grounded in racism, capitalism and sexism can repent and change?" Chavis also praised Louis Farrakhan: "Another unique religious aspect of the rainbow coalition is the active participation of the Nation of Islam under the effective leadership of Minister Louis Farrakhan." Such praise for the author of numerous antisemitic statements prompted strong letters of protest; in response, both Chavis and CALC refused to take a position on Farrakhan, either pro or con.[19] Debra X. Cook, a member of Farrakhan's Nation of Islam and a staff member of the Lane County Oregon CALC, is co–chair of the Human Rights and Racial Justice Task Force for the National CALC.[20]

CALC has numerous links with other radical left–wing groups. It is a sponser of virtually all of the mobilizations and rallies organized by the left such as the April 1985 Actions in Washington. It has participated actively with CISPES on Latin American issues. CALC is part of the Central American Peace Action Plan which has prepared to resist US intervention in the region with nonviolent occupation of congressional field offices and demonstrations at the White House. CALC was one of the early endorsers of the Soviet–dominated World Youth Festival in Moscow in the summer of 1985. Co–director John Collins endorsed the 1981 national conference of the US Peace Council, a major communist front group. Reverend Tony Watkins, disarmament coordinator for CALC in 1985, also serves as Religious Circles Coordinator for the United States Peace Council; in 1986 he taught a course at the Communist Party's People's School for Marxist Studies.

In 1982 CALC approved a statement endorsing a two–state solution to the Israel–Arab conflict. The only party to the conflict it condemned, however, was Israel for its settlement policy. It denounced all acts of violence and terror.[21] CALC has participated in the Campaign for Peace with Justice in the Middle East and the "Breaking the Silence" seminars for organizers along with such organizations as MFS and AFSC, which, while conceding Israel's right to exist, place most of the responsibility for events on it and avoid condemnation of the PLO.

Notes

1. Reverend George Webber, "CALC: The Anti–War Years," *CALC Report,* August–October 1985.
2. Barbara Fuller, "Power Plays in Southeast Asia," *CALC Report*, April 1979.
3. Barbara Fuller, "Crisis in Southeast Asia Continues," *CALC Report*, January–February 1980.
4. "Response to Baez," *CALC Report*, July 1979.
5. "Human Rights and the Energy Quest," *CALC Report,* November 1979.
6. Sidney Lens, "Deadly Connection," *CALC Report*, February 1985.
7. William Sloane Coffin, "Loving Your Enemy," *CALC Report,* February 1985.
8. Karen Collins, "Working for Peace in the Soviet Union," *CALC Report,* February 1985.
9. "Editor's Page," *CALC Report*, February 1985.
10. Jack O'Dell, "The Mass Movement and Electoral Politics," *CALC Report,* December 1984.
11. James Cockcroft, "Iranians Strive for Islamic Ideals,"*CALC Report,* April 1979.
12. "CALC Statement on Crisis in Iran," *CALC Report,* January–February 1980.
13. Don Luce, "Report from Havana," *CALC Report,* October 1979.
14. *Guardian*, October 24, 1984.
15. *Alert*, July–August 1984.
16. *Militant*, September 24, 1982.

17. *Alert,* July–August 1984.
18. *Militant*, May 7, 1982.
19. Reverend Benjamin Chavis, "The Theological Importance of the Presidential Campaign of the Reverend Jesse Jackson," *CALC Report,* September 1984; "Letters to the Editor," *CALC Report*, October–November 1984.
20. Debra X. Cook, "To Be a Black, Muslim Woman in the Struggle," *CALC Report*, June 1985.
21. "CALC Statement on Israeli–Palestinian Relations," *CALC Report,* November–December 1982.

9

Mobilization for Survival

Mobilization for Survival (MFS) has quickly come to play a key role on the American left within a decade of its founding. Set up in 1977 to publicize the first United Nations Special Session on Disarmament, which met in May 1978, it has expanded its interests and activities far beyond the boundaries of anti–nuclear work. Today it serves as a coordinating center for a variety of groups and individuals interested in topics ranging from Central America and the Middle East to the draft and the environment. Unlike many of the Marxist–Leninist groups with whom it shares many policy commitments, MFS by and large avoids their strident, off–putting rhetoric and sectarianism. It also avoids their rigid centralization, pursuing many of the same goals through loosely organized "affinity groups."

One of the Mobe's national leaders, Leslie Cagan, has stated that the group's goal is to build a movement "that is strong enough to really challenge power."[1] MFS's background, ideology and focus all provide evidence of the goals of that movement. At MFS's seventh conference in 1984, Marv Davidoff of the Minnesota Honeywell Project noted that most people present "have the consciousness that the roots of war come from racism, sexism and the capitalist system."[2]

The MFS owes its origin to the initiative of a number of groups and individuals with long histories of radical organizing. The ideological impetus for MFS came from an article on nuclear doomsday by Sidney Lens. A long–time radical, Lens had drifted out of the Trotskyist movement and for years had been involved in numerous united fronts with Marxist–Leninists. He was a key figure in the anti–Vietnam movement. Lens and Sidney Peck, a one–time Communist Party organizer and another prominent anti–war activist, were preparing a call to action around that issue when Peggy Duff, a leader in the British disarmament movement and active in the Soviet–controlled World Peace Council, urged Americans to publicize the UN Special Assembly on Disarmament scheduled for May 1978 in New York. Norma Becker of the War Resisters League convened a meeting in March 1977 at which fifty activists agreed to work to abolish nuclear weapons and stop the arms race, deal with nuclear waste, work for human needs and focus on human survival. A month later 118 people from forty-nine organizations gathered in Philadelphia and formed Mobilization for Survival.[3]

Among the key early leaders of MFS, in addition to Peck and Lens, were Norma Becker and Dave McReynolds of the War Resisters League, Terry Provance of the American Friends Service Committee and representatives from a variety of other groups. In addition to traditionally pacifist organizations and anti-nuclear groups, MFS also came to include a number of communist front organizations. The CPUSA itself was a constituent unit, as were the US Peace Council, Southern Organizing Committee for Economic and Social Justice, and other party fronts. The third major component of MFS was a host of local environmental groups.

Individual communists and their supporters also played a role in MFS, particularly in its early years. Many of its small group of union representatives were people long associated with the Party like Abe Feinglass and Jack Spiegal. Perhaps not coincidentally, the chair of the Labor Task Force was Gil Green, a long-time leader of the CPUSA. One of the featured speakers at the Mobe's second national conference in 1978 was Frank Chapman, then of the AFSC and now a leader of the Party-controlled National Alliance Against Racist and Political Repression.[4]

MFS has engaged in a variety of protest activities since its founding. One thread has been efforts against nuclear power and nuclear weapons. NY Mobe led a campaign to place a referendum on the City ballot to prevent basing of nuclear-missile ships at Staten Island. Boston Mobe supported a failed referendum to ban nuclear weapons research within the city limits of Cambridge. MFS coordinated the International Day of Nuclear Disarmament Protests on June 20, 1983 at fifty sites around the country, many against corporations involved in nuclear weapons production. Almost a thousand members of the Livermore Action Group, an MFS affiliate, were arrested at one demonstration. MFS has also opposed the deployment of missiles by the US, including the MX, Trident, Cruse, Pershings and space weapons. It has also opposed Star Wars research and called for "appropriate unilateral initiatives by our government as a first step toward worldwide disarmament."[5]

MFS has some two hundred affiliates, many of them small, locally-based environmental or anti-nuclear groups with such names as the Three Mile Island Alert or Citizens for a Non-Nuclear Future. Most are in the East and Midwest. The largest affiliates on the West Coast are the Abalone Alliance and the Livermore Action Group. The latter is composed of more than two hundred affinity groups of from five to twenty people that has specialized in non–violent civil disobedience to block access to the Liver-more Laboratory. One of LAG's participants—the group disclaims lead-ers—has noted that among its major groupings are radical Christians anxious to question the sanctity of private property and the importance of the nuclear family, church–going Christians, witches—"who have an influ-ence on the organization's culture that is out of proportion to their num-bers"—environmentalists, feminists and anarchists. There is also a small group of Marxists.[6]

Most local groups are rather small but can enlist larger numbers for demonstrations or petitions on specific issues. Boston Mobe, for example, had about six hundred members in 1984, while NY Mobe, one of the more active affiliates, claimed more than a thousand and a mailing list of twelve thousand people.[7]

While MFS is decentralized and its local groups enjoy a great deal of autonomy, the national organization establishes national priorities each year at an annual meeting. There are also specific task forces organized around specific issues such as Anti–Intervention, Lesbian and Gay Net-work, Direct Action, Emergency Response, Anti–Racism, and so on.

While attempting to build a coalition of protest groups, MFS has been inching towards more traditional political participation. Many MFS mem-bers, particularly in such local groups as the Livermore Action Group, are anarchists and scornful of elections. MFS discussed whether to endorse Jesse Jackson in January 1984 but was split and no endorsement was issued. By October, however, MFS had joined with a number of groups, including CISPES, CALC, WRL, SANE, and the USPC to establish the Organizing Committee of the Rainbow Peace Caucus under the guidance of Jack O'Dell. Late in 1984, despite internal opposition, MFS set up an internal Rainbow Task Force to establish a liason with the Rainbow Coali-tion.[8]

MFS has become one of the key organizations in an emerging coalition that challenges numerous aspects of American policy. While it takes the lead in anti–nuclear issues, it cooperates with anti–intervention groups like CISPES, pro–Palestinian groups like the Palestine Congress of North America, and numerous other activist groups on other issues. MFS was a member, for example, of the November 12th Coalition in 1983, whose demands included no American intervention in Central America, Jobs, Peace and Justice, and an end to both nuclear and conventional arms build–ups. In addition to CISPES and MFS, the National Lawyers Guild, American Friends Service Committee, War Resisters League, Clergy and Laity Concerned, National Black United Front, Operation Push, Peoples Anti–War Mobilization, SANE, Women's International League for Peace and Freedom and US Peace Council signed the call.[9] Leslie Cagan of MFS was national chair of the steering committee of the April Actions Coalition for Peace, Jobs and Justice that organized demonstrations in 1985 around four demands—no intervention, build a just society, freeze and reverse the arms race, and oppose apartheid and end racism.

Mobilization for Survival is not controlled by communists. Its leadership, however, willingly works with communists and apparently sees no incongruity in alliances with them. When Sandy Pollack, a key communist leader, died in a plane crash in 1984, Leslie Cagan, national facilitator of MFS, was one of those eulogizing her. Cagan noted that the two had served together in the first Venceremos Brigade in Cuba in 1970.[10] Cagan herself has been described as a "feminist and open Lesbian" and a socialist.[11] Cagan is also quite critical of opposition to communism. She complained that the 1984 elections revealed "anti–communism as a way of life internationally and domestically."[12]

Some people in MFS, such as David McReynolds, one of its early leaders, claim to have no illusions about the Soviet Union. McReynolds, however, almost invariably places primary blame for world tensions on the United States, "the greatest single part of the problem." McReynolds believes that "imperial capitalism has much greater need for armies than the Soviet bloc."[13]

While MFS has included ritual equations of American and Soviet intervention in Europe in its literature, its focus has always been on the former. At its 1984 conference a sharp dispute broke out over whether it ought to build ties to peace groups in the Soviet Union and Eastern Europe not controlled by their governments. The conference decided to inaugurate internal education on the issue in 1985. No written policy had emerged by the 1985 conference. According to one account in a radical newspaper, the issue was too "divisive" to be resolved.[14]

The dominant sentiment in MFS appears to be far more critical of the United States than the Soviet Union. Norma Becker has ridiculed "the Soviet threat" and argued that the relative merits of communism and capitalism are irrelevant in the search for peace; the USSR, she noted at one conference in 1982, "is certainly no worse than the governments that our government is presently subsidizing with our tax money."[15] Leslie Cagan of MFS was one of the speakers at a New York rally celebrating the tenth anniversary of the "liberation" of Vietnam.

While it has popularized the danger of "the deadly connections" between intervention abroad and the risk of nuclear war, MFS has focused its concern almost exclusively on the actions of the United States. Soviet intervention in Afghanistan or Eastern Europe, Cuban intervention in Africa or Central America or Vietnamese intervention in Cambodia do not appear to be in the same league as American intervention in Central America or the Caribbean or Israel's war with those sworn to destroy it.

Israel, in fact, has been a constant preoccupation of MFS. Although advocates of the deadly connections theme claim that it was the 1982 Israeli invasion of Lebanon that inspired them to link the peace movement with the anti–intervention movement, MFS had previously been actively involved with the Middle East issue. MFS has justified its focus on the Middle East in terms of the danger the area presents for sparking a nuclear holocaust between the superpowers, drawn into conflict by their respective allies. In many of its public statements and educational materials, MFS insists that it supports a solution to the conflict that takes into account the interests of both Israeli and Palestinian peoples and that it accepts Israel's right to exit. The focus of the Mobe's attention, however, is to pressure Israel alone to make concessions, to pressure the American government to force Israeli concessions and to blame Israel for blocking any solution to the problems of the Middle East. Moreover, MFS has joined in demonstrations with organizations and individuals who deny Israel's very right to exist. Its literature often demonstrates a distinct and strong anti–Israeli and anti–Zionist bias.

For several years Mobilization for Survival has been trying to put the Middle East issue higher on the agenda of the peace movement. One of Mobilization for Survival's first efforts to express its Middle East views came in late 1980 with the organization of the Coalition for Justice and Peace in the Middle East. In addition to MFS, its sponsors included the National Lawyers Guild, Women's International League for Peace and Freedom, United States Peace Council, Clergy and Laity Concerned, American Friends Service Committee, Palestine Human Rights Committee, National Association of Arab–Americans and the War Resisters League. Among the individual members were Daniel Berrigan; Dr. George Webber, president of the New York Theological Seminary; Reverend Richard Deats, executive director of the Fellowship of Reconciliation; Reverend William Jones, president of the Progressive National Baptist Convention; David Dellinger; Randall Robinson of Transafrica; Jack O'Dell of Operation Push, Ramsey Clark, and Edward Said.

The Coalition called on the United States to help create conditions making it possible for Palestinians and Israelis "to live in justice and peace within secure and recognized borders." To that end it called for the replacement of the Camp David peace accords with a comprehensive peace plan and recognition of the PLO as the legitimate representative of the Palestinian people. All of the group's listed demands focused on Israel and the United States, and it favored the creation of a Palestinian state "within the context of a comprehensive peace that provides security for all existing states in the region." Paul Mayer, convener of MFS' Religious Task Force, noted that some "progressive" Jews were unable to sign the statement because it did not explicitly call for Israel's right to exist and did not condemn terrorism; he found a balance in that some Arab advocates could not sign a statement that suggested that Israel should have secure and recognized borders. A more appropriate comparison might have been that the statement explicitly called for a Palestinian state but not an Israeli state.[16]

MFS pursues the same "even–handed" tactic in other coalitions and publications. It published a series of papers as a resource guide for "peace and anti–nuclear groups to use in an internal discussion about the Middle East."[17] The respective treatment accorded Jewish and Palestinian nationalism is instructive. One of the discussion units, written by Jacob Bender of New Jewish Agenda, defended Israel from a left–Zionist point of view and warned against efforts to "separate Israel from the Jewish people." Critical of Israeli policies, Western imperialism, and "reactionary elements of the Jewish community" for "obscene" political use of the Holocaust, Bender nonetheless warned that attempts "to organize Jews against the current Israeli government" must "take into account the history and feelings of the Jewish people."[18]

By contrast, the article in the same packet on Palestinian nationalism, by Samih Farsoun, is a paean of praise for the PLO. Farsoun charged that Palestinians living in Israel proper "have been turned into an exploited, segregated, internal colony." Israel had imposed "an increasingly repressive and bloody occupation" on the West Bank and Gaza. His article included such historical inaccuracies as: "British support for Jewish immigration during and after WWII led to a swelling of Jewish population." He praised the PLO and its policies.[19]

Another article in the same packet, dealing with the Israeli peace movement, dated its founding to some Israelis' "shock" at seizing land after the 1967 war. The article never mentioned the adamant refusal of the PLO or Arab states to negotiate with or recognize Israel; its theme was that Israel's refusal to accept generous PLO offers has been the obstacle to Middle Eastern peace.[20]

The tone of MFS views on Israel and Zionism can be gleaned even more clearly from its recommendations on a Resource List for organizations. It suggested that *MERIP Reports*, a stridently anti–Zionist journal, was "an excellent progressive magazine." The four books on Zionist history that it recommended were either extremely hostile to or critical of Zionism. They included Hannah Arendt's *Eichman in Jerusalem*, Uri Avnery's *Israel Without Zionists*, Maxime Rodinson's *Israel—A Colonial Settler State?*

and Amos Elon's critical but pro–Zionist *The Israelis*. By contrast, the four books recommended on Palestinian history are all favorable. The list also recommended films and speakers from the National Emergency Committee on Lebanon, whose major goals were to end American aid to Israel.[21]

While asserting that mutual recognition of national rights by both the Israelis and Palestinians is the route to Middle Eastern peace, Mobilization for Survival has allied itself with organizations and individuals with far less savory records and views on Israel. In January 1985 MFS was part of a coalition—the Committee to Protest Sharon's War Crimes—that included the November 29 Committee on Palestine, a front for the Popular Front for the Liberation of Palestine; the John Brown Anti–Klan Committee, a fanatically anti–Zionist front for the Weather Underground Organization; a host of Arab groups such as the Committee for a Democratic Palestine, Palestine Aid Society, Arab–American Anti–Discrimination Committee, and radical groups like the Socialist Workers Party. Most adamantly oppose Israel's right to exist.[22]

In 1981 Mobilization for Survival was a cosponsor of the Middle East Teach–In Committee, which held teach–ins on the dangers of war in the region during the Salute to Israel Parade in June. Other sponsors were the Palestine Congress of North America, Palestine Solidarity Committee, and the communist–dominated US Peace Council. One of the leaflets produced by the group noted that a just peace could be built on the Palestinian right to self–determination, to an independent state and the right of refugees to return to their homes. In the interim MFS has come to pay lip service, but nothing more, to Israel's right to exist.[23]

Nor were these the only examples of MFS cooperation with extremist anti–Israel groups. For example, a July 1982 leaflet prepared for a rally, sponsored by the National Emergency Committee on Lebanon, to demand that Israel get out of Lebanon and for an end to American arms sales to Israel, listed Mobilization for Survival and the Peoples Anti–War Mobilization, a front for the Marxist–Leninist Workers World Party, as contacts for information and more leaflets and also advertised a teach–in by the November 29 Coalition, a front for the WWP and the Popular Front for the Liberation of Palestine.[24]

MFS was also part of a June 6 Coalition that protested both American and Israeli actions in Lebanon, including American "support for the Zionist regime in Israel" and called for "democratic and secular states in Lebanon and Palestine." Other coalition members included the All–Peoples Congress, Committee for Democratic Lebanon, Committee for Democratic Palestine, Jews for Justice in the Middle East, M'Tai, the US Anti–Imperialist League, and Women for Women in Lebanon.[25]

The National Emergency Committee on Lebanon, formed in June 1982 to call for withdrawal of Israeli troops from Lebanon, no American arms to Israel and no US troops in the Mideast, also called for US talks with the PLO, the sole legitimate representative of the Palestinian people and American pressure on Israel to end its occupation of Palestinian land. The executive committee included Larry Ekin of the United Methodist Church office at the UN, Sara Flounders of the Peoples' Anti–War Mobilization, Jawad George of the Palestine Congress of North America, Sandy Pollack of the USPC, Gail Pressberg of AFSC, Stuart Schaar of Jews Against the Israeli Massacre, Mounir Zahr, a supporter of the Lebanese Movement, and Jackie Gelb of MFS.[26]

In its effort to initiate long–term organizing around the Middle East, MFS has engaged in internal education and "raise(d) questions about continuing US military and economic involvement in the region." This is a polite way of saying that MFS seeks to disassociate the United States from Israel. In spite of its claims of even–handedness, MFS and its partners in these endeavors focus their complaints and criticisms on only one side in the conflict—Israel. They also complain about American support for Israel. Dan Petegorsky of Boston MOBE noted in 1984 that "the major obstacles to peace are the US and Israel."[27]

In recent years, the Campaign for Peace with Justice in the Middle East has been the major vehicle for achieving MFS's goals. Its other sponsors include the American Friends Service Committee (AFSC), Catholic Connection, and Lebanon Emergency Committee. Since the latter two groups are quite small, the Campaign has been largely a product of the AFSC and MFS.

One of the group's projects has been to publish a set of pamphlets, including one on "How to Organize an Event on the Middle East." While the pamphlet talks about the need to understand both Jews and Arabs, it warns that the "tragic" history of Jews is "used to obscure or avoid careful analysis of developments in which the Jews are not victims." Among the warnings thoughtfully provided are that it is hard "to get people to see that the role of the United States is not benign," that debates on the Middle East issue at such events can be "unproductive" and that providing more than one side of the dispute is "absurd."[28]

The reading guide provided by the Campaign is heavily sprinkled with articles from *MERIP Reports*, which it characterizes as "an indispensible source of information [for] activists." It also praises *Palestine Focus*, the journal of the November 29 Committee and recommends films by the North American Friends of Palestinian Universities, MFS and the Lebanon Emergency Committee. Similarly, the resource organizations it lists included a variety of Arab organizations, MFS and only one group at all supportive of Zionism, the New Jewish Agenda.[29]

The Campaign for Peace with Justice held its organizing conference in February 1984 at MIT. Two hundred fifty people attended. Mel King, defeated candidate for mayor of Boston, opened the gathering by charging that American Mideast policy was formulated in the interests of "monopoly capital." The only speaker who presented an "Israeli" viewpoint—Uri Shlonsky—was an advocate of a binational state. The anti–Zionist tone angered members of New Jewish Agenda, who protested afterwards that Israeli security and Jewish national survival were ignored by the speakers.[30]

In a follow–up letter to participants in the MIT conference, Robert Vitalis urged their participation in future events, noting that the Campaign for Peace with Justice in the Middle East was cosponsoring a session on "US Foreign Policy Towards the Developing Countries" in May 1984 with Central American and South African Solidarity groups. He also noted a series of events were planned for the first ten days of June to commemorate the Israeli invasion of Lebanon, the 1967 invasion of Egypt and the 1981 attack on the Iraqi nuclear reactor. A suggested petition called for Palestinian self–determination but made no mention of Israel's right to exist. Vitalis' letter warned about the danger of "maintaining the silence about the US role in the Middle East."[31]

Despite all this noise, late in 1984, still another group of left–wing organizations took the lead in sponsoring a series of conferences on "Breaking the Silence" about the Middle East. MFS included a workshop with that title at its National Conference in November. In February 1985 it held a seminar for community activists along with the American Friends Service Committee. A representative of the American–Arab Anti–Discrimination Committee (ADC), asserted that at the seminar "the Palestinian cause was more clearly in the moral ascendancy than ever before in previous peace movement gatherings."[32]

Gatherings with similar titles were held in 1985 in Philadelphia, New York, St. Paul, and San Francisco. In Minnesota, the sponsoring organizations, gathered under the rubric of Twin Cities Peace and Justice Coalition, included the ADC, Clergy and Laity Concerned, Communist Party, Minnesota Council of Soviet–American Friendship, National Lawyers Guild, Nicaragua Solidarity Committee, Office of Social Justice, Catholic Charities and Women's International League for Peace and Freedom. Although MFS was not listed as a sponsor, Jackie Gelb of the MFS National Office delivered two speeches. Other speakers included Eqbal Ahmd and Elaine Hagopian, well–known pro–Palestinian advocates, and Munir Fasheh, a Palestinian educator, and Dov Yermiya, an Israeli peace activist.[33] In San Francisco, the Bay Area Peace Council, an affiliate of the communist–dominated US Peace Council, took the lead in holding a "Breaking the Silence" meeting in June, at which the keynote speakers were Osama Doumani of the ADC and Rob Prince, a Communist active in the US Peace Council. Other speakers from the FDR–FMLN, November 29 Committee, General Union of Palestinean Students and New Jewish Agenda presented material "on the Israeli–South African axis; Israel and Central America; the Iran–Iraq war; the West Bank and Gaza situation; the subjugation of the Palestinean people; and the Israeli invasion and occupation of Lebanon and the Lebanese civil war."[34]

Its views on Israel demonstrate Mobilization for Survival's role in a host of coalitions working to erode American support for Israel and its willingness to cooperate with organizations seeking to delegitimize Zionism. It has played a central role in the emerging deadly connections network linking extremist organizations.

Notes

1. *Mobilizer*, Fall/Winter 1984.
2. *Guardian*, February 8, 1984.
3. Sid Peck and Kathy Mathews, "A Question of Survival," *WIN*, July 28, 1977; Rael Jean Isaac and Erich Isaac, "The Counterfeit Peacemakers: Atomic Freeze," *American Spectator*, June 1982.
4. Patrick Lacefield, "Mobilization Meets to Chart Future Course," *WIN*, October 5, 1978.
5. *Mobilizer*, Fall–Winter 1984.
6. Barbara Epstein, "The Culture of Direct Action: Livermore Action Group and the Peace Movement," in *Socialist Review*, 1985.
7. *NY Mobilizer*, April 1985.
8. *Mobilizer*, Fall–Winter 1984; *Guardian*, October 24, 1984; *Frontline*, December 3, 1984.
9. *Frontline*, October 3, 1983.
10. *Daily World*, February 6, 1985.
11. *New York Native*, March 12, 1984.
12. *Mobilizer*, Fall–Winter 1984.
13. David McReynolds, "Disarmament: The Politics of the United Nations Special Session," in *WIN*, May 25, 1978.
14. *Frontline*, November 25, 1985.
15. Joseph Gerson, ed. *The Deadly Connection: Nuclear War and US Intervention* (Cambridge, Mass: AFSC), 1983.
16. Religious News Services, November 6, 1980; Paul Mayer, "Waging Peace in the Middle East," *WIN*, February 15, 1981.
17. "In Whose Interest? The Middle East and American Foreign Policy," in Mobilization for Survival Packet.
18. Jacob Bender, "The Idea of the Jewish State," in MFS Packet.
19. Samih Farsoun, "Palestinean History and the Growth of the Palestinean National Movement," in MFS Packet.
20. Allen Solomonow, "Israel: Approaches to Peace," in MFS Packet.
21. "Middle East Resource List," in MFS Packet.
22. "Protest Sharon's War Crimes," Leaflet, 1985.

23. "Teach–In on the Danger of War in the Middle East," Leaflet, 1981.
24. National Emergency Committee on Lebanon Leaflet, 1982.
25. "No to War," June 6 Coalition Leaflet, 1984.
26. Leaflet, Winter 1982.
27. *Boston Phoenix*, April 24, 1984.
28. "How to Organize an Event on the Middle East," in *Middle East Peace Resource.* (Campaign for Peace with Justice in the Middle East).
29. "A Basic Reading Guide on the Middle East," in *Middle East Peace Resource.*
30. *Genesis 2*, April 1984, *Boston Phoenix*, April 24, 1984.
31. Campaign for Peace with Justice in the Middle East, Circular of March 21, 1984.
32. *ADC Times*, April 1985.
33. "Breaking the Silence" Conference brochure.
34. *People's World*, June 15, 1985.

10

National Lawyers Guild

The National Lawyers Guild (NLG) is one of the most active professional groups involved in radical activities. There is scarcely a radical cause in which its members cannot be found, nor a radical issue in which the NLG is not active. Its concerns range from nuclear weapons to immigration, from the environment to political repression. It has active programs in such areas as American intervention abroad, the sanctuary movement, solidarity with third–world revolutionary movements, gay rights, military law, plant closings, and so on. The NLG consistently praises radical regimes. It has also been a vociferous critic of Israel.

The NLG is an affiliate of the Soviet–controlled International Association of Democratic Lawyers (IADL), founded in 1946. Expelled from France in 1949, the IADL is now headquartered in Brussels. Over the years it has steadfastly supported every twist and turn in Soviet foreign policy, including the invasions of Hungary, Czechoslovakia and Afghanistan. The American Association of Jurists, the regional affiliate of the IADL, is headquartered in Havana. Its president, Ann Fagan Ginger, is a long–time NLG activist. The NLG was founded in 1937 by a coalition of liberal and radical lawyers concerned by the conservative role played by the American Bar Association. In addition to a number of prominent and respected New Dealers, its members included many Communist lawyers. Following the Nazi–Soviet Pact in 1939, most of the liberal lawyers resigned from the NLG. By the early 1950s, only a handful of liberals and radical non–communists were left. The NLG reached its nadir in the late 1950s, following the Soviet invasion of Hungary, falling to fewer than six hundred members.

The organization began to revive in the 1960s when its civil rights activities in the South enabled it to once again attract socially committed attorneys. By 1967 it had become the legal arm of the New Left and was intimately involved in radical activities. Many of the new recruits to the NLG made no effort to hide their political sympathies. The 1971 NLG program boldly asserted that "there is no disagreement among us that we are a body of radicals and revolutionaries." NLG activists delighted in proclaiming their goal. William Kunstler explained that "I want to bring down the system through the system."[1]

By the early 1970s the NLG was largely under the influence of younger lawyers influenced by the New Left. It accepted law students, paraprofessionals and "jailhouse lawyers" as members so that, by one estimate, as many as one–half of the NLG was composed of non–lawyers.[2] The NLG's growth was not without costs; by the early 1970s conflicts among the communists, Maoists, Trotskyists and other assorted radicals became more intense. While the Old Guard pursued more traditional legal tactics on behalf of radical causes, many younger members emulated their movement comrades. One faction active in prison–reform work—consisting largely of efforts to revolutionize prisoners—argued that "many people within the Guild consider the strategy of armed struggle to be an integral part of any revolutionary struggle. The Guild itself has not only defended but actively supported the armed actions at Attica and Wounded Knee."[3]

Some Guild members did more than merely represent revolutionaries and terrorists in court. NLG members were active in the Weather Underground Organization (WUO), the Prairie Fire Organizing Committee and the May 19th Communist Organization. Bernadine Dohrn, a leader of the WUO, was the NLG national student organizer in 1967. Stephen Bingham, an NLG lawyer, was a fugitive for more than a decade after being indicted for furnishing guns to George Jackson, a black militant killed along with three guards and two other inmates in a jail break from San Quentin prison. He was found innocent in a 1986 trial. Russ Neufield, editor of *Midnight Special*, an NLG journal for prisoners, was a WUO member. Another staff–member was Judith Clark, now serving a lengthy prison term for participation in the Brinks robbery–murder in Nyack, New York in 1981.

Most Guild members eschewed such violent activities. They could, however, be found in other radical activities. William Schaap, who served as president of the Washington, DC branch of the NLG, was a founder of *Covert Action Information Bulletin,* a journal specializing in exposing American intelligence activities and agents. Arthur Kinoy, a long–time Guild leader, has played a leading role in various efforts to organize new revolutionary parties, including the Mass Party Organizing Committee in 1973, which supported armed struggle of national liberation movements against American imperialism. Another leading Guild figure, Abdeen Jabara, has close ties to the PLO and its support groups in the United States.

In recent years, the NLG has moved closer to the communist vision of the world as the New Left influence has waned and the Maoist and

Trotskyist sects have fallen on hard times. Membership in 1985 was around seven thousand. Portions of the New Left ethic remain, however. The Guild newsletter complained in 1985 that even in NLG law offices "capitalist work relations exist," albeit enlightened ones.[4]

In 1973 the NLG convention affirmed that "the main component of the socialist revolution in the United States will be an organized revolutionary working class."[5] In support of such a goal, the NLG provided assistance to revolutionaries. William Kunstler noted in 1975 that "the thing I'm most interested in is keeping people on the street who will forever alter the character of this society: the revolutionaries."[6] The then vice–president of the Guild, John Quigley, affirmed in 1978 that "the Guild is not Amnesty International. Its aim is not to ferret out human rights violations wherever they exist. As an anti–imperialist organization, its aim is to aid national liberation struggles."[7]

The Guild has been true to that credo. It has been unconcerned about human rights violations in Soviet–bloc countries and highly critical of alleged violations in Western nations or their allies. For example, the NLG's newspaper has noted that "Washington is the Pretoria of the world . . . The spiritual links between the world's most racist regime and its major supporter reflect shared values, not of democracy, but of militarism, repression and privilege."[8] In 1985 the Guild charged the British government with having "illegally occupied" Ireland, attacked its tactics there and called for withdrawal and the immediate release of all Republican political prisoners.[9]

On the other hand, the Guild is enormously solicitous of communist repression. An NLG delegation visited Vietnam late in 1978 and released a statement asserting that "the policies of reconciliation and reunification have been so widely and wisely applied that they will serve as a model for the progressive peoples of the world who have yet to overthrow their oppressors."[10] Another delegation, returning from Kampuchea in the summer of 1984, found "a firm commitment to guaranteeing a system of legality and individual rights" with "a constitution containing human-rights guarantees similar to our own."[11]

The pro–Soviet bias of the Guild led to the formation of a Democratic Caucus that charged in 1978 that "the leadership has conducted Guild affairs as though we were a committed Marxist–Leninist entity." The Caucus claimed that the NLG had totally identified with "socialist" countries and that foreign observers and speakers at its meetings "have almost always represented the Marxist–Leninist sector of that country's politics."[12] When Alan Dershowitz, a prominent attorney, requested that the NLG send an observer to the Soviet trial of Anatoly Sharansky, a Jewish dissident, as it had done in the case of a Palestinean accused of terrorism by the Israeli government, John Quigley declined, noting that since many Guild members supported the Soviet Union, they would not want to criticize one of its judicial proceedings.[13]

While the Guild carefully avoided speaking out on behalf of Soviet Jews, it has not hesitated to invoke the memory of the Holocaust to gain support for its own political views. In a July 1985 letter designed to aid Salvadoran refugees seeking to avoid deportation, Barbara Dudley, the executive director, insisted that "not since the Gestapo terrorized the Jewish communities of Europe have we heard of such brutality and cruelty."[14]

The Guild is far less solicitous of live Jews than of those victimized by Nazis. Until 1977 it took no official position on the Middle East conflict; in 1975, in fact, the NLG abstained when the IADL adopted a resolution supporting PLO terrorism against Israel as a legitimate tactic. In 1976, however, the NLG's Middle East Sub–Committee undertook a study of human rights violations allegedly committed by Israel. A delegation from the NLG, led by Abdeen Jabara, visited the Middle East in the summer of 1977. The trip was partly financed by the PLO and most of its members identified themselves as anti–Zionist. John Quigley noted that the delegation was convinced the Israelis used torture on Palestinian prisoners; one member of the delegation later charged that the former prisoners making those charges were interviewed at PLO headquarters in Beirut with armed PLO guards present.[15]

At its 1977 convention the NLG, acting on the basis of this report, passed a resolution calling for a Palestinian state and declaring the PLO the sole legitimate representative of the Palestinians. The resolution also called for mutual recognition by Israel and this Palestinian state. The Guild's position has become more extreme over the years. At its 1985 convention it approved a resolution holding Israel alone responsible for having "thwarted" the search for peace by policies that violate Palestinian rights. One such right was described as the right of those displaced in 1948 to return to their homes—which implicitly negates the NLG's call for mutual recognition between Israel and a Palestinean state. The resolution also calls on the United States to end all aid to Israel that is used to violate the rights of the people of Palestine, Lebanon and Syria.[16]

The Jesse Jackson campaign for the presidency led the Guild to reconsider its long–standing opposition to endorsing political candidates. While the National Executive Committee defeated a motion to endorse Jackson, it did urge NLG members to support the movement being generated by Jackson's campaign. The New York NLG praised his campaign as "a qualitative step forward for progressives" but worried about his "slur" against New York and Jews—Jackson had called New York "Hymietown." Local chapters, however, have endorsed candidates. The Chicago chapter endorsed Harold Washington's successful candidacy for mayor; he in turn gave the keynote speech at the 1983 NLG convention. The New Mexico chapter was active on behalf of the successful gubernatorial campaign of Tony Anaya.[17]

In recent years the Guild has been active in Central American work. This has involved not only aiding the sanctuary movement but, along with the Center for Constitutional Rights, National Conference of Black Lawyers and La Raza Legal Alliance, putting the United States government on trial in war crimes tribunals around the country. Held in the fall of 1984 in a variety of cities—the largest, in New York, drew four hundred people and included Judge Bruce Wright, Rosa Parks and Paul O'Dwyer as judges— they were designed to provide evidence of American military and covert activities in Central America, influence public opinion, and build the anti- war movement.

A number of NLG members took the lead in establishing the Center for Constitutional Rights (CCR) in the 1960s. CCR functions as a litigation center. Its staff members and cooperating attorneys around the country participate in a variety of legal cases of interest to radicals. Marilyn Clem- ent is director. Among CCR's volunteer staff attorneys are Arthur Kinoy, William Kunstler and Peter Weiss.

A smaller organization, with some five to six hundred members, the National Conference of Black Lawyers (NCBL), shares many of the same political and ideological perspectives as the NLG. The NCBL is affiliated with the IADL. Several of the leading figures in the NCBL have close ties with the Communist Party or its front groups, including Judge Margaret Burnham, the daughter of prominent communists and an active figure in the National Alliance Against Racist and Political Repression; and Gerald Horne, a frequent contributor to *Freedomways*, a black journal allied with the CPUSA. Lennox Hinds has served as the IADL's representative at the United Nations; he has also been a vice–chairman of the Communist– dominated National Alliance Against Racist and Political Repression.

Founded in 1968 the NCBL has actively participated in a number of communist–sponsored conferences in Cuba. Many of its public statements demonstrate its support for communist regimes. Condemning the Amer- ican invasion of Grenada in 1983, Margaret Burnham, then national direc- tor of the NCBL, warned that it represented "a critical threat to the gains of the Nicaraguan and Cuban peoples, and the struggles of the people of El Salvador, Guatamala, and the rest of Central America and the Carib- bean."[18]

In 1976 it sent Hope Stevens as its representative to an International Conference on Racism and Zionism in Libya. Stevens approvingly re- ported that the gathering had unanimously approved resolutions applauding the UN "Zionism is Racism" charge, linked Zionism with imperialism, condemned Israel for racial discrimination and alliances with South Africa and "demanded the elimination of Zionism from the Holy Land." Stevens insisted that the conference carefully differentiated between Zionism and Judaism. She also praised Libyan dictator Muammar Gaddafi for "imposing a people's regime which is demonstrably placing the broad interest's (sic) of the Libyan population ahead of everything else."[19]

In November 1984 Adrien Wing, a member of the NCBL, addressed the Palestine National Council meeting in Amman. Claiming to be speaking for the NCBL, she expressed support for Yasir Arafat and the PLO and pledged "undying support for the Palestinian Revolution." Although the NCBL insisted that she was not speaking for the organization, its subsequent statements indicated that there was no conflict between Wing's remarks and the NCBL position. While claiming to support a two-state solution to the Middle East conflict, the NCBL has called for a distinction "between the Jewish people themselves and the Zionist policies pursued by the Israeli government."[20] Following the trip of an NCBL delegation to the Middle East in 1985, executive director Gerald Horne attacked Israeli "repression" and charged that the airlift of Ethiopian Jews to Israel was motivated by a desire to replace Arabs on the West Bank with Jews. The delegation later produced a slide show to draw parallels between the Israeli treatment of Arabs and the conditions of blacks in South Africa and the US.[21]

Notes

1. *New York Times,* August 2, 1971.
2. Alan Dershowitz, "Can the Guild Survive Its Hypocrisy?" in *American Lawyer,* August 11, 1978.
3. Position Paper of NLG's San Francisco Bay Area Prison Task Force, quoted in *Congressional Record,* December 9, 1981, p. E5726.
4. *Guild Notes,* Summer 1985.
5. Quoted in *Revolution Target: The American Penal System,* Internal Security Committee, House of Representatives, 93rd Congress, 1st Session, H.R. #93–738.
6. *Moneysworth,* September 1975.
7. Quoted in *Congressional Record,* March 3, 1978, p. E1023.
8. *Guild Notes,* Spring 1985.
9. Ibid.
10. *CALC Report,* February 1979.
11. *New York Times,* December 19, 1984.
12. Quoted in *Congressional Record,* May 9, 1979, p. E2172.
13. *American Lawyer,* August 11, 1978.
14. Fundraising letter signed by Barbara Dudley, July 1985.
15. ADL Statement on NLG dated January 1983.

16. *Guild Notes,* Spring 1985.
17. "Editorial: The Jackson Candidacy," *Blind Justice,* April 1984.
18. NCBL Press Release, October 26, 1983.
19. Hope Stevens, "Report on The International Conference on Racism and Zionism," Mimeograph.
20. *Guardian,* January 23, 1985.
21. *New York Voice,* April 20, 1985.

11

The Rainbow Coalition

The radical left has rarely influenced electoral politics in the United States. Burdened by an extreme ideology and rigid positions, Marxist–Leninist candidates running under their own banners won miniscule numbers of votes. Even those people sharing similar political views have been reluctant to waste their votes on protest candidates with no chance of victory. Unable to win support under their own colors, radicals have rarely been willing to enter the two–party system. Most have seen both the Democratic and Republican parties as hopelessly compromised tools of capitalism.

The election year 1984 was an exception. Significant segments of the radical left not only participated in the Democratic Party's presidential primaries but also helped to shape one of the campaigns. The overwhelming majority of Jesse Jackson's votes and support came from the black community but the radical left provided an important component of his effort as well.

Many radicals saw the Jackson campaign as an opportunity to gain a foothold for the first time in a significant electoral movement. Much as communists swarmed into the Henry Wallace campaign in 1948, radicals entered the Jackson campaign in 1984. Manning Marable, a black socialist, approvingly noted that the early absence of traditional black politicians from the campaign meant that "the vacuum was filled, in part, by Black, Latino, and white Marxists and liberal–leftists." He noted that figures from the Communist Party, National Black United Front, All–African Peoples Revolutionary Party and others held "key roles" at the state and local levels of the campaign. In California, the CPUSA, WWP, DWP, LOM and November 29 Movement for Palestine were active in the Jackson effort. While the national leaders were often "bourgeois," Marable noted, "many of the actual cadre and local leaders of the movement were to the left of the candidate himself" and gave the campaign "a left–social democratic tone, and at later instances, even became forthrightly anti–imperialist and anti–corporate."[1]

In addition to the individual Marxist–Leninists who worked for the Jackson campaign, there was considerable support from Marxist–Leninist groups themselves. With the exception of the small Trotskyist sects, most of the Marxist–Leninist groups of any consequence in the United States gave at least tacit support to Jackson; many endorsed him. The CPUSA explained that he was the only Democrat "offering a bold, rounded–out program." The WWP praised his campaign for its contribution to the fight against racism and pledged that it would withdraw its presidential candidate if Jackson won the democratic nomination. The CWP gave critical support to Jackson. LOM vociferously backed the campaign and claimed that it had the potential for unleashing a "progressive social force" that "particularly from among the Black masses" could "shake the entire country." The National Committee for Independent Political Action, a group of unaffiliated radicals that included among its leaders David Dellinger, Arthur Kinoy and Anne Braden, supported Jackson, as did the AAPRP, whose leader, Bob Brown, was a full–time organizer for the campaign. So did *Unity*, published by the League for Revolutionary Struggle.[2]

What attracted these groups and individuals to Jackson when they had so long scorned traditional electoral politics was both his constituency and his program, particularly his foreign policy views. For most radicals, blacks are a key component of any successful left–wing movement in America. They saw Jackson's campaign as an opportunity to reach that constituency and a chance to begin to break it away from the Democratic Party. Additionally, however, many radicals were enthralled with Jackson's "Third World" perspective on American foreign policy, seeing it as an alternative to the traditional anti–communist views of both the Democratic and Republican parties.

Jackson has praised and apologized for many of the radical left's favorite figures. He has called Yasir Arafat "my friend and the friend of justice and humanity." Of the Irish Republican Army he proclaimed that "I feel an identity with its mission." He explained that "I feel a kinship" with Syria's President Assad. Commenting on the Khmer Rouge's genocide in Cambodia, he asserted that, "unfortunate, sometimes the best of people lose their way." He has proclaimed that the Sandinistas are "on the right side of history and they are leading Nicaragua to democracy," a view he finally qualified in the summer of 1986 after the Sandinistas expelled a Roman Catholic bishop from the country and closed down the only opposition newspaper. On a visit to Cuba in 1984 Jackson enthusiastically praised Fidel Castro and Che Guevera. In a *Playboy* interview, he explained that

"America is not known for her capacity to love and heal but for her capacity to organize and kill."[3]

Jackson has not hesitated from expressing his foreign policy views at openly pro–Soviet forums. He delivered an address to the Third Vienna Dialogue–International Conference for Disarmament and Detente in January 1985. The Dialogue was sponsored by the International Liaison Forum, an arm of the Soviet–controlled World Peace Council. The two groups share the same president and secretary. The head of the Soviet delegation to the gathering noted that "roughly 80 percent of the delegates at this forum were communists."[4] The reports of the various sessions closely hewed to official Soviet positions on all foreign policy issues, ranging from condemnation of the United States for its policies through attacks on Israel as "an aggressive instrument of imperialism." There was concern about "increasing tendencies of revanchism" in West Germany, "satisfaction at the peace policy of the Cuban government," denunciation of Brazil for building up a military industry, support for Puerto Rico's "liberation from US colonial domination," praise for the PLO, and dismay at the Iran–Iraq war, "which benefits only the US warmongers."[5]

At this gathering, Jesse Jackson praised "the cause of peace" that was being served by the dialogue. He spoke of "our movements for peace and justice" and "our adversaries who profit from war, racism and the deprivations of colonialism." He asked for "your help in mobilizing public opinion [in the United States] against the gunboat diplomacy and militarism that is creating a war situation in Central America." Jackson did criticize the Soviet Union in the mildest terms—along with the United States—for not doing enough to ban nuclear weapons. More of his speech, however, was an attack on the Reagan administration for its Star Wars proposal and its domestic policies.[6]

Summing up the basis of his and the Rainbow Coalition's foreign policy views in April 1986, Jackson argued that the United States "cannot be blinded by anti–communist obsessions." He had sounded the same theme in 1985 after President Reagan's trip to Bitburg, Germany to lay a wreathe in a cemetery containing the graves of SS men; the US was "obsessed with communism" to the point that it ignored other issues.[7]

A number of Jackson's advisors and associates are certainly not obsessed with communism or blinded by opposition to it. Sheila Collins was National Rainbow Coordinator for the Jackson for President campaign. In an article written after the campaign she attacked middle–class American feminists for minimizing "the impressive gains (however incomplete) that women have made in a short period of time in countries which have undergone or are undergoing national revolutions against Western imperialism in places like Cuba, Nicaragua, Mozambique."[8]

The strongest link between the Rainbow Coalition and the radical left in the United States, however, is Jack O'Dell. He has served as international affairs director for Operation Push and is a key member of the staff of the Coalition. O'Dell has a long history of involvement with the Marxist–Leninist left. He was a district organizer for the Communist Party for several years in the 1950s in the South and, according to the FBI, served on the Central Committee of the Communist Party. Both Robert and John Kennedy warned the Reverend Martin Luther King, Jr. that O'Dell's presence on the staff of the Southern Christian Leadership Conference could, because of his communist background, tarnish the civil rights movement. O'Dell remains close to communist causes. He was an editor of *Freedomways,* a journal that hewed closely to the Party line until its recent demise. He has been active in the World Peace Council.

More importantly, O'Dell frequently and vocally defends the Soviet Union and its policies. In an exclusive interview with *Frontline,* published by the Marxist–Leninist group, Line of March, O'Dell defined the goal of the Rainbow Coalition as "fundamental change." He suggested that it was struggling against the same force that the rest of the world was—capitalism. He criticized segments of the American left for having "characterizations of the two–party system that are often undialectical."[9]

Speaking to a meeting celebrating the 68th Anniversary of the Bolshevik Revolution, held in Berkeley, California in November 1985, O'Dell attacked anti-Sovietism as "an integral part of the belief system of racism and western national chauvinism" ever since World War II. Charging that opposition to communism served US corporations and militarists, he commended Russia for supporting peace and disarmament and assisting liberation struggles around the world. "The Russians are a threat to our security because they seem to be friendly toward all these people and of course they stand for socialism—which we all know means taking away from the hard–working middle class and feeding these lazy welfare chiselers," he noted. He concluded by calling for renewed bonds with America's allies, "among whom first and foremost are the heroic people of the Soviet Union."[10]

In addition to providing rhetorical support to radical causes, both Jackson and the Rainbow Coalition have been actively involved in numerous united fronts with radical organizations. The Rainbow Coalition was on the steering committee of the 1985 April Actions for Peace, Jobs and Justice, along with a host of radical groups, including the CPUSA, USPC, NLG, NAARPR, WILPF, MFS, and so on. Jackson and Vernon Bellecourt of the American Indian Movement led the march to the Capitol.

The 1985 demonstration was not the first time the Rainbow had built alliances with radical activists. In October 1984 the organizing committee of the Rainbow Peace Caucus was set up. Among the groups represented were MFS, CISPES, CALC, WRL and USPC. Jack O'Dell, speaking at the meeting, urged the members to work for the defeat of President Reagan but held out the vision of the coalition eventually taking over or replacing the Democratic Party. Jackson has also endorsed, spoken at or otherwise supported a number of radical causes. Early in 1985 he was the keynote speaker at a fundraiser for the Center for Constitutional Rights.[11] He endorsed the communist–controlled Twelfth World Festival of Youth and Students in Moscow in the summer of 1985.[12] He attended the New York meeting in 1985 celebrating the "reunification" of Vietnam under Communist rule and told the gathering that "our only joy is that the military occupation of that land is over."[13]

Jesse Jackson's views on the Middle East, Israel and Jews have been extraordinarily controversial. Jackson has shared with the radical left a view of Israel as a predatory, imperialist and racist power. While insisting that he supports a secure Israel within accepted borders, he has also denounced Zionism, apologized for terrorists and terrorism and refused to come to the aid of Ethiopian Jews. At the same time, Jackson's comments about Jews have led to charges that he is, at best, insensitive to antisemitism and, at worst, an antisemite himself.

Jackson's prickly relations with American Jews date back to the resignation of Andrew Young as ambassador to the United Nations in 1979. Accusing American Jews of having forced Young from office, Jackson soon led a trip to the Middle East where he embraced Yasir Arafat and was quoted as being "sick and tired of hearing about the Holocaust." Jackson has insisted that this statement was taken out of context, but he was publicly quoted on the same trip making belittling assertions about the Holocaust.[14] While he claims to have counseled the PLO leader to resist violence, Jackson continues to apologize for Palestinian terrorism. In a recent interview in the *Journal of Palestine Studies* he said that "those who would fight against the occupation there [the occupied territories] would be called terrorists."[15]

In the past, Jackson claimed that his views about Israel could and should be distinguished from his views about Judaism. In a 1980 speech he said that "Zionism is a kind of poisonous weed that is choking Judaism." As late as 1984 he said that "Zionism is rooted in race . . . to the extent to which the prophecy of Judaism is made silent by the policies of Zionism, it is a threat to the glorious flower of Judaism."[16]

During Jackson's 1984 presidential campaign, however, there were insistent charges that Jackson harbored animus against Judaism just as severe as his hostility to Zionism. After a long delay, he acknowledged referring to

Jews as "Hymies" and New York as "Hymietown." He apologized for his remarks, but soon was involved in more controversy over the comments and views of one of his close supporters, Louis Farrakhan, leader of the Black Muslim movement, who praised Hitler, threatened American Jews, and called Judaism a "gutter religion." Jackson finally repudiated not just Farrakhan's views but the man himself.

After the 1984 election, Jackson sought to mend his relationship with the Jewish community. He professed to have achieved a new understanding of the meaning of the Holocaust after talking to Eli Wiesel. He journeyed to Vienna during the Reagan–Gorbachev summit meeting in 1985 and confronted the Soviet leader about his country's treatment of Jews. When the airlift of Ethiopian Jews to Israel was halted by the government of Sudan, however, stranding thousands of black Jews, Jackson refused an appeal for help from Teddy Kolleck, mayor of Jerusalem. He wanted to know if the Ethiopians would serve in the Army, thus becoming a military asset to Israel, or would settle on the West Bank. He even cast doubt on the value of the rescue itself; the airlift "saved them from starvation in Ethiopia but they should not be saved from starvation this year to face a war on the West Bank next year." Moreover, he told one newspaper: "it was a military mission even though it had humanitarian goals."[17]

The National Rainbow Coalition held its founding convention in April 1986. It was designed to give a permanent organizational form to the movement initiated by the Reverend Jackson during the 1984 presidential campaign. In addition to creating an organizational structure for their cause, the 765 delegates attending the meeting sought to establish a "progressive agenda" and planned how to promote candidates during the 1986 elections. The radical newspaper, the *Guardian,* said the gathering's goal was "to create a significant left force in the Democratic Party."[18]

The founding convention drew relatively little representation from the south. The largest delegations were from New York, California and Illinois. Among those present were several members of the congressional black caucus, including Congressmen Conyers, Hayes and Savage, Mayor Richard Hatcher, Governor Toney Anaya of New Mexico and Barry Commoner. A number of farmers, including Merle Hansen, leader of the North American Farm Alliance, and union leaders William Winspisinger and Kenneth Blaylock also attended.[19]

Although more time was devoted to organizational matters than to policy discussions, Jackson did call for a non–internventionist foreign policy and a nuclear–free world. He condemned American support for contra rebels in Nicaragua and Angola. Jackson also denounced the American air raid on Libya, charging that the United States government funded, practiced and taught terrorism elsewhere in the world and, therefore, that the president did not have the moral authority to condemn terrorism in the Middle East.

The radical left does not control the Rainbow Coalition and Jesse Jackson is not a Marxist–Leninist. But his movement has provided the radical left with its first opportunity in many years to play a role in mainstream American politics, an opportunity that the left has gladly seized.

Notes

1. Manning Marable, "Jackson and the Rise of the Rainbow Coalition," *New Left Review,* January 1985.
2. *Guardian,* April 4, 1984; *Frontline,* October 1, 1984.
3. Dennis Praeger, "Jesse Jackson and the Meaning of Anti–Semitism," *Ultimate Issues*, Winter 1985.
4. FBIS–SOV–85–022 Vol. III, No. 022.
5. "Third Vienna Dialogue–International Conference for Disarmament and Detente," Reports.
6. Jesse Jackson, "An Address to the Third Vienna Dialogue," January 27, 1985.
7. *Guardian,* April 30, 1986.
8. Sheila Collins, "Feminism and White Racism: Time for Redemption," *CALC Report*, June 1985.
9. *Frontline*, October 15, 1984.
10. *Frontline,* November 25, 1985.
11. *New Alliance,* February 1, 1985.
12. *Daily World,* February 15, 1985.
13. *New York Daily News,* May 27, 1985.
14. Arch Puddington, "Jesse Jackson, the Blacks and American Foreign Policy," *Commentary*, April 1984.
15. "Jesse Jackson: Afro–Americans and the Palestinians," *Journal of Palestine Studies,* Winter 1986.
16. Puddington, op.cit.
17. "Jesse Jackson," *Journal of Palestine Studies,* Winter 1986; "Washington Diarist," *New Republic*, February 11, 1985; *Washington Times,* March 20, 1985.
18. *Guardian,* April 30, 1986.
19. Ibid.

12

Institute for Policy Studies

A variety of organizations devoted to a host of specific aims or constituencies form a radical network devoted to altering in fundamental ways American policies and goals. These groups cooperate with one another in organizing demonstrations, sharing information and assisting foreign radicals. The Institute for Policy Studies, a radical think tank located in Washington, DC, plays an important role in this network. It serves as an intellectual nerve center for the radical movement, providing sustenance and support for a variety of causes, ranging from nuclear and anti–intervention issues to support for Marxist insurgencies. IPS brings together activists and academics and provides a place where they can mingle with congressmen and other policymakers and public figures.

Like other think tanks, IPS rarely if ever takes an institutional position. In response to one attack on its activities, director Robert Borosage and Peter Weiss, chairman of the Board of Trustees, noted that "the views and opinions of the Fellows vary widely" and the IPS "takes no corporate positions, but certifies the excellence of the work of its scholars."[1] Thus, IPS is unlike political parties or organizations that take political positions. Unlike a university, however, IPS makes scant effort to recruit disinterested scholars with varying points of view. It clearly selects fellows whose interests and political beliefs are compatible with the ideological vision of the institution. That vision has been and remains radical. IPS describes itself as "a source of radical scholarship."[2] In a *New York Times Magazine* study of IPS, Joshua Muravchik wrote: "while IPS does not include liberals in its programs the spectrum of opinion among its officers and full–time scholars is rather narrow. All are on the left. Few, if any, are liberal; most, if not all, are anti–anti–communist."[3]

IPS is a loose-knit, chaotic place. In a profile of the group in the *Washington Post* (July 30, 1986), Sidney Blumenthal wrote, "Amid such persistent accusations that the institute is a conspiratorical nest of Marxist–Leninists, the place more nearly resembles the stateroom scene in the Marx

Brothers 'A Night at the Opera' in which the purposeful, the alienated and the merely curious crowd themselves into a small cubicle. . . . The paint in the building is peeling, the elevator doesn't work—and hasn't for years . . . The declasse style that meant political commitment in the 1960s remains in fashion here . . . . Youthful assistants, attired in jeans and work shirts, dash from floor to floor (no elevator), clutching the latest pamphlets. . . ." Some see IPS's radicalism as simply, in Blumenthal's words, "a romanticism that clouds perception." But a tougher assessment came from Robert Leiken, a fellow at the Carnegie Endowment for International Peace formerly associated with IPS. He told Blumenthal: "They are absolutely pro–Sandinista. I have not heard a critical word."[4]

Many of IPS's activities are quite similar to those of other think tanks. It sponsors numerous conferences, provides resources for its fellows to write books and articles, and encourages the widest possible dissemination of their labors. Fellows appear frequently on television, have produced documentary movies and are frequent contributors to such forums as the Op–Ed page of the *New York Times*. The IPS also runs the Washington School, whose courses attract a wide range of students and are taught by prominent figures. The Washington School course list in 1983 included "Matthew, Marx, Luke and John: Theology of the Oppressed," an examination of "Liberation theologies—particularly Black, feminist and Latin American—[which] provide an ideological counterthrust on behalf of the insurgent resistance." The course covered ancient and medieval precedents, parallels in feminist and Latin American theology, the Catholic Bishops' letter on war and peace and "the future of the Christian alliance with Marxism." Also offered was a "Liberation Theology Lecture Series," presenting "three of the most prominent voices in liberation theology today," on "Liberation Theology . . . a powerful voice of radical Christianity, the inspiration for a growing social movement which has actively identified itself with the poor, the disenfranchised and the causes for social justice and world peace." Some courses at the school, it should be said, do not reflect this partisanship.

IPS has achieved considerable success in attracting liberals as well as radicals to its functions. It aspires to influence policy and policymakers. If a roster of those who have participated in its activities is any indication of its success, then IPS has done well. Its twentieth anniversary reception in 1983, for example, was chaired by Paul Warnke and the Anniversary Committee included Senators Dodd, Hart and Hatfield, ex–Senators Abourezk, Bayh, Church, Fulbright, McCarthy and Nelson, Representatives Aspin, George Brown, Burton, Crockett, Dellums, Edwards, Harkin, Kastenmeir, George Miller, Ottinger, Panetta, Reuss, Schroder, Seiberling, and Weiss.

IPS was formed in 1963 by Richard Barnett and Marcus Raskin, both disgruntled government employees. It rapidly became a major center for opposition to the Vietnam War. Barnett and Raskin viewed the war as a logical corrollary of the national security state and regarded those who waged it as war criminals. Raskin developed the concept of the "national security state," which he defined as "the actualizing mechanism of ruling elites to implement their imperial schemes and misplaced ideals." Raskin writes, "In the modern–day United States, neither a democracy nor a republic exists in operation. The state helps the powerful. The emergence of large–scale armed forces and corporate capitalism colonizes people into huge organizational structures." The United States, according to Raskin is a "modern tyranny," defined as "the maintenance of organized power in the hands of the state, its military and bureaucratic apparatus, and its corporate system." Raskin maintains that a president cannot act on behalf of the disadvantaged without "doing battle with capitalism and imperialism. He would be required, therefore, to fashion a new set of symbols from the American landscale of myths and dreams which would cause direct confrontation with the bloated genocide-preparing military system." This system "menaces the freedom and well–being of its citizenry" and "poses a danger to world civilization."[5]

After those who wanted IPS to become more of an activist center departed in 1977, Barnett and Raskin steered it toward a think tank orientation. Most of IPS's financial support has come from private foundations, including the Samuel Rubin Foundation. Cora Weiss, Rubin's daughter, and her husband Peter Weiss have played a major role in a number of radical organizations. She is now the director of the Riverside Church Disarmament Program. Peter Weiss is vice-president of the Center for Constitutional Rights.

IPS has a European offshoot, the Transnational Institute (TNI), set up in 1974 and headquartered in Amsterdam. Director Robert Borosage has asserted that most TNI fellows come out of the Marxist tradition. In fact, some TNI fellows had far less savory connections. Tariq Ali was a member of the Trotskyist United Secretariat of the Fourth International, which supported terrorism in Latin America. Ali regarded the use of violence as a tactical question "depending on the degree of opposition we encounter in our struggle for socialism."[6]

Orlando Letelier, director of the TNI, was assassinated in 1976 in Washington by Chilean intelligence agents. In the course of the ensuing investigation, the contents of Letelier's briefcase at the time of his death were revealed to the press. They indicated that Letelier had been receiving funding from Cuba via its diplomatic pouch and had been in touch with Cuban intelligence agents. Letelier's defenders at the IPS have maintained that the money came from supporters in Europe and vigorously denied that he was involved with Cuban intelligence.

Another controversial figure once associated with TNI and IPS is Philip

Agee, one-time CIA agent who specialized in identifying and undermining CIA operations and agents around the world, while cooperating with Cuban intelligence.[7] (Agee wrote in *Esquire* in June 1975: "I aspire to be a communist and a revolutionary.") Agee was expelled from Great Britain in 1977 for disclosing information harmful to British Security and for associating with foreign spies. Agee had held dozens of meetings with the Cuban intelligence service DGI and its station chief, as well as other Cuban and Soviet–bloc agents. Agee was refused residence by all other NATO countries until the Netherlands decided to admit him. (They later reversed their decision as well.) TNI's Amsterdam center provided him a place to stay while he figured out where he would live. Agee resided on the premises of TNI from October 25 to November 22, 1977.[8]

Dutch journalist J. Emerson Vermaat has written that

> Agee's work in Holland also brought him into direct conflict with the usually tolerant Dutch government. Agee wanted to set up a databank of CIA agents and their contacts in order to reveal their names. Agee's claim that his research would be based solely on public domain documents contrasted with a *Newsweek* interview in which Agee refers to the exposure of *secret* CIA operations in order to render these ineffective.

Agee was asked to leave the Netherlands when the new coalition government of Christian Democrats and liberals assumed power. Vermaat writes that Agee left "in midst of a publicity row followed by a lengthy parliamentary debate in which the government claimed that Agee's activities in Holland had been considered 'wrong' and 'contrary to Dutch interests.'"[9]

IPS has also had connections with other allies of Agee who have sought to undermine American intelligence agencies. Marcus Raskin, then an IPS Fellow, served for two years on the board of the Organizing Committee for the Fifth estate, which published *Counterspy*; in 1975 a CIA station chief in Greece, Richard Welch, was assassinated after being identified in the magazine. IPS also created the Center for National Security Studies, whose goal was to ban all American covert action.[10]

Fred Halliday, a TNI fellow, and formerly assistant European director, is a sharp illustration of the skewed moral bookkeeping of the radical left. For example, although Halliday is mildly critical of the Soviet Union's invasion of Afghanistan, he is a far more vociferous critic of any American response to the Soviet invasion—accusing the United States of "rushing to shore up a crew of petty tyrants and religious obscurantists."[11]

Halliday is not the only person associated with the IPS to exhibit significantly less concern about Soviet or communist violations of human rights or interntional law than of alleged American sins. Michael Parenti, who was an IPS fellow, is a political scientist who frequently writes for *Political*

Affairs, the theoretical organ of the American Communist Party. Parenti has spoken at a dinner honoring communist theoretician Herbert Aptheker, called himself a Marxist, praised Gus Hall and Yuri Andropov and condemned anti–communism.[12]

While critical of Soviet violations of human rights, Richard Barnett has claimed that respect for human rights is improving in Russia while it is declining in America.[13] In 1977 Barnett and Cora Weiss were among the signers of an advertisement defending Hanoi's record on human rights.[14] Two of the most ardent defenders of the genocidal Pol Pot regime in the non–communist world were associated with the IPS. Associate fellow Gareth Porter testified before Congress in 1977 that only a few thousand Cambodians had died at a time when more than two million had been murdered. Representative Stephen Solarz (D–NY) called his testimony contemptible. Porter's book, *Cambodia: Starvation and Revolution,* concluded that the Pol Pot regime had found "a collective framework designed to release the creative energies of the people." Another IPS fellow, Malcolm Caldwell, attacked "reactionary refugees" who allegedly spread false stories of communist bloodbaths in return for economic benefits.[15]

IPS fellows have consistently maintained that the Soviet threat is largely non–existent and a product of the military–industrial complex in the United States. This view encouraged the IPS to demand dangerously steep cuts in American defense efforts and to claim that they would represent no danger to American security. At the request of fifty–six congressmen, IPS made a study of the federal budget in 1977. In addition to recommendations for a socialist housing program and health system, and altering capitalist control over the educational system, the IPS suggested a fifty percent cut in defense spending, an end to the American role in the Middle East, and withdrawal from NATO.

IPS signed an agreement in 1982 with the Soviet's Institute of the USA and Canada, headed by Georgiy Arbatov, for exchanges on peace and disarmament. Since then IPS has sponsored an annual meeting of American experts and Soviet officials. Although portrayed by the Soviets as an "independent" semiacademic "think tank," the Institute of the USA and Canada has been widely identified as an instrument of Soviet foreign policy influence. Located in Moscow, the IUSAC is nominally under the direction of the Soviet Academy of Sciences. In practice, however, it operates under the direction of the International Department of the Soviet Communist Party Central Committee. According to the testimony of John McMahon, then deputy director of Central Intelligence (during the House Selected Committee on Intelligence Hearings on Soviet Active Measures in 1982), the International Department "directs Western dialogue activities of Soviet organizations such as the USA–Canada Institute," with a view toward influencing western perceptions of peace and disarmament. At least one IUSAC official, deputy director Radomir G. Bogdanov, is a ranking KGB officer, while other officials have extensive intelligence backgrounds.

The highest ranking Soviet official to defect to the United States, the Under Secretary General of the United Nations, Arkady Shevchenko, has written of the Institute of the USA and Canada's role in "active measures" (spreading false information and propaganda in behalf of the Soviet Union).[16] In his book, *Breaking With Moscow,* Shevchenko, who worked part–time at the IUSAC during his career with the Soviet Foreign Ministry, wrote that as director of the institute, Georgiy Arbatov "could pretend to be an independent spokesman as those of the Western academic world often are. . . . He can . . . foster the belief in the United States and the West that his Institute is as independent as American academic institutions and think tanks." Shevchenko went on to write that in fact, "Arbatov's institute is . . . a front used by the Central Committee and the KGB for many purposes: collecting valuable information, promoting the Soviet position, recruiting Soviet sympathizers in the United States, and disseminating disinformation. On the last point, they have been particularly successful, since the West sees Arbatov and his institute as the Soviets wish them to be seen."

Prior to signing the agreement in 1982, an IPS delegation went to Moscow in April 1982 for week–long meetings with Soviet officials. The meetings reportedly included five members of the Central Committee (the highest decision–making body next to the Politburo), among them Arbatov and Vadim V. Zagladin, first deputy chief of the International Department (ID) of the Central Committee. (The International Department is responsible for directing active measures, particularly through the use of "International front groups.") A joint statement signed by Marcus Raskin for IPS, Georgiy Arbatov for the IUSAC and a representative of the USSR–USA Friendship Society noted the participants agreed on holding a "citizens conference on the problems of Soviet–American relations and limitations of nuclear arms" in the United States early in 1983.

The first conference, held in Minneapolis in 1983, demonstrated IPS's squeamishness about embarassing its Soviet guests. At a public session, Soviet emigres and Jewish activists sharply questioned the Soviet representatives about Russian policy towards dissidents and on human rights. Most of the American delegation, with the exception of Mayor Don Fraser, were upset, not by the Soviet policies or defenses of them, but by the probing questions. The Reverend Paul Moore was "deeply ashamed" and "deeply humiliated" by criticism of the Soviets. Another American on the IPS delegation was angry because he thought raising human rights could allow the Soviets to talk about political prisoners in the United States. Randall

Forsberg, William Sloane Coffin, Reverend Moore and others were opposed to discussing human rights. Marcus Raskin claimed that human rights in the USSR would improve when the arms race was brought under control.[17]

Richard Barnett was critical of US human rights policy. He stated, "Soviet commentators like to accuse the United States of hypocrisy because the government dwells on human rights violations in the Soviet sphere and ignores or minimizes atrocities on a much more terrible scale committed by such pro–American regimes as Guatemala and Argentina." He concluded that it "is not surprising that Soviet leaders dismiss human rights rhetoric in the United States as nothing more than an ideological weapon."[18]

A central theme which appeared in the papers of leading IPS staff at the conference in Minneapolis depicted a sort of moral equivalency between the superpowers in which both sides were described as imperialist and violators of human rights, and Soviet expansionism was presented as mitigated by the Soviet sense of insecurity, to which the United States has been "insensitive."

Barnett also maintained in his paper, "A Question of Trust," that a perception of a Soviet threat had been concocted for domestic consumption in the United States. He equated Soviet charges that the Solidarity movement in Poland is US–inspired with American charges that the communist–backed Salvadoran insurgency ("a peasant revolution in El Salvador") is supported by the Soviet Union and its satellites. Barnett stated:

> In both superpowers the idea of the enemy plays a crucial domestic political role. The very concept of "national security" is defined in terms of keeping that enemy at bay. Most other perceived threats to the leadership, whether a peasant revolution in El Salvador or a worker's movement in Poland, are attributed to the machinations of the enemy superpower. Thus restrictions on dissent, assembly and movement in the Soviet Union, the privileges accorded to the military–industrial complex in both countries, and the depletion of the two civilian economies to feed the military depend upon painting the other superpower as dangerous.

In Barnett's view both sides are "expansionist," each threatening the other, and sharing similar motivations for their behavior.[19]

A number of people associated with IPS have engaged in controversial activities associated with the Middle East. After critics charged that IPS fellows and associates were linked with organizations and journals hostile to Israel and Zionism and favorable to terrorism, IPS officials indignantly responded that all IPS fellows and associates supported Israel's right to exist. Robert Borosage and Peter Weiss noted that while some people associated with IPS were sympathetic to the plight of the Palestinians, they doubted "whether any other members of the IPS community" believed that Zionism could be equated with racism. They were particularly upset by critical remarks about Eqbal Ahmad, an IPS fellow and once director of the TNI.[20]

Several current and former IPS fellows have been associated with *MERIP Reports,* a journal that has been consistently and unequivocally hostile to Israel, Zionism and American policy in the Middle East. MERIP (Middle East Research and Information project) was founded in 1971. It has distributed PLO publications. In 1972 *MERIP Reports* urged that "we should comprehend the achievements of the Munich action," referring to the slaughter of Israeli Olympic athletes by the PLO. Joe Stork, a one-time IPS fellow, is an editor and frequent contributor to the journal. Fred Halliday, Michael Klare and Eqbal Ahmad have also been associated with *MERIP Reports.*[21]

Ahmad's views on the Middle East have been praised by IPS officials. But although he has acknowledged that concern for Israel is legitimate, he has an even longer record of virulently anti–Zionist and anti–Israeli remarks. In 1969 Ahmad declared that "Zionism is the product of Western racism, colonialism and imperialism—forces which are now represented by the United States of America." [22] As late as 1984 he had not changed his mind. Writing in *Race and Class,* the TIN's publication, Ahmad charged Zionism with collaborating with Nazism and discouraging resettlement of victims of fascism outside of Israel. "Both policies on the part of Zionist organizations caused undoubted augmentation in the number of Holocaust victims." Not content with blaming Jews for their own destruction, Ahmad went on to link present–day Israel with Nazism, accusing it of ethnocide: "the Arabs under occupation today live in the nightmarish world of a thousand and one krystelnachts." He condemned Arab governments for letting Arab Jews emigrate. He also attacked Israel for launching "an elaborate campaign to alienate the Soviet Jewry from its patrimony and to induce the immigration of Russian Jews to Israel."[23]

Race and Class has consistently supported international revolutionary movements. In 1976 it contained an editorial opposing any Arab–Israeli accord, since that would defuse Arab nationalism. The same included a paper by the Popular Front for the Liberation of Palestine expressing hope that Jews would begin to see Zionism as the source of their oppression.[24]

The summer 1986 issue of *Race and Class* contained a lead article by Noam Chomsky, entitled "Middle East Terrorism and the US Ideological System." In his article, Chomsky described President Reagan and Israeli Prime Minister Peres as "two of the world's leading terrorist commanders." Chomsky stated that "Israel has chosen to become a mercenary state serving the interests of its provider"—the United States, and speaks of "the extraordinary commitment of the American intellectual establishment to US–Israeli rejectionism and violence." He wrote:

> It should be noted that Israel is not alone in enjoying the right of piracy and hijacking. A Tass report condemning the Achille Lauro hijacking in October 1985 accused the United States of hypocrisy because two men who hijacked a Soviet airliner, killing a stewardess and wounding other crew members, were given refuge in the US, which refused extradition. The case is not exactly well–known, and the charge of hypocrisy might appear to have a certain merit.

Stating that "The record of Israeli terrorism goes back to the origins of the state—and indeed long before . . ." Chomsky wrote that:

> When the leading contemporary US terrorist took over the presidency in 1981, Israel's prime minister and foreign minister were both notorious terrorist commanders. . . .
>
> Even terrorism against Americans is perfectly tolerable . . . such as the attempt to sink the US spy ship Liberty in international water in 1967 by Israeli bombers and torpedo boats. . . . Each new act of terrorism if noted at all, is quickly dismissed and forgotten, or described as a temporary deviation from perfection, to be explained by the hideous nature of the enemy which is forcing Israel to depart, if only for a moment, from its path of righteousness.[25]

IPS does have a loose structure, and some of those associated with it go their own independent way. But it is somewhat ingenuous of IPS spokesmen and supporters to deny a certain underlying ideological uniformity of views. The evidence is clear that IPS has been a forum and catalyst for the radical left in the United States over the last two decades.

Notes

1. "The Fight Around the Institute for Policy Studies," *Midstream*, February 1981.
2. IPS Annual Report, 1979–80.
3. Joshua Muravchik "The Think Tank of the Left," *New York Times Magazine*, April 26, 1981.
4. Washington *Post*, July 30, 1986.
5. Marcus Raskin, *The Politics of National Security*, (New Brunswick, NJ: Transaction Books, 1979); Raskin, *Notes on the Old System* (New York: David McKay, 1974); in Adam M. Garfinkle, *The Politics of Nuclear Freeze* (Philadelphia: Foreign Policy Research Institute, 1984).
6. David Kelley, "For Socialist Alternatives," *Barron's*, August 23, 1976.

7. J.A. Emerson Vermaat, "The Transnational Institute: The Cuban Connection," *Midstream*, February 1986.
8. Ibid.
9. Ibid.
10. Muravchik, "The Think Tank of the Left," *op. cit.*
11. Fred Halliday, "Wrong Moves on Afghanistan," *The Nation,* January 26, 1980.
12. *Daily World,* December 23, 1981; Michael Parenti, "Thinking Along with Marx—A Personal Reflection," *Political Affairs,* September 1983 and Michael Parenti, "Two Faces of the Capitalist State," *Political Affairs,* June 1984.
13. Muravchik, "Think Tank of the Left," *op. cit.*
14. *New York Times*, January 30, 1977.
15. Muravchik, "Think Tank of the Left," *op. cit.*
16. In their book, *Dezinformatsia,* Richard Schultz and Roy Godson write that "Active measures may entail influencing the policies of another government, undermining confidence in its leaders and institutions, disrupting relations between other nations, discrediting and weakening governmental and non-governmental opponents."
17. *Washington Times,* May 26, 1983.
18. Richard Barnett, "A Question of Trust." Paper presented at the Minneapolis Peace and Disarmament Conference, University of Minnesota, May 26, 1983.
19. *Ibid.*
20. "The Fight Around the Institute for Policy Studies," *Midstream,* February, 1981.
21. Murovchik, "Think Tank of the Left," *op. cit.*
22. *Christian Science Monitor,* December 16, 1969.
23. Eqbal Ahmad, "Pioneering in the Nuclear Age: An Essay on Israel and the Palestinians," *Race and Class,* Spring 1984.
24. A. Sivanandan, "Editorial," *Race and Class*, Winter 1976.
25. Noam Chomsky, "Middle East Terrorism and The American Ideological System," *Race and Class,* Summer 1986.

Conclusion

Despite its relatively small size, the American radical left has a number of resources as it prepares for the post–Reagan years. Tireless, dedicated and, frequently, capable organizers, many of them with years of experience in the radical movement, are ready to give their time and effort to the cause. The probability that the United States and its allies will face continued challenges abroad from regimes and "liberation movements" aligned with the Soviet Union and hostile to democratic values promises to produce issues upon which radicals will seize. Future economic difficulties at home may offer radical groups potential new recruits.

It is unlikely that any of the myriad of communist splinter groups discussed in Part II of this book will ever have much impact on a larger American stage. Many of them will continue to exist and occasionally burst into public view. Their very extremism, however, will bar them from any legitimacy in American political life.

The Communist Party, on the other hand, is a far more sophisticated organization. Its slow but steady growth in the last decade and its ability to increase its influence even during a conservative era in American life suggest that it will remain the largest and most important force on the radical left for the foreseeable future. The Party will continue to pose a challenge to Americans committed to democracy; to eliminate or correct those defects in our own society that sometimes make communist claims seem plausible to some people and to defend and strengthen democratic institutions.

One facet of that effort is to oppose communism and its influence as forcefully and vigorously as possible. It is no violation of civil liberties to expose communist fronts for what they are, to warn citizens committed to decent and legitimate values and causes that they taint them and endanger them by cooperating with the Communist Party, to remind Americans that, their rhetoric to the contrary notwithstanding, communists are no friends of democracy and liberty.

The evidence to support that claim is overwhelming. It is as plain as the nature of the regimes around the world that call themselves Marxist–Leninist or communist. It is as voluminous as the records of those persecuted and oppressed by those regimes. American communists have not denied their ties to such oppressive societies. On the contrary, they trumpet their support for the Soviet Union, East Germany, Bulgaria, Afghanistan, Cuba and other regimes that have waged war on their own citizens. Moreover, they have attacked and slandered those forces in communist countries, such as the Solidarity movement in Poland, that have valiantly sought greater freedom.

The United States and the Soviet Union have a mutual interest in preventing their differences from endangering world peace. But recognizing the need to reach mutually advantageous agreements with the Soviet Union should not mean ignoring the enormous gulf separating Marxist–Leninist and democratic governments and ideologies. No communist regime has ever allowed free elections or real intellectual freedom. None has permitted a free press. When political organizations praise such repressive societies abroad as democratic, their protestations of support for democracy at home ring very hollow.

The groups discussed in Part III of this book do not call themselves Marxist–Leninist. Nevertheless, they identify themselves with many of the same causes and movements. They willingly cooperate in political undertakings with Marxist–Leninists. And, they see opposition to communism only as a ploy to distract Americans from the task of radically altering American society. For example, Sidney Lens, a founder of Mobilization for Survival, insisted that opposition to communism only contributed to a cold–war mentality.[1]

Many radicals assume that combatting communism or containing it is immoral. Walden Bello, an associate fellow of the Institute for Policy Studies and co–director of the Philippine Human Rights Lobby, recently attacked liberal Democrats for trying to "out–Reagan Reagan" by going "down the anti–communist road."[2] No one has epitomized that view more than Jack O'Dell, who has linked anti-communism with racism and chauvinism.[3]

Others on the radical left maintain just as forthrightly that it is the United States that is the major source of evil and repression in the world. Many of these people and the groups they lead proudly assert that they are not even–handed in their treatment of the United States and the Soviet Union because the two superpowers bear differential responsibility for the Cold War. Norman Solomon, disarmament director of the Fellowship of Reconciliation, has asserted that "during the past four decades, the US political process has functioned as the world's greatest threat to the future existence of humanity."[4]

The radical left airily dismisses the notion that a commitment to democratic values might require opposition to communism. Just as Stalinists of an earlier generation insisted that opposition to the Soviet Union tainted a person, a new generation of radicals is accepting the belief that hostility towards such an anti–democratic ideology is a moral blight.

While assailing American support for repressive regimes abroad, members of the radical left praise Soviet support for "revolutionary" regimes ranging from Cuba, Angola and Ethiopia to Afghanistan, Vietnam and Laos.

Many of the leading figures in these groups have long denounced Zionism and castigated Israel in the most extreme language. David Dellinger, a leading figure in the anti–Vietnam war movement, now active in the anti–nuclear movement, is also a participant in several radical organizations supporting the PLO. Dellinger compared South Lebanon to Vietnam and the West Bank to Nazi Germany in the course of a diatribe accusing Israel of "systematically and intentionally bombing schools, churches, mosques and attacking civilians on the grounds that they are so-called 'terrorists.'"[5] At a conference in Kuwait in 1971, sponsored by the PLO, Sidney Lens noted that "all of us there, including myself, were already convinced that Zionism was an expansionist force," but complained that some of those in attendance were blind to the evils of Arab reactionaries and "British or American imperialism." Insisting that "Israel cannot survive as a Jewish state," Lens called for a binational state as a transitional step towards a "democratic revolutionary society" in the Middle East.[6] Father Daniel Berrigan made a notorious speech to the Association of Arab University Graduates in Washington, DC in 1973 calling Israel a "criminal Jewish community" and castigating American Jews for their support for it.[7]

The radical left in the United States is not bashful about identifying its enemies. Those who value democracy and liberty need to be just as alert to who their enemies are. The United States is far from a perfect society. Criticism of America or its policies is not only a constitutional right but an important way to improve our society. Organizations committed to Marxism–Leninism, however, are devoted to a very different agenda, one whose destructive results can be viewed in every regime ever governed by communists. Groups that trumpet their committment to democracy and freedom while praising regimes hostile to both values have only themselves to blame for the opprobrium that results. Democracies do not have to make intellectual peace with those who praise the foes. One of the marks of the health of a democratic society is its willingness to tolerate those who oppose it. Another is its ability to recognize their dangers. When citizens understand the views and goals of the radical left, they will reject them.

Democratic societies have shown a remarkable resilience in this century. Critics and commentators have periodically written their epitaphs, suggesting that they lack the vision, the will and the discipline to combat their foes. Less than twenty years ago American society seemed on the verge of chaos, its cities aflame, its young disaffected and its political system under attack. Those who confidently predicted the imminence of revolution were once again proved wrong.

Past success does not, however, immunize democracies from new challenges. Preserving and protecting democratic institutions and processes requires continued effort and vigilance by an informed citizenry.

Notes

1. Sidney Lens, "Preventing World War II," *Progressive,* August 1985.
2. Walden Bello, "Little Reagans," *Progressive,* January 1986.
3. *Frontline,* November 25, 1985.
4. *Guardian,* October 23, 1985.
5. *Chicago Defender,* November 12, 1980.
6. *Chicago Daily News,* February 16, 1971; Sidney Lens, "Letter from Kuwait," *Progressive,* June 1971.
7. Daniel Berrigan, "The Middle East: Sane Solution," *Liberation,* February 1974.

Index

Name Index

191

Subject Index

Camp David Agreement, US communists against, 33, 34, 45, 79
Capitalism, the left and, 16–17, 19, 64, 75, 78
Center for Constitutional Rights (CCR), 165
Central America, 60–61; US communism and, 32, 34, 61, 64–65, 66, 69, 75, 79, 84, 135–41; radical left and, 135–41, 165
Challenge, 88, 89
China, US communism and, 93–94, 97
CISPES. *See* Committee in Solidarity with the People of El Salvador
Clergy and Laity Concerned (CALC), 143–47; and the USSR, 145; and Vietnam, 144
Comintern (Communist International), 4–5
Committee for a Just Peace in the Middle East, 46
Committee in Solidarity with the People of El Salvador (CISPES), 135–41
Communist Party USA/Provisional (CPUSA/P), 121–22
Communist Party of the United States of America. *See* CPUSA
Communist Workers Party (CWP), 98–102, 170
Congressional Black Caucus, 40
CPUSA (Communist Party of the United States of America), 3–51; *passim*, 57, 87, 103–4; and blacks, 39–43; clubs, 10–11, 13; and democratic centralism, 12, 13; doctrine of, 44; finances, 11–12; history of, 3–7; and international affairs, 24–25, 28–29; and US Jews, 43–47; anti-Maoism, 23; membership in, 9–10, 13; anti-monopoly strategy of, 14–15; and the NAARPR, 42; and related organizations, 48–50; and peace, 26–27, 32; publications of, 50–51; and the USSR, 3, 5, 13, 23–25, 26, 31, 32, 44; and US politics, 13–14, 15–17, 18, 26; and women, 47–48; youth organization of, 37–39, and Zionism, 43–44. *See also* United States Peace Council.

Daily World, 11, 15, 24, 42, 44, 50
Democratic centralism, 12, 13

Economic Notes, 18–19, 20
Emergency Committee Against Racism, 77

"Entrism," 60, 77

FBI, 62, 72, 76, 110, 136, 172
FMLN/FDR, 135–36
Fourth International, 60, 61, 67–68, 69
Fourth International Tendency (FIT), 68
Freedomways, 172
Freiheit, 44
Frontline, 69, 103, 104, 172

Guardian, The (independent Maoist newspaper), 92, 174

Hitler in historical context, 80
Institute for Policy Studies (IPS), 177–85
Institute of the USA and Canada (IUSAC), in Moscow, 181–82
International Association of Democratic Lawyers (IADL), 161, 164
International Committee, 76
International Committee Against Racism, (InCAR), 88, 89–90
International Committee of the Fourth International, 74
International Department of the Soviet Communist Party of the Central Committee, 181, 182
International Workers Party (IWP), 123
IPS. *See* Institute for Policy Studies
Iran, US communism and, 49, 65, 73, 145–46
Israel: Jesse Jackson, and 173; radical left against, 137, 138, 146, 153, 154–55, 156, 164, 166, 183–85; US communism against, 43–47, 67, 75, 77, 83, 91, 103, 110, 126. *See also* Zionism

Jackson's presidential campaign: US communism and, 15, 15, 40, 47, 66, 67, 70, 78, 80, 81, 95, 100–101, 102, 104; US radical left and, 146, 164, 169–75; and Zionism/Judaism, 173–74. *See also* Rainbow Coalition
Jewish Affairs, 45, 46, 47
Jewish Americans for World Peace (JAWP), 46
Jews: Jesse Jackson and, 173–74; US communism and, 43–47, 66–67, 80, 83, 154
John Brown Anti-Klan Committee, 110–11, 112, 114, 115